AMPHIBIAN DEVELOPMENT

ENCYCLOPAEDIA OF DEVELOPMENTAL BIOLOGY-II

AMPHIBIAN DEVELOPMENT

By

Manju Yadav
Lecturer
Department of Zoology
M.M.H. College
Ghaziabad (U.P.)
(India)

DISCOVERY PUBLISHING HOUSE PVT. LTD.
NEW DELHI-110 002

First Published-2008

ISBN 978-81-8356-298-0

Published by

DISCOVERY PUBLISHING HOUSE PVT. LTD.
4831/24, Ansari Road, Prahlad Street,
Darya Ganj, New Delhi-110002 (India)
Phone: 23279245 • Fax: 91-11-23253475
E-mail: dphbooks@rediffmail.com
dphtemp@indiatimes.com

Printed at:

Sachin Printers, Delhi

Preface

The present title **Amphibian Development** is an important link between almost all biological sciences, and is assuming more and more importance in fields such as medicine and agriculture. Molecular biology has began fulfilling its long anticipated role of linking genetics and embryology and many questions of embryology that had lain dormant for decades have been taken up with new molecular tools and strategies. While our knowledge of the molecular aspects of development has so drastically increased during the time, our applications of developmental phenomenon in evolution and ecology has also expanded. It is becoming impossible to study any area of biology without some background in developmental biology.

This title integrates the descriptive, experimental and biochemical approaches into a conceptual framework for the analysis of development. All important points are illustrated diagrammatically. It is well balanced, completely accessible presentation of principles and application of embryology. In order to create a book which is written within the economy as well as the physical group of the student, only the main essentials of each topic have been presented. It does this with the aid of careful selected examples—some recent and other classic of the field and with numerous illustrations. The aim is to enthuse the reader with this active and exciting area of research and to lay a solid foundation on which further study of its various facts may be based.

To make the work more comprehensive and informative, the author has consulted many authoritative books, research journals, abstracts, monographs etc. He is grateful to all those great scholars whose work are cited or substantially reproduced.

There can be no claim to originality except in the manner of treatment and much of the information has been obtained from the books and scientific journals available in the different libraries.

The author expresses his thanks to his friends and colleagues whose continue inspirations have initiated him to bring out this book.

The author expresses his gratitude to Mr. Wasan and staff of M/s Discovery Publishing House for their whole hearted co-operation in the publication of this book.

Author

CONTENTS

1

Introduction

THE MALE REPRODUCTIVE ORGANS

Sexual Characters

In frog sexual dimorplus is not well distinct. However during breeding season some characters appear. The female is bigger the male. The identifying features of male which distinguish it from the female are *a darkened thumb pad* which changes thickness and colour intensity as the breeding season approaches; a distinct low, guttural *croaking sound* with the accompanying swelling by air of the lateral vocal sacs located between the tympanum and the forearm; a more slender and *streamlined body* than that of the female; and the *absence of coelomic* cilia except in the peritoneal funnels on the ventral face of the kidneys. Males of many species carry additional features such as brilliant colours on the ventral aspects of the *legs (R. sylvatica),* black chin *(B. fowlerz),* or the size of colour of the tympanic membrane.

The Testes

There is a pair of testes present just above the dorsally placed kidneys and remain suspended by a double fold of peritoneum known as the *mesorchium.* This mesentery surrounds each testis and is continuous with the peritoneal epithelium which covers the ventral face of each kidney and lines the entire body cavity.

The testes are whitish and ovoid bodies lying ventral to and near, the anterior end of each kidney. The *vasa of ferentia,* ducts from the testes, pass between the folds of the mesorchium and into the mesial margin of the adjacent kidney. The number of vasa efferentia leaving the tesits is about a dozen. During the breeding season, or after slight compression of the testis of the hibernating frog these ducts become the more apparent due to the presence in them of whitish masses of spermatozoa in suspension. The ducts are very small in diameter, tough walled, and interbranching. They are lined with closely packed cuboidal cells. All vasa efferentia of one testis unit together. inside the kidney of the related side and form a cerenal duct the *Bidders Canal* that transports sperms through the kidney. The Bidder canal is a longitudinal tube situated along the median edge of the kidney communicated with the writer by transverse collecting tubes. The presence of spermatozoa in the kidney also can be achieved artificially be injecting the male frog with the anterior pituitary sex-stimulating hormone.

The spermatozoa are produced in inside *seminiferous tubules.* Thesc arc closely packed, oval-shaped sacs, which are separated from each other by thin partitions (septula) of supporting (connective) tissue known as *interstitial tissue.* This tissue presumably has some endocrine function. The thickness of this tissue is much reduced immediately after breeding or pituitary stimulation. The interstitial tissue is continuous with the covering of the testes known as the tunica *albuginea.*

Spermatogenesis

When the photoperiodism is appropriate during breeding season the given cells undergo spermatogenesis but shortly after the breeding season the *spermatogonium,* which has ceased all mitotic activity, enters upon a period of rest but not inactivity. During this period the nucleus passes through a sequence of complex changes which represent an extended prophase. This is in anticipation of the two maturation divisions that finally produce the haploid spermatid which metamorphoses into a spermatozoon.

The Spermatogenia show several cytolosical charges. The nucleus of the spermatogonium contains chromatin which appears as relatively coarse lumps distributed widely over an achromatic reticulum. Both the cytoplasm and the nucleus grow and the

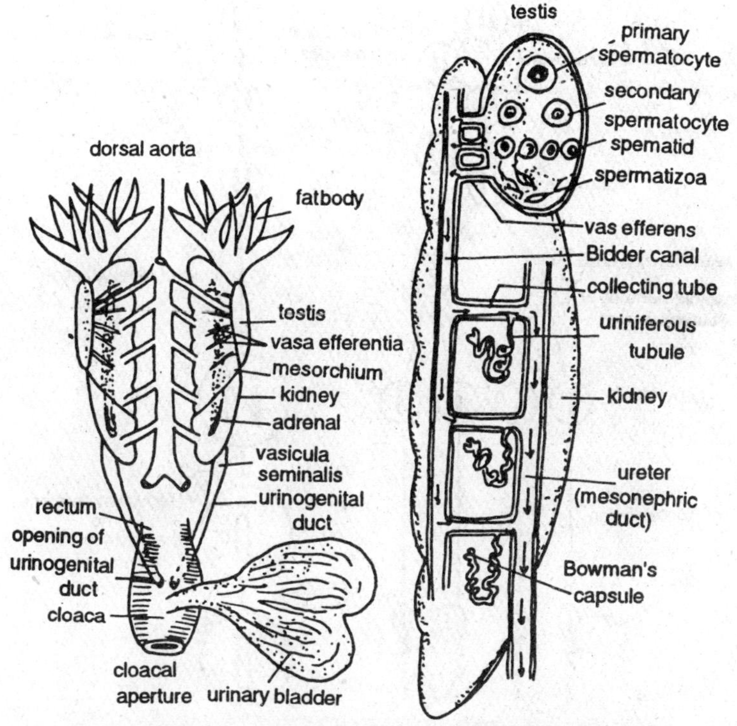

Figure 1.1 : Frog. Urinogenital organ of male.

chromatic granules become finely divided and arranged into contiguous rows, bound by an achromatic thread, together known as chromosomes. This is the *leptotene stage* of spermatogenesis. Shortly the chromosomes become arranged in pairs which converge toward that side of the nucleus where the centrosome is found. The opposite ends of the paired chromosomes merge into the general reticulum. This is the *synaptene stage* or *boughal stage.* The chromatin granules become telescoped together on the filaments so that the aggregated granules, known as *chromosomes,* appear much shorter and thicker. Pairs of chromosomes become intertwined and the loose terminal ends become coiled and tangled together. This is the contraction or synizesis *stage.* Then the members of the various pairs become laterally fused. While there is no actual reduction in total chromatin, there is a temporary and an apparent reduction in the total number of chromosomes to

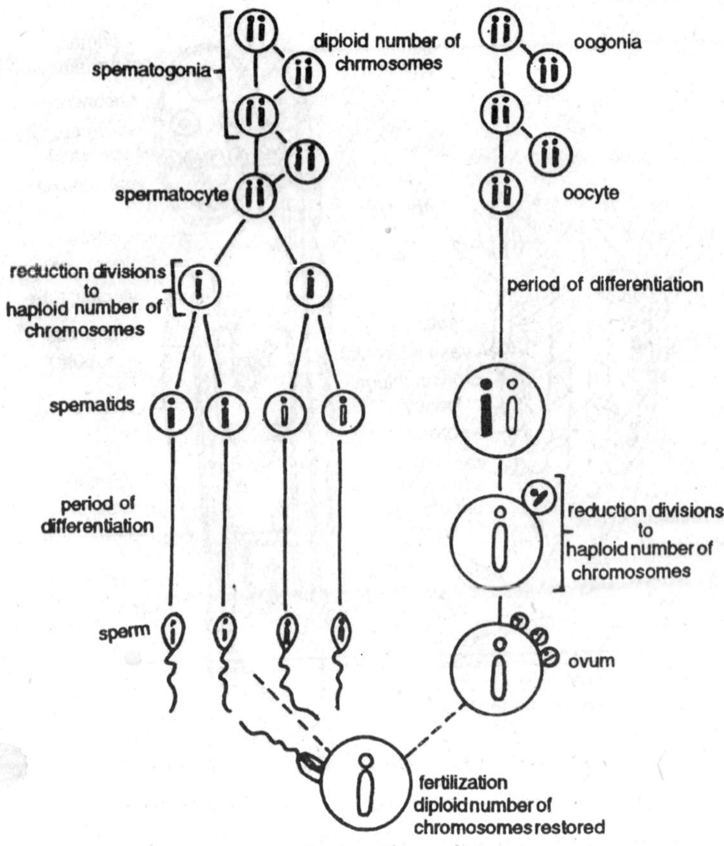

Figure 1.2 : Diagramatic representation of gametogensis.

the haploid condition, because of this fusion. There is no actual reduction in the total amount of chromatin material, nor is there any permanent reduction at this stage in the number of chromosomes. Their identity is lost only temporarily. This is known as the *pachytene stage.* The members of each pair then separate again. It must be remembered, however, that (a) the separation need not be along the original line of fusion and that (b) an exchange of homologous sections of the chromosomes may occur without any cytological evidence. In any case, the diploid number of chromosomes reappears and this is then known as the *diplotene stage.*

During these changes in the chromatin material of the nucleus, the volume of the nucleus and the cytoplasm are considerably increased, the nuclear membrane breaks down, and the chromosomes assume bizarre shapes and various size. They may be paired, curved, or straight; W" and "C" and reversed "L" shapes, figures 8's, and grouped as tetrads. This is known as the *diakinesis stage:* The chromosomes are then lined up on a spindle in anticipation of the first of the two maturation divisions.

Frog is a seasonal breeder and the spermatogenesis in is completed within the testes. The walls of the seminifcrous tubules produce *spermatogonia* which go through mitotic divisions and then the series of nuclear charges without mitosis. This results in the appearance, toward the lumen of each tubule, of clusters of mature *spermatozoa.* The spermatogonia are found close to the basement membrane of the seminiferous tubule. These then await their turn to undergo, the maturation changes necessary for the production of spermatozoa which will be ready for the breeding season. The elongated and filamentous tails of the clustered mature *spermatozoa* project into the lumen of each seminiferous tubule.

At the peak of spermatogenetic activity, all the stages of maturation from the spermatogonium to the spermatozoon are present. The spermatogonia are always located around the periphery of the seminiferous tubule and are small, closely packed cells, each with a granular, oval nucleus. In between the spermatogonia may be found occasional very large cells, the *primary spermatocytes.* These tend to be irregularly spherical, possessing large and vesicular nuclei. The cells are so large that they may be seen under low power magnification of the microscope. Apparently they divide to form secondary spermatocytes almost immediately, for they are so few and far between. The *secondary spermatocytes* are about half the size of the primaries, and lie toward the lumen of the tubule. They generally have a darkly staining nucleus, and the cytoplasm may be tapered toward one side. The *spermatid,* following another division, is even smaller and possesses a condensed nucleus of irregular shape. Clusters of spermatids appear as clusters of granules, the dark nucleus being almost as small as the cross section of a sperm head. The metamorphic stages from spermatid to spermatozoon are difficult to identify with ordinary magnification, and are often confused with the spermatids themselves. During this change the inner of two spermatid centrioles passes into the nucleus while the outer one gives rise to the tail-like flagellum.

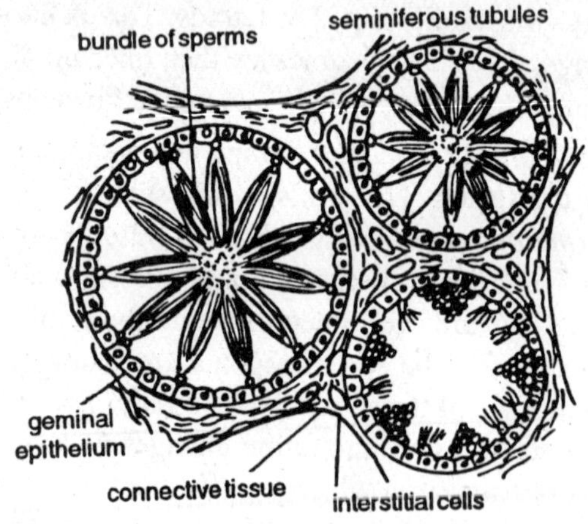

Figure 1.3 : Frog. T.S. of Testis.

The mature *spermatozoon* averages about 0.03 mm. in length. It has an elongated, solid-staining head (nucleus) with an anterior acrosome, pointing outwardly toward the periphery of the seminiferous tubule. The short middle piece generally is not visible but the tail appears as a gray filamentous extension into the lumen, about four or more times the length of the sperm head.

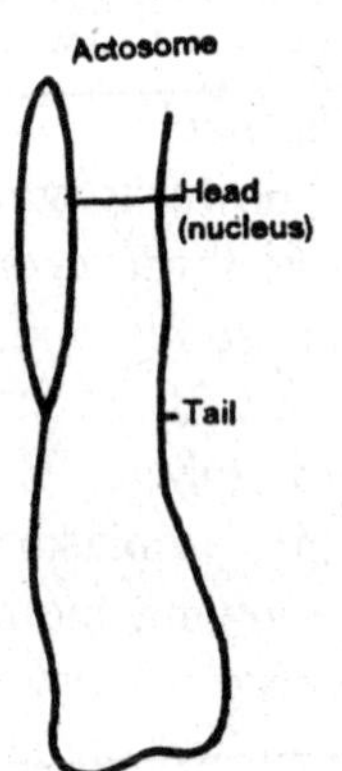

Figure 1.4 : Frog spermatozoon.

In any cross section of this testis, bundles of sperm heads or tails may be cut at right angles or tangentially, giving misleading suggestions of structure. The mature spermatozoon is dependent upon external sources of nutrition so that it joins from 25 to 40 other spermatozoa, all of whose heads may be seen converging into the cytoplasm of a relatively large, columnar-type basal cell known as the *Sertoli cell.* This is functionally a nurse cell, supplying nutriment to the clusters of mature spermatozoa until such time as they may be liberated through the genital tract to function in fertilization.

REPRODUCTIVE BEHAVIOUR

It has been proved definitely that the anterior pituitary hormone causes the release of the mature spermatozoa from the testis. But this hormone also releases other maturation stages. It is therefore probable that there are smooth muscle fibers, either among the interstitial cells or in the tunica albuginea of the testes, which fibers contract to force the spermatozoa from the seminiferous tubules. It would be as difficult to physiologically demonstrate the presence of these fibers in the testis as it is simple to demonstrate them in the contracting cyst wall of the ovary.

Responding to sex stimulation, the spermatozoa become free from their Sertoli cells and are formed from the lumen of the seminiferous tubule into the related *collecting tubule.* These collecting tubules are small and are linked with closely packed cuboidal cells. They join the *vasa offerentia* which leave the testis to pass between the folds of the mesorchium and thence into the *Malpighian corpuscles* of the kidney. From this point the spermatozoa pass by way of the excretory ducts, the uriniferous tubules, and into the *mesonepheric duct* (ureter) which may be found attached to the lateral margin of the kidney. Within the excretory system the spermatozoa are immotile, due to the slightly acid environment. They are carried passively down the ureter to the slight dilation near the cloaca, known as the *seminal vesicle.* Within the vesicle the spermatozoa are stored briefly in clusters until amplexus and oviposition occur. At oviposition the male ejaculates the spermatozoa into the neutral or slightly alkaline water where they are activated and then are able to fertilize the eggs as they emerge from the cloaca of the female.

During the normal breeding season amplexus is achieved as the females reach the ponds where the males are emitting their sex cells. During amplexus there are definite muscular ejaculatory movements on the part of the male frog, coinciding with oviposition on the part of the female. Amplexus may be maintained by the male for many days, even with dead females. As soon as the eggs are laid and the male has shed his sperm, 'he goes through a brief weaving motion of the body and then releases his grip to swim away. The frogs completely neglect he newly laid eggs.

ACCESSORY REPRODUCTIVE ORGANS

In the male frog the ureter is not directly connected with the *ladder,* as it is in higher vertebrates. It is possible that the ladder in the Anura may be an accessory respiratory and hydrating organ, particularly in the toads, where water may be stored during migrations onto land.

The male frog also has a duct, homologous to the oviduct of the female, known as the "rudimentary oviduct" or *Mitllerian duct.* This duct normally has no lumen, and is very much reduced in size so that it may be difficult to locate. There is experimental evidence that this duct may be truly a vestigial oviduct since it respondents to ovarian or female sex hormones by enlarging and acquiring a lumen. At the anterior end of the testes of some Anura (e.g., toads) there may be found an undeveloped ovary known as *Bidder's organ.* This structure is said to respond to the removal of the adjacent testis or to the injection of female sex hormones by enlarging to become structurally like an ovary. Occasionally isolated ova have been found within the seminiferous tubules of an otherwise normal testis, suggesting the similar origin and the fundamental similarity of the testis and the ovary.

Finally, attached to the anterior end of the testis of the hibernating frog may be seen finger like *fat bodies* (corpora adiposa) which represent stored nutrition for the long period of hibernation, and for the pre-breeding season when food is scarce. Under the microscope these fat bodies appear as dusters of vacuolated cells, and are not to be confused with the mesorchium. It is believed that they, as well as the gonads, arise from the genital ridges of the early embryo. The fat bodies tend to be reduced immediately after the breeding season, only to be built up again as the time for hibernation approaches.

THE FEMALE REPRODUCTIVE ORGANS

Secondary Sexual Characters

The mature female frog is generally larger than the male of thee same age and species, the *Rana pipiens* female measuring from 60 to 110 mm. in length from snout to anus. The sexually mature female has a body length of at least 70 mm. It can be identified by the absence, at any season, of the dark thumb pad; the inability to produce lateral cheek pouches resulting from the croaking reaction; a flabby and distended abdomen; and the presence of peritoneal cilia. These cilia are developed in the female in response to the prior development and secretion of ovarian hormones.

The Ovaries

There is a pair of large flat, irregular multi-lobed ovaries attached to the dorsal body wall by a double-layered extension of the peritoneum known as the *mesovarium.* This peritoneum continues around the entire ovary as the *theca externa.* Each lobe of the ovary is hollow and its cavity is continuous with the other 7 to 12 lobes. The ovaries of the female are found in the same relative position as the testes of the male but the peritoneum extends from the dorso-mesial wall rather than from the kidneys, as in the male.

The size of the ovary varies with the seasons more than does the size of the testis. From late summer until the spring breeding season the paired ovaries will fill the body cavity and will often distend the body wall. They may contain from 2,000 *(Rana pipiens)* to as many as 20,000 ova *(Rana catesbiana),* each measuring about 1.75 mm. in diameter *(Rana pipiens).* The mature ova are highly pigmented on the surface of the animal pole, so that the ovary has a speckled appearance of black pigment and white yolk, representing the animal and the vegetal hemispheres of the ova.

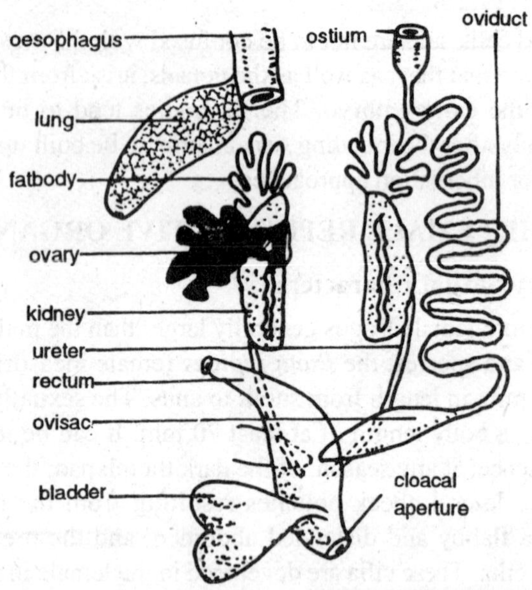

Figure 1.5 : Frog. Urinogenital system of female.

All reproductive organs undergo cyclic changes. There is no appreciable change in the size of the ovary during hibernation, nor is there any observable cytological change in the ova. However, if a female is forced to retain her ova beyond the normal breeding period by isolating her from males or by keeping her in a warm environment and without food, the ova will begin to deteriorate (cytolize) within the ovary. Immediately after the spring breeding season, when the female discharges thousands of *mature ova,* the remaining ovary with its *oogonia* is so small that it is sometimes difficult to locate. There is no pigment in the tissue of the ovary (in the stroma or in the immature ova), and each growing *oocyte* appears as a small white sphere of protoplasm contained within its individual *follicle sac.*

The history of the ovary shows that within its outer peritoneal covering, *the theca externs,* are suspended thousands of individual sacs, each made up of another membrane, the *theca intern* or cyst wall, which contains smooth muscle fibers. This theca interna is derived from the retro-peritoneal tissue. The theca interna surrounds each ovum except for the limited area bulging toward the body cavity, where it is covered by only the theca externa. This is the region which will be ruptured during ovulation to allow the ovum to escape its follicle into the *body cavity*. The theca interna, plus the limited covering of the theca externa, and the

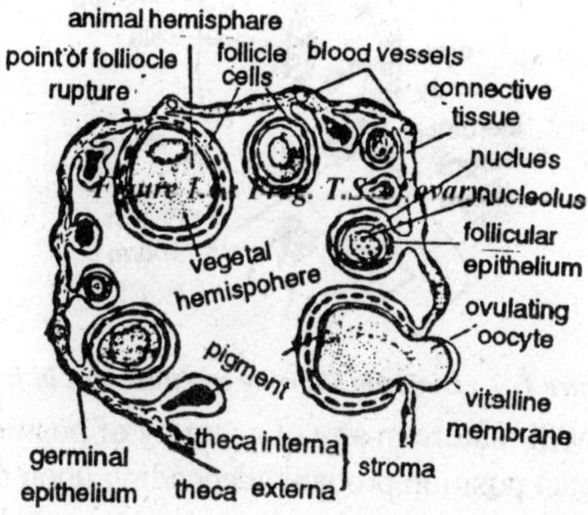

Figure 1.6 : Frog. T.S. of ovary.

follicle cells together comprise the *ovarian follicle*. These two membranes make up the rather limited *ovarian stroma* of the frog ovary, and they contain both blood vessels and nerves. Within each follicle are found *follicle cells,* with their oval and granular nuclei, derived originally from oogonia. These follicle cells surround the developing oocyte and are found in close association with it throughout those processes of maturation which occur within the follicle. Enclosed within the follicle cells, and closely applied to each mature ovum, is the non-cellular and transparent *vitelline membrane,* probably derived from both the ovum and the follicle cells. This membrane is developed and applied to the ovum during the maturation process so that it is not seen around the earlier or younger oogonia. Since the bulk of the ovum is yolk, this membrane is appropriately called the *vitelline membranes*. It is sometimes designated as the primary egg membranes. After the ovum is fertilized this membrane becomes separated from the ovum and the space between is then known as the *perivitelline space,* filled with a fluid. The fluid may be derived from the ovum which would show cd npensatory shrinkage. As the oocyte matures and enlarges, the follicle cells and membranes are so stretched and flattened that they are not easily distinguished.

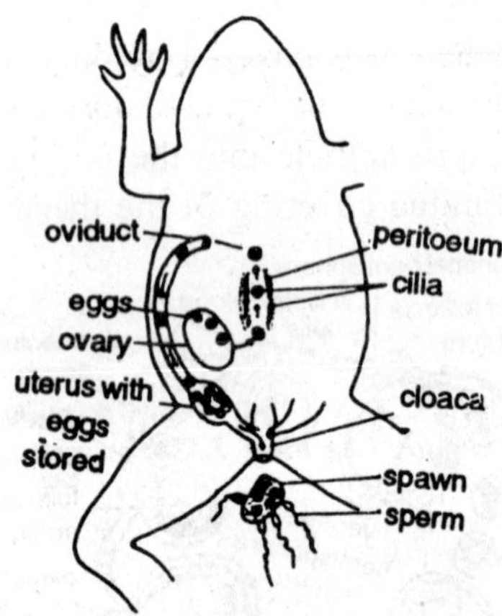

Figure 1. 7 : Diagram showing egg transport in frog.

The ovum will mature in any of a variety of positions within its follicle, the exact position probably depending upon the maximum blood supply. As one examines an ovary the ovum the will be seen in all possible positions, some with the *animal hemisphere* and others with the *vegetal hemisphere* toward the theca externa and body cavity. It is believed that the most vascular side of the follicle wall will tend to produce the animal hemisphere of the ovum and hence give it its *fundamental* symmetry and polarity.

The frog's egg is of *mesolecithal type* having a moderate amount of yolk. The eggs are *telolecithal* having yolk at its lower *vegetal pole.* There is a thin outer layer *of cytoplasm,* more concentrated toward the animal hemisphere and in the vicinity of the *germinal vesicle* or immature nucleus. Surrounding the entire ovum is a non-living surface coat, also containing pigment. This *pigment is* presumably a metabolic by-product. This coat is necessary for retaining the shape of the ovum and in aiding in the morphogenetic processes of cleavage and gastrulation.

The Body Cavity and the Oviducts

There is a pain of oviducts suspended from the dorsal body wall by a double fold of *peritoneum.* Its anterior end is found between the heart and the lateral peritoneum, at the apex of the liver lobe. At this anterior end is a slit-like infundibulum of *ostium tuba* with ciliated and highly elastic walls. The body cavity of the female is

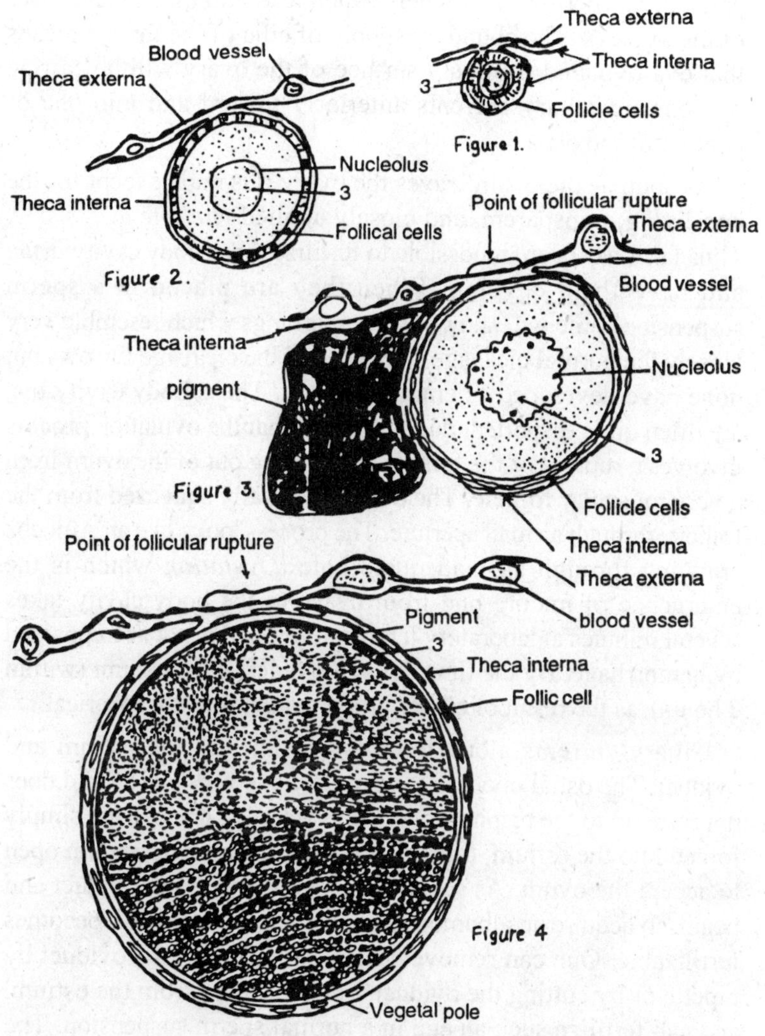

Figure 1.8 : Growing Oocytes of the frog.

almost entirely lined with cilia, each cilium having its effective beat or stroke in the general direction of one of the ostia. These cilia are produced in response to an ovarian hormone and therefore are regarded as secondary sex characters. They are found on the peritoneum covering the entire body cavity, on the liver, and on the pericardial membrane. There are no cilia on the lungs, the ntestines, or the surface of the kidneys except in the ciliated peristomial (peritoneal) funnels which lead into the blood sinuses of the kidneys. The abundant supply of cilia of the female means that ova ovulated from any surface of the ovary will be carried by constant ciliary currents anteriorly toward and into one or another of the ostia.

As soon as the ovum leaves the ovary it is nude except for the non-living, transparent, and closely applied *vitelline membrane.* Thus far it has been impossible to fertilize these body cavity *ovum* and have them develop. When they are placed in a sperm suspension some will show surface markings which resemble very closely the normal cleavage spindles and the cleavage furrows but none have developed as embryos as yet. These body cavity ova are often quite disported, due to the fact that the ovulation process involves a rupture of the follicle and forcing out of the ovum from a very muscular follicle. The ovum is literally squeezed from the follicle, through a small aperture. The process looks like an Amoeba crawling through an inadequate hole. *Ovulation* which is the emergence of mature one from ovary to the body cavity takes several minutes at laboratory temperatures, and is not accompanied by hemorrhage. By the time the ovum reaches the ostium (within 2 hours), as the result of ciliary propulsion, it is again spherical.

Ciliary currents alone force the ovum into the ostium and oviduct. The ostial opening is very elastic is very elastic and does not respond to the respiratory or heart activity. The ova are simply forced into the ostium, from all angles, stretching its, mouth open to accept the ovum. As soon as the ovum enters the oviduct and begins to acquire an albuminous (mucinjelly) covering, it becomes fertilizable. One can remove such an ovum from the oviduct by pipette or by cutting the oviduct 1 inch or more from the ostium, and can fertilize such an egg in a normal sperm suspension. The physical (or chemical) change which occur between the time the ovum is in the body cavity and the time it is removed from the oviduct, which make it fertilizable, are not yet understood.

As soon as the ovum is propelled through the oviduct by ciliary currents, it receives coatings of *albumen* (jelly). The initial coat is thin but of heavy consistency, and is applied closely to the ovum.

The ovum is spiraled down the oviduct by its ciliated lining so that the application of the jelly covering is quite uniform. There are, in all, three distinct layers of jelly, the outermost one being much the greater in thickness but the less viscous. The intermediate layer is of a thin and more fluid consistency. There is hyperactivity of the glandular elements of the oviduct just before the normal breeding season, or after anterior pituitary hormone stimulation, so that the duct is enlarged several times over that of the oviduct of the hibernating female.

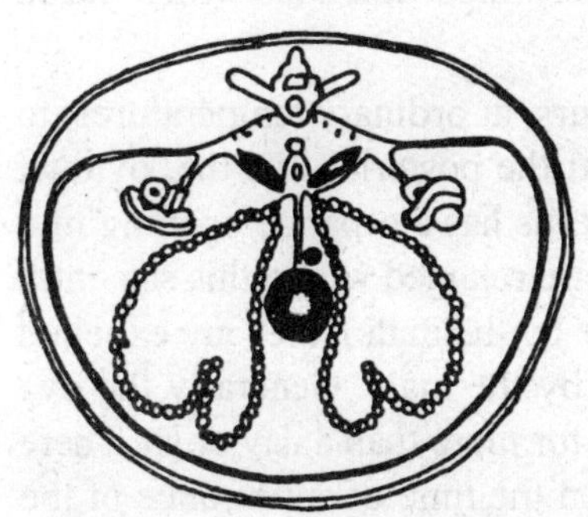

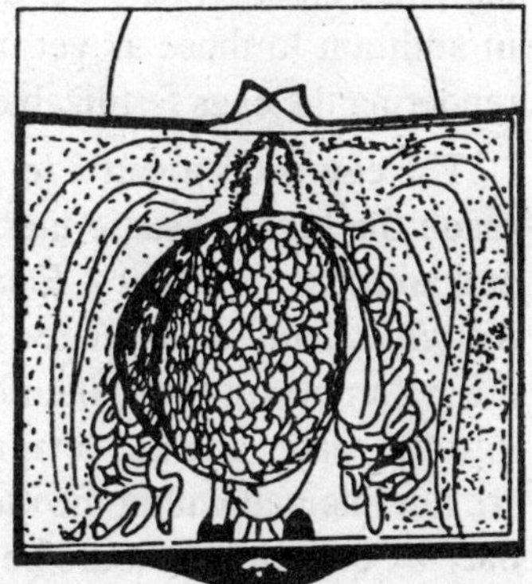

Figure 1.9 : Distribution of coelomic cilia within the body cavity of the female frog. (Left) Schematic section through the level of the ovaries. (Right) Schematic drawing of the open body cavity. The cilia in the body cavity of the female develop in response to the elaboration of an ovarian hormone, and function in propelling the eggs to the two ostia.

The presence of the jelly layers on the oviducal or the uterine egg is not readily apparent because it requires water before it reaches its maximum thickness. Ova sectioned within the oviduct show the jelly as a transparent coating just outside the vitelline membrane. As soon as the ovum reaches the water, however, imbibition swells the jelly until its thickness becomes greater than the diameter of the ovum.

The function of the jelly is to protect the ovum against injury, against ingestion by larger organisms, and from fungus and other infections. Equally important, however, is the evidence that this jelly helps the ovum to retain its metabolically derived heat so that the jelly can be said to act as an insulator against heat loss. *Bernard* and *Batuschek (1891)* showed that the greater the wave length of light the less heat passed through the jelly around the frog's egg, in comparison with an equivalent amount of water and under similar conditions. Originally, and erroneously, the jelly was thought to act as a lens which would concentrate the heat rays of the sun onto the ovum, but the since jelly is largely water, which is a non-conductor of heat rays, this theory is untenable. One can demonstrate that the temperature of the ovum is higher than the temperature of the immediate environment, even in a totally darkened environment. So, the jelly has certain physical functions in addition to those as yet undetermined functions which aid in rendering the eggs fertilizable.

The egg takes about 2 to 4 hours, at ordinary temperatures, to reach the highly elastic uterus, at the posterior end the, oviduct and adjacent the *cloaca.* Each uterus has a separate opening into the *cloaca,* and the ovulated ova are retained within this sac until, during amplexus (sexual cmbrace by the male), they are expelled into the water and are fertilized by the male. Generally the ova are not retained within the uterus for more than a day or so. There may be quite a few hours between the time of appearance of the first and the last ova in the uteri.

Oögenesis

The process farming ova is called oogenesis. During the process the ova develop from oogonia which divide repeatedly. These pre-maturation germ cells divide by mitosis many times and then come to rest, during which process there is growth of some of them without nuclear division. These become ova while those that fail to grow become follicle cells. However, there are pre-prophase changes of the nucleus of the prospective ovum comparable to the pre-prophase changes in spermatogenesis. The majority of oogonia, therefore, never mature into ova, but become follicle cells.

The process of maturation involves contributions from the nucleus and the cytoplasm. *First,* chromatin nucleoli aid in the synthesis of yolk, and *second,* the breakdown of the germinal vesicle allows an intermingling of the nuclear and the cytoplasmic components. Only a small portion of the germinal vesicle is involved in the maturation spindle so that it may be at this time that the nucleus exerts its initial influence on the cytoplasm. All cytoplasmic differentiation must be initiated at a time when the hereditary influences of the nucleus are so intermingled with it.

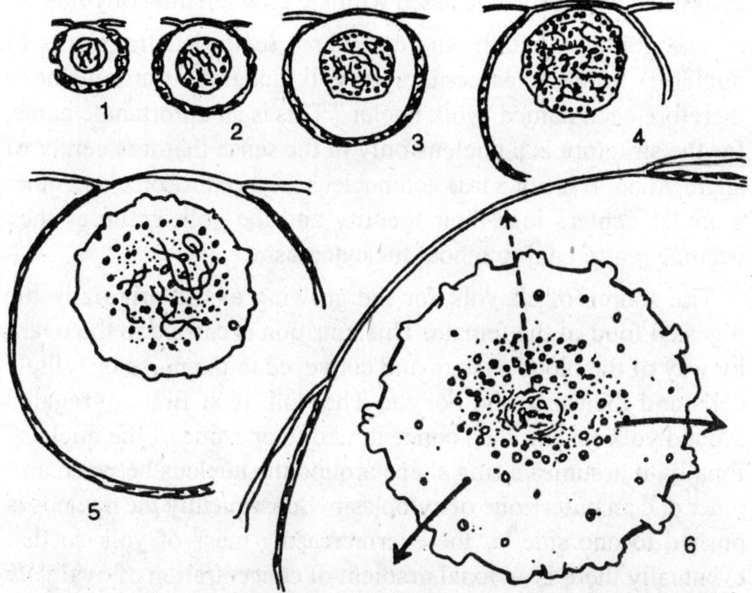

Figure 1.10 : Normal nuclear growth cycle and its role in vitellogenesis.

Growth of the developing oocytes is achieved largely by the accumulation of *yolk.* As soon as growth begins the cell no longer divides by mitosis and is known as an *oocyte* rather than an oogonium. The growth process is aided by the *centrosome,* which is found to one side of the *nucleus,* and around which gather the granules or *yolk platelets.The chromatin* filaments become achromatic and the *nucleoli* increase in number, by fragmentation, and become more chromatic. Many of the nucleoli, which ' are concentrations of nucleo-protein, pass through the nuclear membrane into the surrounding cytoplasm during this period. It is not clear whether this occurs through further fragmentation of the nucleoli into particles of microscopic or sub-microscopic **size, and** then their ejection through the nuclear membrane. It may occur by the loss of identity (and chromatic properties) by possible chemical change and subsequent diffusion of the liquid form through the membrane to be resynthesized on the cytoplasmic side of the membrane. During the growth of the oocyte, further nucleoli appear within the nucleus, only to fragment and later to pass out into the cytoplasm. The presence of chromatic nucleoli in the cytoplasm is closely associated with the accumulation of yolk.

The granules within -the cytoplasm (extruded fragments of nucleoli) function as centers of yolk accumulation and have therefore been named "yolk nuclei." This is an unfortunate name, for the structure is a nucleus only in the sense that it is center of aggregation. It is not a true cell nucleus. The centrosome and other granular centers lose their identity and the yolk granules then become scattered throughout the cytoplasm.

The source of all yolk for the growing ova is originally the digested food of the female. This nutrition is carried to the ovary by way of the blood system and conveyed to the nurse or follicle cells and thence to the oocyte. The yolk is at first aggregated around yolk nuclei, then concentrated to one side of the nucleus. Finally, it assumes a ring shape around the nucleus between an ' inner and an outer zone of cytoplasm. Subsequently the nucleus is pushed to one side by the everincreasing mass of yolk so that eventually there is an axial gradient of concentration of oval *yolk platelets* from one side of the egg to the other. The smaller platelets are found in the vicinity of the nucleus, in the animals hemisphere. The larger platelets are located toward the vegetal hemisphere. There is an increase averaging from 200 to 700 per cent in the total lipoid substance, neutral fat, total fatty acids, total cholesterol, ester cholesterol, free cholesterol, and phospholipin content of the ovaries of *Rana pipiens* occurring during the production and growth of ova. The primary oocyte may show a slight flattening of the surface directly above the region of the nucleus.

These growth changes and the unequal distribution of pigment, yolk, and cytoplasm are the first indications of *polarity* or a gradient system within the ovum. When the polarity is well-established, the cytoplasm, the superficial melanin or black pigment, and the nucleus are all at the animal hemisphere. The light coloured yolk is more concentrated toward the vegetal pole. The eggs is then regarded *as a telolecithal* egg. During this phase of egg maturation there is a drain on the metabolism of the frog which requires an excess of food intake because the materials for the growth of ovum must be synthesized from nutritional elements received from the vascular system of the female. For *Rana pipiens* this period of most active feeding comes during the summer when the natural foods, insects, worms, etc., are the most abundant.

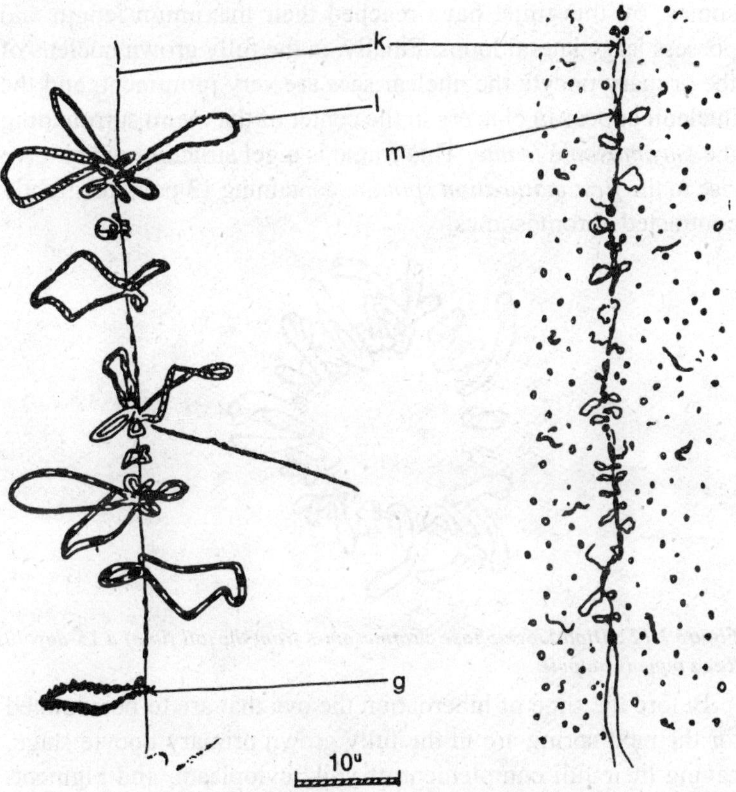

Figure 1.11 : Lateral loops of the amphibian chromosome.

During the growth of the oocyte in general there are important changes occurring within the nucleus (germinal vesicle) of the ovum. Thirteen pairs of *chromosomes* may be seen in synizesis (contraction), converging toward the centrosome at the "yolk nucleus" stage. A little later the nuclear membrane develops saclike bulges, the *nucleoli* are scattered, and there is a colloidal chromosome core which almost fills the entire nucleus. The chromosome themselves are small and almost invisible. When the *primary oocyte is* about half its ultimate size, there appear definite sacs on the nuclear surface. The fragmented nucleoli are located at the periphery of the lobulated nuclear membrane, and the chromosome frames have become relatively large. The chromosomes, by this time, have reached their maximum length and possess large lateral loops. Finally, in the fully grown nucleus of the primary oocyte the nuclear sacs are very prominent, and the nucleoli appear in clusters in the center of the ovum surrounding the *chromosome frame.* This frame is a gel structure which give rise to the *first maturation spindle,* containing 13 pairs of slightly contracted chromosomes.

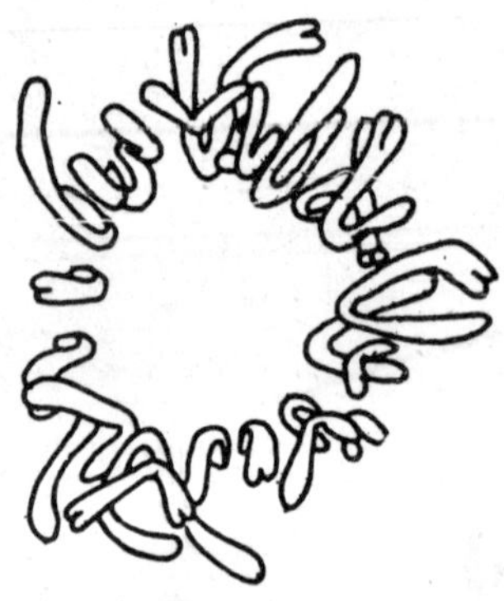

Figure 1.12 : Diplid metaphase chromosomes from the tail fin of a 15-dayold Rana pipiens tadpole.

Before the time of hibernation the ova that are to be ovulated for the next spring are in the fully grown primary oocyte stage, having their full complement of yolk, cytoplasm, and pigment. Externally more than one-half of the ovum appears densely black, due to surface pigment granules, while the rest is creamy white. The nucleus is prepared for the maturation divisions. Such an ovum measures about 1.75 mm. in diameter. The surface layer of the amphibian ovum is formed before fertilization and it is definitely not hyaline, as it is in some Invertebrate eggs. It contains many small yolk grains and irregular accumulations of spherical, black

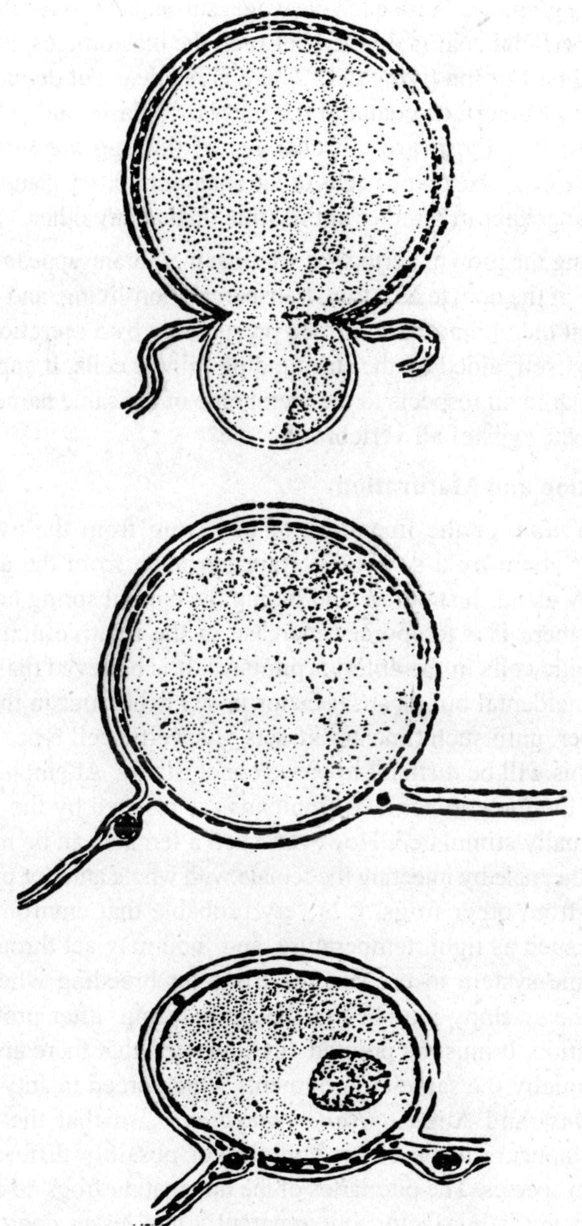

Figure 1.13 : Showing the process of ovulation.

pigment granules. With each cleavage, subsequent to fertilization, this superficial coat is divided between the blastomeres, being an integral part of the living cell. There is no clear-cut demarcation between this surface coat and the inner cytoplasm and yolk. It is believed that these growth changes of the egg are under the influence of the basophilic cells of the anterior pituitary gland, which cells are greater in number at this time than at any other.

During the growth period the vitelline membrane appears on the surface of the oocyte as a thin, transparent, non-living, and closely adherent membrane. It is formed presumably by a secretion from the egg itself; aided by the surrounding follicle cells. It appears to be similar in all respects to the membrane of the same name found around the eggs of all vertebrates.

Ovulation and Maturation

Ovulation, or the liberation of the ovum from the ovary, is brought about by a sex-stimulating hormone from the anterior pituitary gland. Just before and during the normal spring breeding period there is a temporary increase in the relative number of addophilic cells in the anterior pituitary. It is believed that this is not coincidental but a causal factor in sex behaviour in the frog: However, until such time as extracts of specific cell types can be made this will be difficult to prove conclusively. Attempts on the part of the male to achieve amplexus are resisted by the female not sexually stimulated. However, such a female can be made to accept the male by injecting the female with whole anterior pituitary glands from other frogs. it is very probable that environmental factors such as light, temperature, and food may act through the endocrine system to prepare the frogs for breeding when they reach the swampy marshes in the early spring, after protracted hibernation. It must be pointed out, however, that there are frogs in essentially the same environments which breed in July *(Rana clamitans)* and August *(Rana catesbiana), so* that the causal factors appears to be either complex or possibly different for different species. The pituitaries of the hibernating frogs do contain the sexstimulating factor, but apparently to a lesser degree than the glands of frogs approaching the breeding season. The injection of 6 glands from adult female frogs will cause an adult female of Rana *pipiens* to ovulate as early as the last week in August, some 8 months before the normal breeding period. One or two such glands will accomplish the same results if used early in April. Another explanation for this may be offered, namely that the ovary itself may become more sensitive to such stimulation as the breeding season approaches.

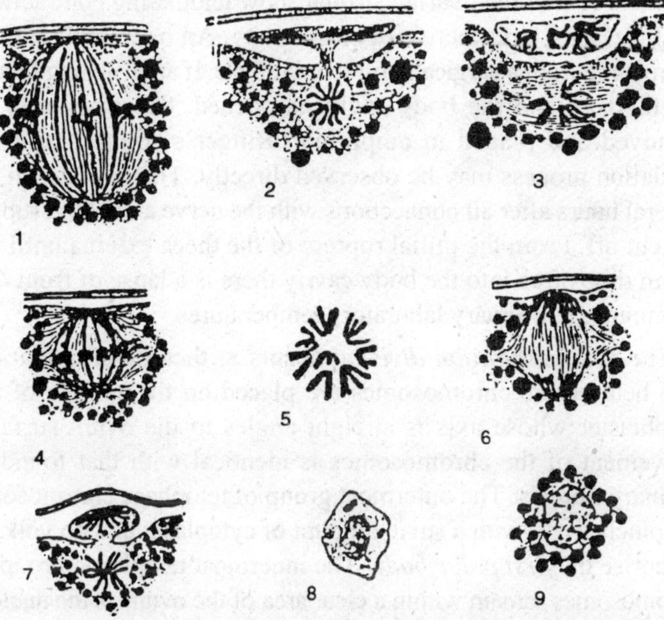

Figure 1.14 : The maturation divisions in the female (Axolot). (1) First polar spindle with heterotypic chromosomes. (2) Extrusion of first polar body. (3) Appearance of second polar spindle. Longitudinal division of chromosomes in egg and in first polar body. (4) Second polar spindle radial. Homoeotypic chromosomes' on equator (metaphase). (5) Polar view of the same. (6) Anaphase. (7) Extrusion of second polar body. (8) Second polar body with resting nucleus. (9) Female pronucleus in resting condition, closely surrounded by yolk granules.

The process of ovulation involves the rupturing and the emergence of ova from their individual follicles. The surface of the ovum separated from the body cavity by only the nonvascular *theca externa,* is first ruptured and then the ovum slowly emerges through the small opening. Since the ovum is know contain a peptic-like enzyme, it is believed that the pituitary hormone may activate this enzyme to digest away the tight and non-vascular covering. Then by stimulation of the smooth muscle fibers of the cyst wall *(theca interna) the* process of emergence is completed. The relation of the pituitary to smooth muscle activity has long been established clinically.

It is true that the ovarian stroma show undulating contractions at all seasons, irrespective of sex activity. An ovum will emerge at any time from a surgically ruptured follicle. If an ovulating female is etherized and the body cavity is opened, the ovary may be removed and placed in amphibian Ringer's solution and the ovulation process may be observed directly. This will go on for several hours after all connections with the nerve and blood supply are cut off. From the initial rupture of the theca externa until the ovum drops free into the body cavity there is a lapse of from 4 to 10 minutes at ordinary laboratory temperatures.

The *first maturation division* occurs at thetime.of ovulation. The heterotypic chromosomes are placed on the spindle of the amphiaster whose axis is at right angles to the ovum surface. Movement of the chromosomes is identical with that found in ordinary mitosis. The outermost group of telophase chromosome are pinched off, with a small amount of cytoplasm and no yolk, to comprise the *first polar body.* The innermost telophasic group of chromosomes remain within a clear area of the ovum as the nuclear mass of the secondary oocytc. These changes occur as the ovum leaves the ovary and before it reaches the oviduct. Possibly the same forces which bring about follicular rupture also influence this maturation process.

The *second maturation division* begins without any intermediate rest period for the chromosomes, at about the time the ovum enters the oviduct. There may be a variation in time up to 2 hours for ova to reach the ostium; depending upon the region the body cavity into which they are liberated. Thus the stage of maturation of different ova within the oviduct may vary considerably. There is a longitudinal division of the chromosomes of the ovum which are lined up in metaphase on the *second maturation spindle,* the axis of which is at right angles to the ovum surface. Since the spindle is primarily protoplasmic, and is made up in part of fibers the space occupied by the spindle will be free of yolk. Since it is peripherally placed, and represents a slight inner movement after the elimination of the first polar body, the surface layer of the ovum is slightly de-pigmented just above the spindle region. This situation is exaggerated in aged ova a relatively large depigmented area of the cortex appearing toward the center of the animal hemisphere.

Maturation is not completed until or unless the ovum is activated by sperm or stimulated by parthenogenetic means. However, every ovum reaching the uterus is in methaphase of the second' maturation division, awaiting the stimulus of activation to complete the elimination of the *second polar body.*

2

Breeding Behaviour

It is in spring that the average person is most conscious of the amphibian. The Spring Peeper, *Hyla crucifer,* is considered by many to be more reliable harbinger of warm weather than is the robin. One old saying is that there will be but three more freeze-ups after the peepers are heard calling. This is akin to the superstition that if a ground hog sees his shadow on the second of February, there will be six more weeks of winter. Though the peepers are weather prophets far superior to our finest meteorologists, unfortunately they are not so expert that they can forecast just how many more frosts will occur before it is safe to set out the tomato plants.

A great many amphibians breed in the spring, but by no means all of them do. Some breed in the summer, some in the fall, some in the winter. However, in the North we are most apt to notice the breeding activity in the spring. Spring must be interpreted very loosely, for sometimes the peepers and Wood Frogs are calling before March 21st even as far north as New England. The nights are often cold and frosty, and you may wonder why **these** little creatures have come out of hibernation so early.

We do not begin to recognize all the conditions that cause the amphibians to emerge from hibernation and to commence courtship and mating, any more than we understand all the reasons behind bird migration. But though there is much to be learned on this subject, it is interesting helpful to discuss a few of the factors that have an important bearing on the matter.

The prime factor governing the amphibian's emergence form hibernation is the weather. If the ground is frozen solid, the animal hibernating beneath the frost line would not be able to break through the frozen crust, even should he so desire, which he does not. For those that hibernate in the detritus of pond bottoms, ice on top prevents their escape. But the amphibian is a cold-blooded creature, whose internal temperature is nearly the same as his external surroundings, and very cold surroundings make him sluggish and incapable of the violent movement necessary to burrow out of hibernation. Therefore, until the temperature of the earth or pond water rises to a certain level, the amphibian remains in the dormant condition known as hibernation, where heartbeat and respiration are slowed to the minimum.

All amphibians are extremely sensitive to temperature changes, and notice the slightest gradations that are imperceptible to us. Furthermore, each amphibian has a temperature at which he must live for optimum comfort and activity. This varies from species to species, and helps to explain why the Spring Peeper emerges form hibernation and begins to breed earlier than the toad.

The temperature of the water is important not only because it must be warm enough to arouse those sleeping beneath it to activity but also because it must be warm enough so that *any* eggs laid *in* it will not be frozen and killed.

Humidity also plays a tremendous part in determining courtship and mating time. You will always find that the peak of breeding activities in all species occurs on evenings of high humidity - the choruses of peepers, toads, treefrogs, and frogs are at their loudest on rainy overcast days and especially nights. Naturally, the humidity of the air has more influence on those amphibians who are more terrestrial than on those who are partially or completely aquatic. But it affects them all to some extent. Perhaps there is considerable truth in the fisherman's adage that fish bite better on a rainy or dull day. Certainly it would be true if one fished for amphibians.

The weather does not, of course, completely govern courtship and mating. It is also regulated by the animal's ductless glands-especially the anterior lobe of the pituitary gland. The secretions of this gland stimulate the sexual glands, which in turn rouse the animal to mate.

We usually think of ponds and lakes as being the place where amphibians congregate to mate and lay their eggs. It is true that the great majority of all amphibians do deposit their eggs in water. The salamanders may choose a quiet pond, as do the Newt and many Mole Salamanders. They may prefer the swift-running water of a brook, as do many Lungless Salamanders. Or they may select a moist place in the woods or in the mud. Doubtless, this dry-land laying is a surprise to many. And no wonder, for it is far more difficult to find a few eggs under a stone or log in the woods than it is to *see* the thousands upon thousands clustered in various parts of the pond. It may be even more of a surprise to learn that some salamanders lay their eggs in trees.

Frogs and toads lay, in much the same places as do the salamanders. There are pond layers, river layers, and even tree layers, though none of our native frogs lays in trees. With the frogs and toads, courtship is always conducted very close to the place where mating and egg laying will occur. How do they court one another? Let us take a specific example, the Spring Peeper.

The peepers hibernate in the woods, beneath the earth. When the ground becomes thawed, they emerge from their winter burrows and head for ponds and swamps. On dull afternoons and in the evenings, the male sits on the bank of the pond and utters his sweet birdlike call. He takes air into his lungs and closes his mouth and nostrils. He sends the air into the vocal sacs located in the throat region. They balloon out into a glistening bubble that is almost as large as the body of the peeper. The air is sent back and forth between lungs and vocal sacs, causing the vocal chords to vibrate. An enormous sound for so small a creature emerges: *Preep, peep, peep* ... he sings sweetly. Other males join in, and soon there is a deafening chorus of peepers all calling to the females. A female approaches one of the singing males. She is silent, for only the males sing in the breeding season. But the male senses her approach. He turns toward her, climbs on her back, and embraces her, placing his arms just behind hers in her "armpits." The couple are now ready to enter the pond and lay the eggs. Courtship in frogs and toads consists mainly of the male's calls. The female approaches the calling male. He may be so intent on his singing that she may even have to touch him to make him aware of her. Female toads frequently nudge males, though in other species of frogs and toads, movement in the vicinity of a calling male is sufficient to make the male cease his calling and turn to embrace the moving object.

Since the peak of the breeding activities are carried out at night, sight plays no part in the recognition of a mate. Sound and hearing and feeling are the things that count. The females are guided to the males by their calls. The males hear or feel a nearby female. "But," you may ask quite reasonably, "how do the males know they are embracing a female and not another male? And how can they be sure that they have a mate of their own species, and not a female of another species, if they cannot see her?

First of all, the males distinguish the females by their silence. Should a male embrace another male—and this happens quite frequently - the male who is thus treated squeaks or croaks in protest, and struggles to free himself or such unwanted attentions. The female, however, is completely silent during the breeding season. Some female frogs can call at other times of the year, but when the breeding season comes they are mute.

Second, different species breed at different times. They are not all in or around the ponds at once. However, there are several separate species there at the same time. The males of like species tend to congregate in groups apart from others. Since each species has its own distinct song, the females naturally go toward the sound of their own kind calling.

Should the male embrace a female of a different species, however, he can tell by feel that she is not of his own kind. She must be the correct size - larger than he, and swollen with unlaid eggs, but not so large that she is of a different species. The way she moves when he embraces her may also tell him whether or not she is of his own kind.

It sometimes happens, however, that mistakes are made in the excitement of the moment. Toads, whose nuptial embrace is strong, have been known to grasp a fish and not let go until the fish was crushed to death. This is rare, but it is probably due to the fact that there weren't enough females to go around and that the urge to reproduce was so strong that the male seized the first object that nudged him.

About the only romantic part of the courtship of frogs and toads from a human standpoint are their songs. These may be as sweet as are the calls of birds, and many people mistake the trill of the American Toad and some of the treefrogs for birds. They may be plaintive, as is the lamblike bleating of the Narrowmouth Toad. They may be insectlike, as are the calls of the Cricket Frogs. They may be squirrel-like, or like the noise of riveters; they may sound like a banjo, like a snore, or like a foghorn. It all depends upon the species, and there is but one male frog in all the world that, so far as we know, lacks a voice with which to call to his mate. This curious exception; which we shall discuss more fully later, is the Tailed Frog, *Ascapus truei,* found in parts of the northwestern United States.

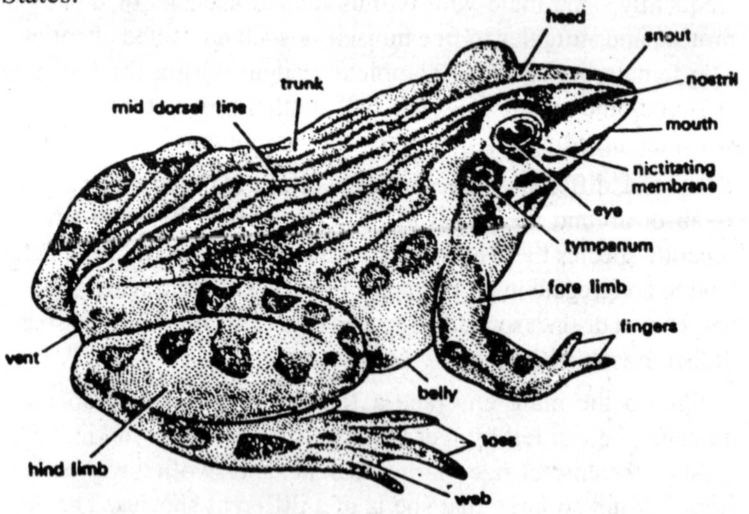

Figure 2.1: Rana tigrana.

When we look at courtship in the salamanders, we perceive an altogether different picture. In the first place, because the salamanders lack vocal chords they are silent. Not for them are the pleasures of serenading a lady love on a warm humid night. Neither have they any ears; they "hear" through their front legs or, in certain aquatic species, the lower jaw, which are especially adapted to receive vibrations from the ground. So even if the males could sing, neither the singer nor the one sung to could hear the sounds. *They* are like the frogs and toads in that sight plays no part in the recognition of a mate. How then do. the salamanders find their mates, and recognize them? So far as we know, scent is the main factor in recognition of sex and species. Females and males smell differently, and each species evidently has its own distinctive fragrance. We humans with our dull sense of smell cannot detect most of the odorus that attract the salamanders to one another. The salamanders have their own built-in perfume factories. The hedonic glands, as these "factories" are aptly named, are located mainly at the base of the tail and on the underside of the head on the males. Though the females lack any readily differentiated glands, their skin secretions evidently possess the odour that enables the males readily to identify them as to species and sex.

But once a salamander finds a mate, he does not embrace her as do the frogs and toads. The salamander has more finesse, and carries on a real courtship, for a very good reason. The courting varies with the species, of course. But in general he rubs his chin against her head so that she may smell his perfume. He caresses her with his tail, and he may even invite her to dance if that is the accepted thing with his particular species. The dance may consist of his transporting her on his back, or of many other "engaged" couples joining together and making various figure eights around each other. In certain species the female may straddle the male's tail, placing her head on the base of the tail, and the two will then waddle off together in this position. It is the male's object to make himself irresistible to the female, and to excite her so that mating may take place.

In most salamanders the eggs are fertilized internally, but internal fertilization is accomplished in a manner far different from that employed by mammals. When the male salamander feels that the female is sufficiently excited, he deposits, either on land or in the water, according to the habits of his species, a small jelly-covered package. This is known as the spermatophore, and each one contains the male's sperm. Next, the female comes and picks up one of these spermatophores with the lips of her cloaca, and it is placed inside her body in a special receptacle, known as the spermatheca, where the sperm remains to fertilize the eggs before they are laid.

The salamander has such an elaborate courtship because if he did not put the female in a receptive frame of mind, she might not pick up the spermatophore. There is nothing to force her to do so. In order that the eggs may be fertilized, the males must court the females.

Many species of salamanders lay their eggs a day or two after they have picked up the spermatophore. But there are others that delay. The Mudpuppy, *Necturus maculosus maculosus,* generally mates in the fall, but does not lay her eggs until the following May or June. The same is true of the Red-backed Salamander, *Plethodon cinereus cinereus, a* terrestrial species.

As we pointed out, most salamanders fertilize the eggs internally. However, there are a few exceptions. In this country there are two families of salamanders that fertilize the eggs externally. The first of these families is the Hellbenders, or Cryptobranchidae. They are completely aquatic salamanders. The male digs out a large nest in the water under a rock. The females enter, and as they lay their eggs the male sheds his sperm over them.

The other family of salamanders, the Sirens, or Sirenidae, so far as is known, fertilizes its eggs externally also. All anatomical evidence points to this conclusion. However, no one has yet observed the Siren breeding. It may seem amazing that no one has yet seen and accurately described these vital statistics of an animal found, not in darkest Africa, but in the United States. On the other hand, anyone who has ever tried to observe animals in the wild will realize how long it takes to obtain data on even the most inconsequential phase of their life cycles.

Mating in frogs and toads is an different matter altogether. Most frogs and toads fertilize their eggs externally. The male frog mounts the female, puts his arms around her, and grasps her firmly either just in back of her arms or in her groin. "Firmly" is a mild word for this nuptial embrace. If you catch a mated pair of toads. you will find it almost impossible to separate them, so tight is the male's grasp and so strong is the clasping reflex. However, it does not seem to bother the female in the least. Possibly, she enjoys this bear hug. In any case, if the pair mate on land they soon enter the water.

The female does not, however, always lay her eggs immediately. She may lay them anywhere from 3 to 26 days after pairing, the couple remaining in amplexus all during this time. What is it that governs when the eggs shall be deposited? Is it some physiological factor? Do some species require prolonged clasping in order to lay? Or does the length of time between coupling and laying depend mainly on the weather? Perhaps all of these have some bearing on the matter.

As the female lays her eggs, the male sheds his sperm on top of them. After all the eggs are laid, the female is considerably slimmer, for she may have had as many as 20,000 eggs inside her body. As soon as she no longer feels so pleasingly plum, the male releases her. Does he return to the bank and recommence his calling in the hope of attracting another female? According to one authority, frogs and toads fertilize the egg complement of but one female each year, but this may be wrong, at least for some species. It is an extremely difficult thing to prove either way.

What of the female who finds no mate? Does she lay her unfertilized eggs just the same? Evidently not. As with many unmated birds, the eggs of the female are gradually resorbed into the body. A few may emerge from the oviduct, but they are never deposited in the characteristic mass of the species as they are when the male clasps the female.

There are several outstanding and interesting exceptions to the way most frogs and toads mate. We shall discuss three of them.

The first example is the primitive aquatic Surinam Toad known as *Pipa pipa.* This large flat-bodied creature lives in the ponds of South America. The mating call is a rapid clicking. This metallic sound is not produced by air vibrating the vocal chords, as in all other frogs, but by the cartilaginous disks of two bones "cracking" as the bones are moved. In much the same manner, some people en "crack" the joints of their fingers, jaws, or knees.

Clasping before laying is prolonged, and lasts at least 24 hours and sometimes longer. During this period the skin on the female's back becomes swollen and puffy. For many years it was believed that *pipa* had a protrusile oviduct that was everted when. laying began. However, it has recently been proved that this is not true. When the couple are ready to lay, the pair roll over and, while they are in an upside-down position, three to five eggs emerge and are fertilized. The pair then right themselves. The entire roll and righting take about 11 to 14 seconds, and the pair is upside-down for about one second of this entire time. When the female is ready to lay more egg, the pair once more roll over, until, after many such turns, the entire complement of from 40 to 114 eggs are laid. The eggs are pressed into the spongy skin on the female's back by the male's ventral surfaces; the first eggs are placed near the anus, later ones successively farther forward toward the female's shoulders. One day after deposition, the eggs are half buried in the skin of the female, and by the tenth day the top membranes of the eggs are level with the skin of the back.

Our own Tailed Frog, Ascapus *truei* is voiceless. Since he does not seem to be able to hear, and since he spends most of his time in swift-running mountain streams, a voice would be of little use to him anyway. He possesses something far more valuable, namely, a tail. Actually, it is not a real tail, though it certainly looks like one. It is an organ for copulation. The male crawls along the bottom of the stream searching for a mate. When he finds a female, he embraces her and then inserts his "tail" into an extension of her cloaca, and thus her eggs are fertilized internally.

The Tailed Frog alone possesses an intromittent organ because of his habitat. External fertilization of eggs would be precarious, to say the least, in the fast-flowing water where the Tailed Frog makes his home. No sooner would the sperm be shed than the water would carry it downstream before it could possibly fertilize all the eggs of the female. So in order that the species may continue to reproduce. Nature has provided the Tailed Frog with a "tail" so that he may fertilize his eggs internally.

There are two African toads with the jawbreaking names of *Nectophrynoides vivipara* and *Nectophrynoides tornieri.* These toads also fertilize their eggs internally. But the mystifying thing in their case is how they go about it. They have no copulatory organ as has the Tailed Frog. Scientists have long been puzzled as to how the sperm is introduced into the female's body. Do they, like the female salamanders, pick up a spermatophore which the male deposits. There is no indication that they do. But scientists know that the eggs *are* fertilized internally because both species give birth to fully transformed young. The entire larval period is spent in the mother's body, and when the young are born they are miniatures of their parents. *Nectophrynoides vivipara* and *Nectophrynoides tornieri* and the only two known species of frogs and toads that are ovoviviparous, though there are several salamanders that are normally ovoviviparous and several that are occasionally so when existing conditions, such as extreme cold or high altitude, make egg laying impractical.

Let us look at some of the external differences between the sexes. With the sole exception of the Tailed Frog, these differences are secondary sex characteristics in frogs and toads. They are to a frog what a beard is to a man. With the Tailed Frog, the male is easily distinguished from the female by his longer "tail." Her "tail" is an extension of her cloaca, and is much shorter and more blunt than is his.

With the rest of the frogs and toads, we find great variety in secondary sex characteristics. About the only secondary sex characteristic that most male frogs and toads possess in common are their vocal sacs—and even here there are one or two exceptions that we shall examine in a movement. These vocal sacs are of different sizes and shapes, according to the species. Thcy may be in throat region and when in use swell out to a glistening bubble, as is true in the peepers and many toads. They may swell out in kidney-shaped masses on the side of the head, as in the Leopard Frog. Or there may be no localized swelling, but a general enlargement of the throat, as in the Bullfrog.

Vocal sacs might seem absolutely necessary to the male frog, as without them he would be unable to call to the females in the breeding season. But that is evidently not so, for some of our frogs, such as the California Toad, *Bufo boreas halophilus,* and a few others, lack vocal sacs altogether. The Tailed Frog lacks them also, but he is believed to be silent. However, the California Toad is known to have a voice - a trill, similar in character to that of our northeastern American Toad, *Bufo americanus americanus,* but lower pitched. Neither does the sound carry so well, but whether this is because of the lack of vocal sacs, as one eminent scientist believes, or because lowerpitched sounds do not seem to carry so well as those that are shrill, has not been proved.

The vocal sacs, even though they are usually present, are not very helpful to us when we pick up a frog and want to know whether or not he is a male. Unless we see his vocal sacs swelled up, we would not even know he had them. The females of some species lack vocal sacs, and in others they are greatly reduced in size. And, as we have said, the females are silent during the breeding season, though at other times of the year they may make calls similar to the males of their kind, but not so loud or so resonant.

Size is a factor in sex recognition *of* frogs and toads. The female is a general rule, larger than the male. It is just as well that she is, because she must carry him about on her back during mating and egg laying. In the . water, though the additional weight does not matter so much, the female nevertheless does the swimming for both. Many males- keep their hind legs drawn up on the female's back, while others allow their legs to float out behind. In a few species, if the couple is alarmed, the male may try to aid the female by using his feet in swimming motion, but their efficiency is impaired by his position on top of her. Many, however, like the

American Toad, make no attempt at all to help the female in her race to escape. It seems curious to us that the male refuses to release his hold on the female and that each does not go its separate way when threatened with danger. But such is not their habit. Some species separate more easily than others, but none does it voluntarily, and often it is almost impossible to force the mated pair apart without injury, so strong is the embrace of the male.

Whereas the female is usually larger in over-all size, the male may have much larger and heavier forelegs. Perhaps, he has need for powerful arms the better to grasp the female. The male toad, *Bufo boreas,* found in the Northwest and in California, has enlarged forelimbs. His are insignificant, however, compared with a South American frog. *Leptodactylus ocellatus,* whose arms are fully three times the size of those of the female!

In some species of frogs, the eardrum or tympanum, of the male is considerably larger than the eye whereas in the female it is the same size. A male Bullfrog can easily be distinguished from a female by this characteristic. Why the male should need a larger ear than the female has never ben explained. You would think that if either of them should have a larger one, it would be the female that would have most use for it. And why, of all species, should the Bullfrog, with his tremendous foghorn cry that can be heard from a distance of half mile or more, need a larger ear. The answer probably lies in the Bullfrog's evolution. At one time male perhaps did need larger ears, and though they are no larger useful they have not as yet been discarded.

In certain species of frogs and toads, the males have much larger thumbs. These may be swollen at the base or at tip. This enlargement of the thumb gives the male betterr gripping power. Does it also help to cushion the female's skin from being overly bruised by the male amphibian's strong grasp? We have never heard this suggested as a reason - it would probably be considered rank sentimentality by most scientist - but we can see no reason why it should not be so.

There is also a difference in the shape of the toe webbing of the two sexes in certain species. A male Wood Frog and be distinguished from a female in the breeding season by his convex toe webs. The female's are concave. Of course, you have to catch the frog and spread his hind toes apart in order to see this. It can't be observed from a distance.

Some reptiles and many birds present striking color dimorphism between the sexes. This is not true of frogs and toads. Colour differences, when they exist, are usually confined to the underparts, and especially the throat region. Some males have darker or more brightly coloured throats than the females of the same species.

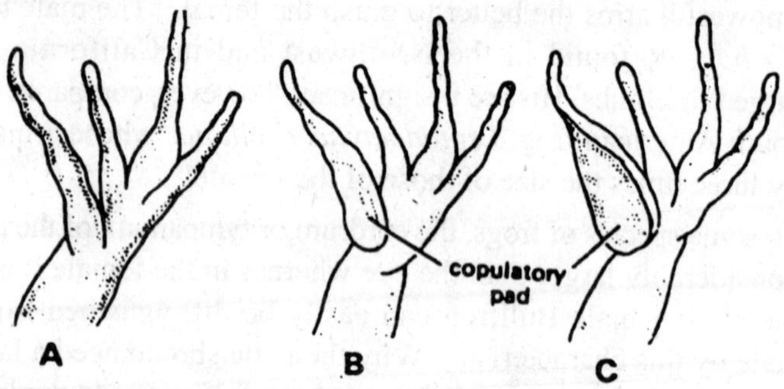

Figure 2.2 : A. Foot of frog showing web, B. Hand of male frog showing nupial or amplexusory pad.

Of all the secondary sex characteristics exhibited by the frogs and toads, none is more startling than those developed by the male Hairy Frog. *Astylosternus robust us,* of Africa. All male frogs and toads need a great deal more oxygen during the breeding season than at any other time. This is due in part to their vociferous calls, and in part to the fact that their metabolic rate is heightened. Most male frogs land toads, therefore, have larger lungs to satisfy the necessary requirements of their bodies for oxygen. But the Hairy Frog is an aquatic frog with very small lungs. Since he is a large fellow, he needs a great deal more oxygen in the breeding season than his diminutive lungs can supply. Therefore, he broadens his skin area at that time, so that he will have a greater surface through which to absorb the extra oxygen needed, by growing long "hair" on his hind legs and lower sides. Of course, they are not really hairs, any more than gills and feathers, which they resemble at times. Scientists call these "hairs" vascular villosities. Be that as it may, they look like hair and they work like gills, enabling the Hairy Frog to obtain the additional oxygen necessary during the breeding season.

All in all, the secondary sex characteristics of frogs and toads are not very useful to us in helping us to tell whether our frog is male or female. It is unfortunate, but in this case there is no short cut. In ord r to distinguish between the sexes, you must know the second sex characteristics of each species.

Fortunately, the same state of affairs does not exist in the salamanders, in the breeding season. There are the larger overall size of the females, the enlarged hind legs and or tail of the male, differences in the colours of the two sexes, and differences in the teeth. These correspond to those secondary sex characteristics in frogs and toads. But in almost all salamanders, there are differences around the vent, especially during the breeding season, though at other times these may be negligible. The male's vent is large, protuberant, and has tiny nipple-like projections. The female's vent is smooth or in folds.

Before we go on to the eggs. Let me urge you to choose a warm humid overcast night in May for an outing. Wear a pair of galoshes, take a strong flashlight, and head for the nearest pond or swamp. You should have an experience that you will not soon forget. Peepers, treefrogs, toads, and frogs will be calling from all sides. You should be able to approach them easily, for they depend mainly on sight to warm them of enemies, and at night they cannot see you. Look in the water. There you will see mated pairs, salamanders and frogs, calling under the water. You will notice species you never knew existed, and species that you rarely if ever catch a glimpses of during the day. You have read how the frogs, toads, and salamanders court and mate but there is nothing that can compare with the thrill of actually witnessing these things with your own eyes and ears. Even if you aren't a keen field naturalist, you will be amazed at all you will discover, and will be very glad that you went. Perhaps you may even be so impressed and enthusiastic that you will want to repeat the experience.

3

Amphiabian Ova

The beginning of most life is hidden from us. We are unable to see the egg being fertilized; its development from one-celled organism to an embryo of many cells is screened from our view until birth or hatching. This is true of the shelled eggs of reptiles and birds. They are fertilized within the parent's body and are then surrounded with a shell before laying. The mammalian egg is shell-less with two exceptions; but it is microscopic in size and inaccessible for observation, since it remains inside the mother's body during its development.

If we really want to find out what happens between laying and hatching we must turn to the amphibian egg. The spermatozoa of the amphibian are microscopic in size, so that we are unable to see (with the naked eye) the egg being penetrated by the sperm. But all stages after fertilization are visible to use; furthermore, most of the changes that occur can be seen without a microscope.

To begin with, the eggs are round, though they do not remain so. They may be black or brown on top. The top part is known as the animal pole; it is the section that is alive and will grow. The vegetal pole at the bottom may be white or yellow. It consists of the food on which the egg "feeds" as it develops, for you must remember that all living things; be they animals or that most miraculous of all living entities, a fertilized egg cell, must have nourishment if they are to grow. The living protoplasm of the animal pole is lighter than the non-living deutoplasm of the vegetal pole. Therefore, it always is uppermost. You can easily test this by turning an amphibian egg so that the animal pole faces down. You will notice that very little time elapses before it has rotated so that the protoplasm is again facing up. A few amphibian eggs are yellow or white, and are called unpigmented eggs. But though the separation of animal and vegetal poles is not readily visible in these, it exists nonetheless.

Because the eggs require a certain amount of insulation from shocks land enemies, as they descend through the female's oviduct they are coated with albuminous jelly. Depending upon the way the oviduct is constructed in different species, there may be one or more jelly envelopes, or envelopes surrounding the eggs may be lacking, and the mass of jelly may constitute the sole protection. You can get a clear picture of what an egg with its jelly envelope looks like if you make a small dot and draw a circle around it. The jelly may be clear, or it may be milky white or greenish.

Once the eggs are deposited in the pond, the jelly swells. The capacity of the jelly to absorb water is a decided benefit to both the layer and the egg. It means that the eggs and jelly, when inside the female amphibian, require little space. But one in contact with the water, the jelly swells to twice or three times its original bulk, giving far greater protection to the egg than would be the case if it did not enlarge. Of course, there are instances on record of frogs that delayed too long in laying their eggs. The water content of the body is absorbed by the jelly, which expands rapidly and beyond all bounds. The female then bursts open and dies. Fortunately such circumstances as these occurs seldom, and may be considered freaks of nature.

The eggs vary in size according to the species that lays them. But the size of the adult is no reliable indication of the size of the egg that will be laid. The Tailed Frog is only about 2 inches long. But it lays one of the largest eggs of all our native-frogs. Each vitellus is approximately 5 mm., or roughly 1/4 inch in diameter. Our larges frog, the Bullfrog, which may be as long as 8 inches, lays small eggs of about 1.5 mm. The smallest egg in this country is laid by the Southern Chorus Frog. *Pseudacris nigrita nigrita* and is approximately .7 mm. in diameter. Wc shall allow you to figure out the equivalent measurement in fractions of an inch. Frankly, it's beyond our mathematical ability, and we are quite content to leave egg measurements in millimeters. The average salamander lays a far larger egg than do the frogs and should you ever wish to watch the development of the amphibian egg, you would be well advised to choose those of a salamander rather than those of a Bullfrog or a toad.

The number of eggs laid also varies greatly, and generally speaking, salamanders lay fewer eggs than do frogs and toads. The Bullfrog and the American Toad lay as many as 20,000. The Rocky Mountain Toad, *Bufo woodhousei woodhousei,* produces upto 25,000 eggs, the largest complement laid by a native salientian. The Robber Frogs of the genus *Syrrhophus* may lay as few as 5 eggs but they are the exception. Most frogs and toads lay eggs in the hundreds. or thousands, while salamanders lay in the tens or a hundred. Because of the salamander's more secretive ways, larger egg size, and internal fertilization, they do not need to lay so many eggs to ensure continuance to the species as do the frogs.

The way the eggs are laid also differs with the species. The Red-spotted Newt lays each egg separately, fastening each on the leaf of a water plant and folding the leaf around it thus hiding it very effectively from enemies. The Spring Peeper also lays its eggs individually, but this species merely deposits each egg on the pond bottom. The Bullfrog and the Green Frog both lay theirs in spreading mass on the surface of the water. The Wood Frog and the Spotted Salamander lay theirs in a round or oval mass attached to submerged vegetation. The American Toad and most other toads lay theirs in two long strings of jelly. The Hellbenden that large aquatic salamander, lays its eggs in rosarylike strings, as does the Tailed Frog. The Spadefoot Toads lay their eggs in bands or cylinders. It is, of course, the jelly that gives the egg mass its shape, for the eggs themselves are round, with the exception of those of the Colorado River Toad who occasionally, though not always, lays wedgeshaped eggs. The form of the jelly is governed in part by the way the oviduct is shaped, and in part by the natural egglaying movements, which differ in the various species.

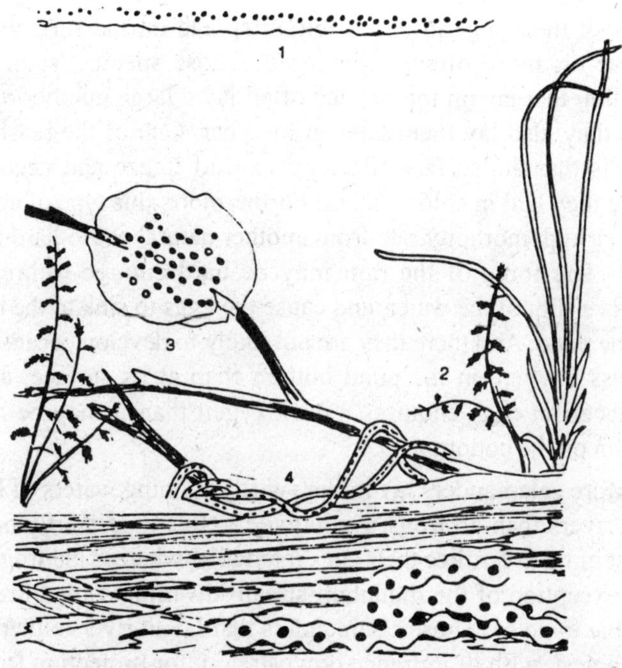

Figure 3.1 : The eggs of some amphibians: 1. The surface mass of the Bullfrog. 2. eggs of the Red-spotted Newt laid individually among plant leaves. 3. The submerged egg mass of the Spotted Salamander. 4. The egg complement in strings laid by the American toad. 5. Eggs in rosary-like strings deposited by the Hellbender.

Eggs of amphibians are identified one from another by their colour, size, number of jelly envelopes, if any; shape of the eggs mass, total complement of eggs, and the places in which they are laid. All of this sounds complicated as do most things scientific at first glance. However, it is not so formidable as it seems, and if you are one who enjoys finding out just exactly what species of amphibian has laid those eggs in the southeast corner of your pond, do not be overawed. Consult one of the two handbooks listed in the Bibliography, and forge ahead. You may not find that you can identify every egg that you discover with complete scientific accuracy, but you will be able to identify most, and make a well-informed guess about the others.

The eggs are laid in many places. A large majority amphibians deposit their eggs in ponds, either spread on the surface of the water or, more often, submerged. Those species, such as the Bulling that lay on the surface often lay a large number of eggs, and they also lay them later in the year. One of the reasons for this is that the surface-film eggs would freeze and decompose were they laid in cold weather. Furthermore, this type of eggs has *a very* high mortality rate from another natural cause-hard pelting rain. The force of the rain may be hard enough to break the surface film of the water, and cause the eggs to sink to the bottom of the pond. And there they are not likely to develop because there is less oxygen on the pond bottom than at its surface, and the surfacefilm eggs enquires more oxygen than it may be able to obtain on the bottom.

More salamanders lay in the swiftly running waters of brooks and rivers than do frogs. Undoubtedly, this is primarily because most of them fertilize their eggs internally, whereas the frogs, with the exception of the mountain-stream-dwelling Tailed Frog, are unable to do so. Those salamanders that lay in rivers either scoop out a nest, with its entrance downstream, for protection from the onslaught of the cascading waters, or they attach their eggs, either singly or in a mass, to the underside of a rock.

In many parts of this country, permanent bodies of water are non-existent. Where this situation occurs, you might think that there would be no water-laying amphibians. But amphibians such as the Spadefoots, the Narrow-mouths, and some of the toads must lay in shallow water, and in dry regions they lay in mud puddles that are formed from a rain that may not recur for a year or more. Naturally, the eggs hatch rapidly, and the tadpoles are transformed in a short time into adults.

The habit of laying in the shallow water of mud puddles and syamps is not, however, confined to arid regions. None of our north-eastern toads will deposit their eggs in deep water even though it is available. If you wish to find toad's eggs, the best place to look is a swamp or a mud puddle. We have even found toad's eggs laid in a large mud puddle in the middle of a road. Lacking swamps in your vicinity, go to a small pond. Search around its shallowest edges, for it is there that you will find the toad's strings of jelly.

Very few people who do not make a study of amphibians are aware that some of them deposit their eggs on moist or dry land. This is not particularly surprising, for the chances of finding these land-laid eggs just by accident are slim, hidden as most of them are beneath rocks or logs. As a matter of fact, diligent hunting is generally required to locate them **even** if you know the most likely spots to search. There are quite a few native salamanders who lay on land. The Marbled Salamander, *Ambystoma opacum,* lays in a moist spot near the water, as does the Dusky Salamander, *Desmognathus fuscus.* The Red-backed Salamander, *Plethodon cinereus, is* woodland salamander, and it lays its eggs in cavities or rotted logs. For some reason the Amphiuma, *Amphiuma means,* though it is an aquatic salamander, also lays its eggs in muddy spots on land. There are many reasons for normally terrestrial amphibians to lay on land, but why a salamander that spends its life in the water should do so is a mystery.

As to frogs, there are fewer of them, and most of them are not so common as the land-laying salamanders. The landlaying frogs in this country are confined to "several species within one family, the Robber Frogs, or Leptodactylidae, of which we will say more in a subsequent chapter.

We have but one native species of amphibian that deposits its eggs in trees. This is the Oak Salamander, *Aneides lugubris lugubris,* of California. It occasionally lays on the ground, but just as frequently lays in trees.

None of our native frogs lays in trees, but there are many foreign frogs that do. All the treefrogs of the family Hylidae that live on the island of Jamaica lay in trees. Perhaps this habit arose because there are very few natural ponds and lakes in Jamaica. The.type of vegetation found in Jamaica and parts of South America favoured its development. The Jamaican hylas all deposit their eggs in bromeliads. Bromeliads are relatives of the pineapple, but, unlike it, thcy are epiphytic; that is, they attach themselves to trees and obtain their sustenance from the air through specially modified aerial roots. The bromeliad leaves from a rosette, just as do those of the pineapple. In the very center of the rosette is a hollow that generally holds a considerable amount of water. It is here that the Jamaican hylas place their eggs, and the tadpoles develop in this water. Even in the driest of seasons, the bromeliad has a store of water in the center of its leaves.

Other foreign frogs, such as the treefrogs of the family Rhacophoridae, found in Asia, deposit their eggs in trees overhanging pools, and upon hatching, the tadpoles fall into the water below and carry on their larval life there. In order to protect the eggs from drying out, the mother first deposits some albuminous jelly without any eggs. This is whipped into a frothy mass by the hind legs of one or both parents until it is as full of air as beaten eggs whites. The jelly-covered eggs are then placed on top and are covered by an additional layer of jelly which is also well beaten. The outside of this nest soon hardens, while the inside liquefies, providing the eggs with a suitable medium in which to develop.

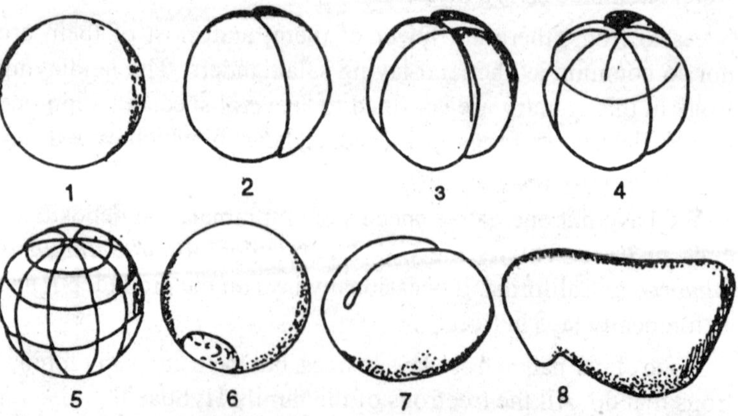

Figure 3.2 : A few stages in the development of a frog's egg: 1. The unsegmented egg. 2. The two-called stage. 3. The four-celled stage. 4. The eight-celled stage, showing the beginnings of cleavage into the sixteen-called stage. 5. The blastula, or many-called stage. 6. The yolk-plug stage. 7. The neuralgroove stage. 8. The embryo.

The changes in the amphibian eggs from the moment it is laid and fertilized to the time it hatches are fascinating to watch. This is how most life begins and develops, from the mammal down to the lowly earthworm. If you go to the nearest pond and collect the largest eggs that you can find, you may watch the entire process with the naked *eye* or with an inexpensive magnifying glass. Suffice it to say here that the eggs changes - divides from one into many cells - lengthens out, and develops, and finally the tadpole or larva wriggles its way out of the confining jelly and hatches. The length of time between laying and hatching varies with the species and the temperature. It may be as short a time as 36 or 58 hours, as in some toads, or as long as 3 or 4 months in some salamanders. In general, salamander eggs are slower in hatching than are those of the frogs and toads.

By and large, amphibians lay their eggs and then desert them, devoting little thought as to the possible fate of the eggs. However, there are many exceptions to this rule, and some of them, especially the foreign ones, are most interesting.

Our first exception is the male Hellbender, native to this county, who, as we mentioned earlier, scoops out a nest on the river bottom, and welcomes the females as they enter to deposit their rosary-like strings. The male is a most faithful father, for he remains with the eggs, guarding the opening of the nest against all intruders, until the eggs hatch out 2½ or 3 months later, while the female goes her own way, her responsibility ended.

The female Three-toed Amphiuma, *Amphiuma means tridactylum,* who lays in the mud, remains with her eggs until they hatch. One wonders why the other subspecies, *Amphiuma means means,* who also lays in the mud, does not remain with hers.

This habit of one or both parents remaining with the eggs laid on land is quite common. We find it true of the Marbled Salamander, the Dusky Salamander, the Oak Salamander, and the Redbacked Salamander. When this habit exists, you may be sure it is necessary, not so much for the protection of the eggs from enemies as from desiccation. The damp body of the parent helps in no small measure to keep the eggs themselves moist. It has also been suggested that the skin secretions and cloacal excretions and / or secretions of the parents may serve as a deterrent to any fungus growths that might destroy the eggs capsule and egg.

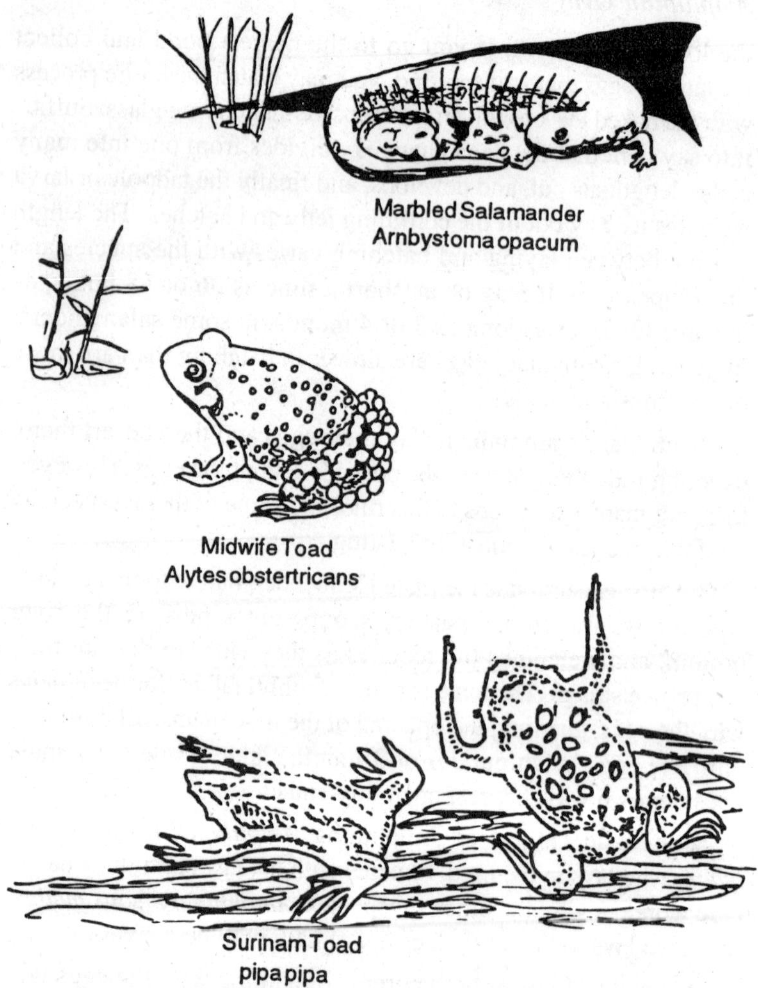

Figure 3.3 : Care of the eggs by some amphibian parents.

Recent research indicates, however, that mold develops only on dead eggs or embryos. The role that skin and cloacal secretions and the brooding habit play in increasing the number of young which survive has not been fully explained to date.

When we come to the foreign species who care for their eggs, we see all manner of strange sights. The male Midwife Toad, *Alytes obstetricans,* found in western Europe, is tied down by his parental duties. The female lays her jelly-covered eggs in long strings; the male then takes these, wraps them around his hind legs, and retires to a damp cavity. Here he remains during the day, coming out at night to bathe the eggs in dew or in a nearby pond. When the tadpoles are ready to emerge, the male goes to the water and the tadpoles hatch One wonders how the male is able to get around at all without crushing the eggs. Perhaps a large number are destroyed, though we have never read anything to indicate it. But whether or not a large percentage of the eggs develop, Nature has amply provided for the survival of the Midwife Toad, for the female lays not once or twice annually, as do most amphibians, but three or four times each year. The male must be quite adept at carrying his burden of eggs, since he obviously gets plenty of practice.

But if you think the Midwife Toad is badly off, you have never heard of *Rhinoderma darwinii,* and others of the genus *Rhinoderma.* The males carry the eggs and tadpoles until they are transformed into fully developed frogs in their mouthsor, properly speaking, in their vocal sacs, which are necessarily quite large and elastic.

Figure 3.4 : X-ray views of two South American amphibians to show the position of the developing embryos and eggs.

In the general *Phyllobates* and *Dendrobates,* found in South America, the male again cares for the young. In his case, he builds a mud dam to trap water for a suitable site for egg laying. Should this artificially made pool dry up before the tadpoles are transformed, their father takes them for a pickaback ride to a nearby stream where they can complete their development. They, in turn, have special suctorial lips with which they can fasten themselves firmly to his back so that they will not be dislodged on the overland journey. Naturally, if they should fall off their life is soon ended, for though they are able to withstand short trips out of water, they are unable, while tadpoles, to live away from an aquatic medium for any extended period.

4

Early Development

An understanding of amphibian development is fundamental to the interpretation of chick and mammal development. Amphibian eggs are easily obtained and may be studied in the laboratory from the moment of fertilization onward. This is not so easily true of the higher vertebrates. The amphibian embryos, also, are relatively straight, not coiled. This makes description easier. Frog eggs are generally used, having been either collected in freshwater ponds in the early spring or obtained by means of induced ovulation at other seasons of the year. Some of the tailed amphibians, however, have eggs which are more satisfactory for observation and experiment than frog eggs, although they are less readily provided. Both frog and salamander eggs are considered in this chapter.

THE DEVELOPMENT OF THE OOCYTE IN THE OVARY

The pre-embryonic development of the eggs of a frog or salamander is a slow process. It requires three seasons during which time it passes through three phases: multiplication, growth, and retention.

Multiplication of Oogonia

During the first or multiplication phase, the oogonia divide several times by mitosis and give rise to "nests" of cells in the wall of the ovary. The nests lie in mesenchyme, sandwiched between the outside epithelium of the ovary (peritoneum) and the inner epithelium which lines the cavity of the ovary. (Birds and mammals do not have an ovarian cavity.) The oogonia are small (about 20 μ in diameter) and scarcely to be distinguished from the spermatogonia of the male.

Meiosis and Growth

When the time comes for meiosis to begin, some of the oogonia move apart and begin to be surrounded by an envelope of follicle cells. This takes place in the tadpole and annually thereafter in the case of older frogs. As the oogonium becomes an oocyte, its chromosomes elongate into threads (leptotene stage) and come together in pairs (synaptene stage). In some amphibians the clusters of chromosomes appear as "bouquets" with their ends all turned toward one pole of the cell.

The second phase involves a process which is unique to oogenesis. Instead of contracting and remaining contracted (as they do in spermatogenesis), the chromosomes expand and develop a fuzzy appearance (diplotene stage). What actually happens is that the chromosomes lengthen greatly and develop pairs of lateral loops, so that each chromosome has the appearance of an old-fashioned lampbrush. The oocytes remain at this stage (diplotene) for more than a year, during which time they grow tremendously. What is the meaning of the lateral loops? The presence of RNA and protein around them indicates clearly that they are an adaptation to facilitate transcription and synthesis.

During this phase the nucleus of the oocyte enlarges mostly by accumulating liquid (nuclear sap). No doubt the liquid is a "pool" rich in nucleotides, amino acids, and other substances used in synthesis. In its inflated condition it is known as *a germinal vesicle.* Nucleoli increase in number within the nucleus and come to lie next the nuclear membrane. Some of them have been observed to burst through the nuclear membrane and discharge their contents into the surrounding cytoplasm. At the same time rRNA is synthesized and ribosomes increase in the cytoplasm, so that the oocyte cytoplasm comes to stain darkly with basic dyes. (It is of interest that these ribosomes of the oocyte are conserved and continue to serve the developing embryo at least until the tail-bud stage.)

Mitochondria also increase in the oocyte cytoplasm. At first they form a "cloud" in the region of the centrioles. Then they scatter and move closer to the periphery. Vesicles appear in the cytoplasm, possibly having derived from the Golgi complex.

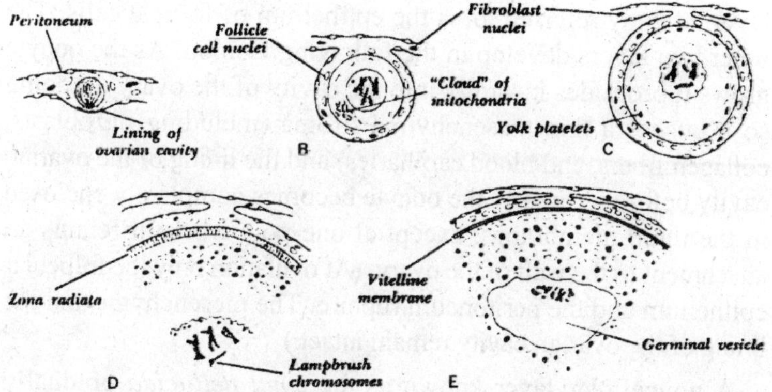

Figure 4.1 : Diagram of oogenesis in amphibians. A. Leptotene and synaptene stages of oocyte, showing the "bouquet" of chromosomes. × 220. B to D. Diplotene stages, showing lampbrush chromosomes. × 130, × 65, and × 65, respectively. E. Diakinesis. × 44. The cytoplasm of the oocyte is stippled; that of other cells is not shown.

Yolk granules (platelets) are not present in the cytoplasm until about the middle of the second summer. By this time the oocyte is about 350 μ in diameter. At first they are located close to the plasma membrane; but as they increase in number they encroach nearer to the nucleus until finally, when the growth of the oocyte is complete, they are present throughout the cytoplasm.

Where do the several proteins and lipoproteins that constitute yolk come from? Radiotracer experiments and experiments using immunological techniques have made it clear that most of them are synthesized in the liver. They circulate in the blood, penetrate past the follicle cells-possibly with their help-and are deposited as organized platelets in the oocyte cytoplasm.The mitochondria and Golgi bodies have something to do with the production of the platelets, but the details are not entirely clear.

The yolk platelets are large and densely packed in the vegetal hemisphere of the oocyte. They are smaller and less consolidated in the animal hemisphere, especially in the region of the nucleus.

A thin layer of dark pigment is laid down in somewhat similar fashion beneath the plasma membrane of the animal hemisphere.

The Envelopes of the Oocyte

Three layers of cells enclose the oocyte in the ovary. The inner layer, already referred to, is the epithelium of follicle cells. The other two layers develop in the following fashion: As the oocyte grows it protrudes inwardly into the cavity of the ovary. In doing so it pushes a thin mesenchymal stroma (including fibroblasts, collagen fibers, and blood capillaries) and the lining of the ovarian cavity before it. Finally the oocyte becomes completely enclosed in the three membranes, except at one pole where it retains an attachment to the wall of the ovary. (At ovulation only the follicular epithelium and the peritoneum rupture. The mesenchyme and the lining of the ovarian cavity remain intact.)

A noncellular layer known as the *zona pellucida* gradually forms between the follicle cells and the plasma membrane of the oocyte. Microvilli grow into it from both the follicle cells and the oocyte, giving it a crossstriated appearance when seen in section.

Hence it is also called the zona radiata. The interdigitating villi presumably facilitate the transfer of nutrients to the growing egg. As the oocyte attains its full size (1,500 to 2,000 μ) the villi are withdrawn, but the zona pellucida remains as the *vitelline membrane* which supports and protects the egg.

Retention in the Ovary

The oocyte reaches its full growth toward the end of the second season, but it is not immediately laid. The third phase, therefore, is one of quiescent retention in the ovary until the next breeding season. Then, sensitized by hormones of the pituitary and stimulated by the clasp of the male, the ova erupt through the peritoneum and enter the body cavity. This is *ovulation.* It is accompanied by the dissolution of the germinal vesicle and the spreading of its liquid contents across the animal hemisphere. The first meiotic spindle forms, and the first polar body is given off. As the egg enters the oviduct, a second meiotic spindle forms, and the second meiotic division progresses as far as the metaphasc. At this stage it pauses, and no further progress is made until and unless the ovum is fertilized.

Laying is a reflex act which is brought about in part by the clasping of the male. Ovulation and then laying can be stimulated artificially in the frog any time from autumn until spring by injecting a pituitary substance into the abdomen of the female and then, two days later applying gentle pressure to her body.

THE NEWLY LAID EGG

Each amphibian egg, as it comes from the cloaca of the female, is a single cell ¾ to 3 mm in diameter. It is surrounded by the vitelline membrane and by several layers of adhesive jelly which were added as it passed through the oviduct. In some species the eggs are laid singly, but in most cases they adhere together in clusters. On reaching water, the jelly layers swell and lose much of their stickiness. The outer layer of jelly becomes firmer, especially in salamanders, while the inner layer remains more fluid.

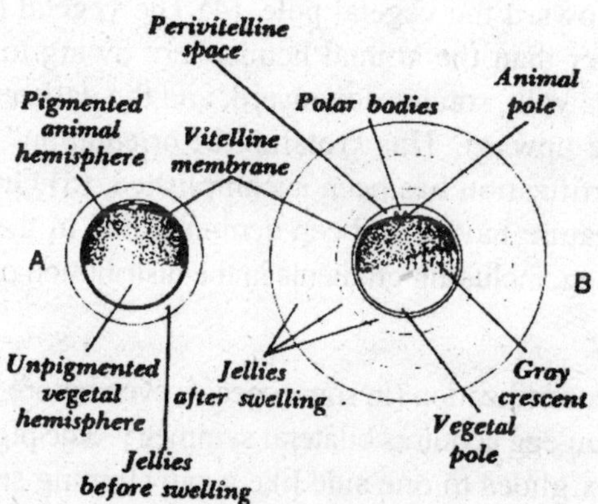

Figure 4.2 : An amphibian egg before and after laying. A. Before laying. B. After laying and fertilization. Seen from the left side. Approximately × 3½.

The eggs of amphihiana are fertilize at the time they are raid. In frogs the male clasps the female (amplexus) and sheds a suspension of sperm over tale eggs as they leave her cloaca. In some tailed amphibians, packets of sperm (spermatophores) are deposited by the male on the bottom of a pond and are picked up by the female and placed in her cloaca. In other tailed amphibians, the male deposits the spermatophores directly in the cloaca of the female In either case., the eggs are fertilized as they pass through the cloaca. Following fertilization, the vitelline membrane (now called the fertilization membrane) rises off the surface of the egg, and the egg becomes free to rotate within its membranes.

The eggs of amphibians are spherical cells quite abundantly supplied with yolk. Some of them are so soft that they would flatten under the influence of gravity if it were not for the support they receive from the vitelline membrane.

Polarity

The amphibian egg shows polarity in several ways: (1) The yolk granules are fewer and smaller in the animal hemisphere and are larger and more packed together in the vegetal region. (2) The nucleus is located nearer the animal pole, and it is here that the polar bodies are given off. (3) A thin cortical layer containing dark pigment granules covers the animal hemisphere and extends downward toward the vegetal pole. (4) The vegetal hemisphere, being heavier than the animal hemisphere owing to the greater density of its yolk, rotates downward, and the darker hemisphere comes to be upward. This "rotation of orientation" serves as a sign that fertilization has been accomplished. (5) Gradients of a chemical 'nature have also been demonstrated in the newly laid amphibian egg, including gradients in the distribution of ribosomes.

Bilaterality

Soon after fertilization (in some species even before fertilization) the amphibian egg acquires bilateral symmetry. The pigmented part of the cortex glides to one side like a cap slipping sidewise on a head. Most commonly it glides to the side on which the sperm entered.

By so doing it uncovers an area of yolk-rich cytoplasm on the opposite side of the egg. Because of its color in the frog's egg, this area is known as the *gray crescent*. It appears, however, as a clear or gleaming crescent in tailed amphibians. Vertical streaks of pigment, torn from the edge of the retreating dark cortex, are sometimes seen strewn across it.

This shift of the pigmented cortex has been called the "rotation of symmetrization," although the inner cytoplasm does not rotate at all. The gray crescent is important because it is the first visible indication of the side which will become the dorsal side of the embryo. The meridian of the egg, which passes through the animal and vegetal poles and the center of the gray crescent, is destined to become the mid-dorsal line of the embryo.

Other influences besides the entrancc of the sperm are capable of affecting the localization of the dorsal side of the embryo, but they are effective only if they act before the eight-cell stage. For example, tilting the egg or compressing it mayy cause the heavier yolk to become rearranged within. In effect, any region, even the ventral side, where white yolk becomes uncovered by the retreat of the pigmented cortex so that it comes to be close to the surface of the egg, can become functionally a gray crescent and give rise to the dorsal side of an embryo. After the eight-cell stage, however, the dorsal side is stabilized and is no longer subject to environmental influences. The ventral side, on the other hand, is still labile. Curtis has found that if a bit of the cortex of the region of the gray crescent (after it is determined) is transplanted to the ventral side of another egg, it will cause dorsal, organs to develop on the ventral side.

Numerous experiments have been performed in which amphibian eggs have been pinched in two, or parts have-$en removed. In general, it has been found thaj any major part of the egg which contains material of the gray crescent has the capacity to develop into a whole embryo of reduced size. One of the first to demonstrate this was Hans Spemann. In 1901 he separated the first two blastomeres of a salamander egg from each other with a hair noose between them. If, as usually happens, the first cleavage plane passed through the gray crescent, then both blastomeres became whole embryos of half size. It is of interest that in this case the embryo which is derived from the right blastomere often showed reversed asymmetry of its heart and viscera. If the first cleavage planc did not pass through the gray crescent, then only the blastomere which received gray crescent material became a whole embryo. The other blastomere became a "belly piece" without dorsal parts of any sort -no neural tube, no notochord, no somites. A similar experiment of Spemann's (1928) in which the noose partially divided an uncleaved egg into halves. The half which at first lacked a nucleus was later supplied when a descendent nucleus migrated across the narrow isthmus of cytoplasm and underwent cell division. The fates of the halves depended upon the materials of the cytoplasm which they possessed, and not upon the source of their nuclei.

The opposite experiment was performed by Mangold and Seidel (1927). They took eggs at the two-cell stage and, after removing the vitelline membrane, placed them on top of each other crosswise. The eggs united and developed as one. If the *gray* crescents of the two eggs were joined together, then a giant embryo of twice the normal size developed. If, however, the gray crescent materials were not adjacent, then double or even triple monsters resulted.

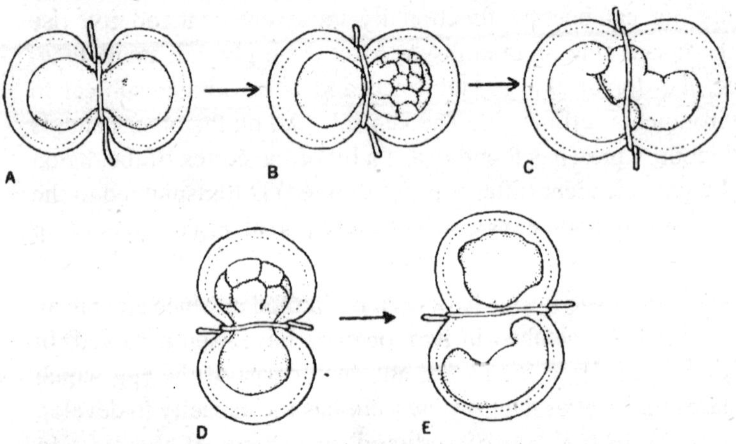

Figure 4.3 : Spemann's experiment in which he partially constricted an uncleaved egg with a hair noose. One of the descendent nuclei crossed the isthmus of cytoplasm, and cleavage became complete on both sides. A to C. When the hair noose passed through gray crescent material, both sides developed as whole embryos of half size. D to E. When one side lacked gray crescent material, it developed into a "belly piece."

The cytoplasm of an amphibian egg contains DNA-enough, so it is said, to supply 5,000 or more nuclei. Apparently, this DNA is inactive during cleavage and is not mobilized until the yolk platelets are digested. Presumably, it has no genetic significance but is nutrient in function, serving as a source of precursors for the DNA and RNA needed later in development.

CLEAVAGE

In amphibians, the first plane of cleavage is meridional; it passes through the animal and vegetal poles. Usually, it passes through the center of the gray crescent. The early experimentalists were misled, however, when they supposed that the first cleavage was a means of separating the potentialities of the right side from the left, for it does not always pass through the center of the crescent.

The first cleavage begins as a shallow furrow at the animal pole and progresses gradually through and around the egg until it reaches the vegetal pole. Normally, it divides the egg into two blastomeres of approximately equal size.

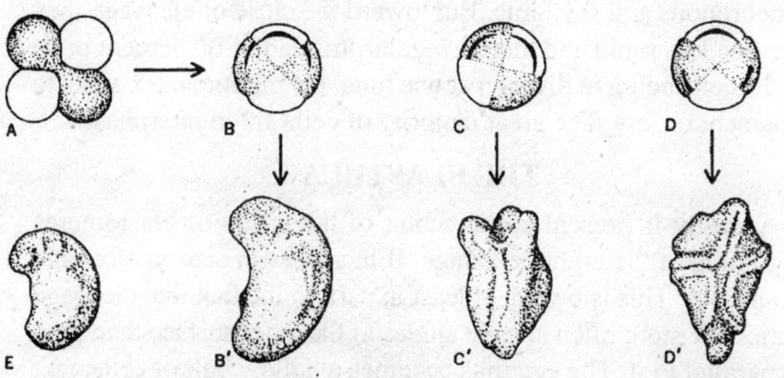

Figure 4.4 : Mangold and Seidel's experiment in which two eggs at the two-cell stage (the vitelline membranes having been removed) were laid crosswise of each other. One egg had been vitally stained with Nile blue sulfate to distinguish it. A. The experiment. B and B'. Giant embryos were produced when the gray crescent material was together. C and C'. Double monsters resulted when the gray crescent material was separated and two blastopores formed. D and D'. Triple monsters were produced when there were three invaginations. E. A normal embryo drawn for comparison.

The second cleavage, like the first, is meridional. It is approximately at right angles to the first. It be ins at the animal pole even before the fir clcavage his complete itself at tthe vegetal pole The result is four nearly equal blastomeres.

The third cleavage is typically at right angles to the first two cleavages, and hence cuts latitudinally, that is, horizontally, when the egg's axis is vertical. It passes well above the equa tor, so that the eight-cell stage commonly consists of four smaller animal balstomeres (micromeres) above and four larger, yolk-laden vegetal blastomeres (macromeres) below There is, however, much variation in the direction of the cleavage planes. As a consequence, the sizes of the cleavage cells vary. It frequently happens that the third cleavage planes are vertical, that is parallel, to the first cleavage planes and at right angles to the second planes. It is evident, therefore, that the particular pattern made by the blastomeres has no significance with respect to the normality of development. Rather, it is the distribution of the materials and the localization of the chemical processes which determine development.

During the early phases of cleavage the cell divisions are synchronous and rhythmic. But toward the close of cleavage they become less rapid and more irregular. Instead of 60 percent or so of the cells being in division at one time, the mitotic index sinks to 5 percent or less. The great majority of cells are in interphase.

THE BLASTULA

A cavity is present at the center of the group of blastomeres beginning at the eight-cell stage. It increases in size as cleavage progresses. This is owing, at least in part, to the fact that cleavage planes cut more often at right angles to the outer surface than they do parallel to it. The egg thus becomes a hollow ball of cells, i.e., a blastula. Its cavity, the balstocoel, ir roughly hemispherical. It has a dome or roof of smaller animal hemisphere cells and a floor of larger yolk rich vegetal cells.

As cleavage progresses, the roof of the blastocoel expands and actually becomes thinner. Its margins push downward on all sides, while at the same time the floor of the yolk-laden vegetal cells bulges upward from below. Cells from the center of the vegetal pole area fountain upward internally until some of them reach the floor of the blastocoel.

Most of them retain connection with the external surface. As a result of these shifts, the blastocoel comes to have the shape of an inverted bowl. These changes are preliminary to the mass movements of gastrulation which follow.

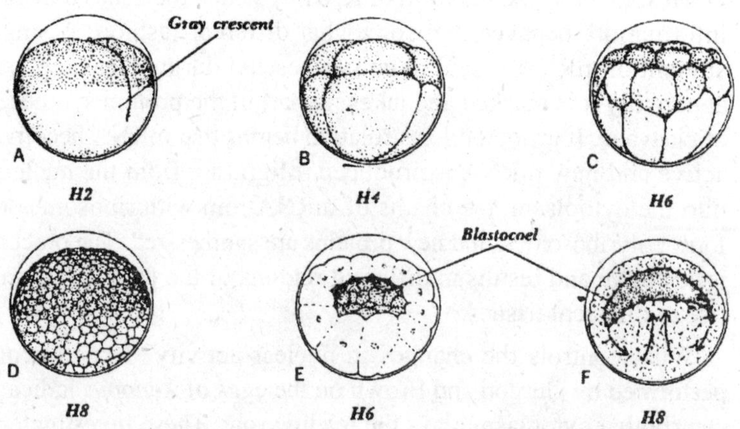

Figure 4.5 : Cleavage and blastulation in amphibians, seen from the left. A to D. Harrison's stages 2, 4, 6, and 8 for Ambystoma. (Compare stages 3, 5, 7, and 8 for Rana pipiens.) E and F. Median sections of stages 6 and 8. The arrows indicate the mass movements of the cells of the vegetal hemisphere according to Schechtman.

The Role of the Nucleus and Cytoplasm during Cleavage

In amphibians the replication of DNA increases sharply beginning about one-half hour after fertilization. But the synthesis of rRNA and tRNA is not resumed until near the end of cleavage. Nucleoli are absent during cleavage stages, and new ribosomes are not produced. The proteins needed for the manufacture of chromosomes and mitotic apparatus are synthesized with the aid of old RNA and ribosomes carried over from the oocyte.

Indeed, it would seem that the store of ribosomes derived from the oocyte is sufficient to provide for the needs of the embryo until the early tadpole stage. Brown and Gurdon have described a mutant form of the South African clawed toad, *Xenopus,* which lacks nucleoli and presumably is unable to produce ribosomes. Only the heterozygotes (mutant X normal) have a nucleolus and are viable. The homozygotes (those without nucleoli) develop as far as the swimming stage and then die. The normal embryo, on the other hand, begins to synthesize new rRNA and tRNA about the time that gastrulation gets under way. It is then that nucleoli reappear.

Messenger RNA, the form of RNA by which the genes transmit information, behaves in a somewhat different fashion. A small amount of mRNA is said to be synthesized during cleavage, but apparently it is masked and takes no part in the protein syntheses of cleavage. It is not until gastrulation begins that mRNA becomes active and new mRNA is produced. Migrating from the nucleus into the cytoplasm, the chains of mRNA join with ribosomes to form polyribosomes, and new proteins are synthesized. The process is selective and results in different regions of the gastrula giving rise to different tissues.

What controls the changes in nuclear activity? Experiments performed by Gurdon and Brown on the eggs of *Xenopus* indicate clearly that cytoplasm plays the leading role. These investigators took nuclei from late stages of development and substituted them for the nuclei of unfertilized eggs. They even used nuclei from differentiated cells of the epithelium of the intestine of swimming tadpoles. Now, if these nuclei had been left in place, only those few genes would have been active which were needed in the functioning of the gut epithelium. The rest would have remained repressed. But when one of these nuclei is implanted into an uncleaved egg, it quickly (within an hour) takes on the character of a zygote nucleus! It increases 30 times in volume; its nucleolus disappears; it ceases to synthesize RNA. Instead, it resumes the replication of DNA. In short, it actually becomes a zygote nucleus. Normal cleavage follows. Then, in due time, gastrulation commences, and the expected chemical changes follow. In a few of Gurdon and Brown's experiments, mature, fertile male and female frogs resulted.

What do we conclude from these experiments as to the roles of the nucleus and cytoplasm? We conclude that (1) any differentiation of nuclei which takes place during early development is reversible; (2) all the genes remain inviolate within the differentiated cells, even though only a few genes are called upon to function; and (3) in some unknown manner the cytoplasm which surrounds a nucleus controls its activity. At the beginning of cleavage, the cytoplasm turns DNA synthesis on and RNA synthesis off. As the time of gastrulation approaches, the cytoplasm turns DNA synthesis off and RNA synthesis on.

Why is it that in so many nuclear transplantation experiments some of the operated eggs failed to develop normally? Gurdon and Brown suggest that possibly the cytoplasm of the uncleaved egg, acting on the nucleus implanted from a differentiated cell, forces the implanted nucleus to divide before it is fully ready. It has not had time to wholly regain the character of a zygote nucleus.

Fate Map of the Blastula at the Beginning of Gastrulation

It will be of great help in describing the mass movements which follow blastulation if we consider the fates of different regions of the tula. If one could mark an individual cell or group of cells, on the surface of the blastula and then follow the mark through the movements of gastrulation and neurulation. one would be able to say that one region is positive brain, that another is prospective epidermis, or muscle segments, etc. Thus, by reasoning backward, one could construct a "fate map" of the blastula, in which each region would be designated, not according to any present difference which it may or may not have, but according to its *prospective significance,* given normal development.

He took small chips of agar, which he had stained with a vital dye, and placed them for a few minutes in close contact with the surface of the egg. Brightly stained spots_ remained on_ the egg's surface. The dyes he used were Nile blue sulfate and neutral red. They colored granules in the cytoplasm, but had little effect on the course of development. Vogt observed the changing positions of the marks and was able to draw his now classic fate map of the surface of the blastula or beginning gastrula. Only minor changes in the map have been made since.

It is very important not to confuse the prospective significance of a cell (given normal development) as recorded on a fate map with its actual capacities for development. If we interfere experimentally with the mass movements of embryo formation so that a cell ends up in a different location from that which it normally would have occupied, or if we transplant a group of cells to a new location in another egg, or, again, if we isolate (explant) a group of cells and so free them from the influence of adjacent cells, then the cell, or group of cells, may become something quite different from what it would normally have become.

A fate map of an amphibian blastula at the beginning of gastrulation such as drawn b vogt, shows three primary zones:

1. The zone of prospective ectoderm (epidermis and neural plate) corresponds roughly to the animal hemisphere of the egg. It might he called the "zone of expansion " for during gastrulation it expands downward and then converges toward the vegetal pole. It gives rise to the entire outer germ layer of the grastula.

2. The zone of *prospective notochord and mesoderm*, often called the *marginal zone*, is roughly a subequatorial belt around the balstula, although it is broader and extends above the equator on the dorsal side. Its dorsal part is approximately the original gray crescent.

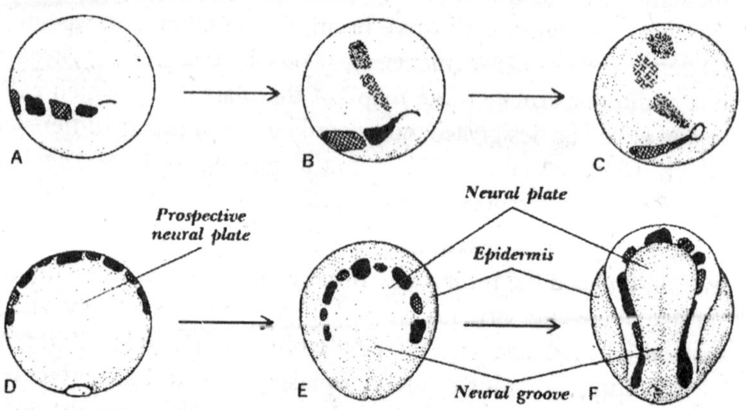

Figure 4.6 : Vogt's method of marking the surface of amphibian eggs with spots of vital die, namely Nile blue sulfate or neutral red. In B and C some of the spots have entered through the blastopore and are seen through the outer layer of cells.

The prospective chorda-mesoderm might be called the "zone of involution, for its fate, as we shall soon see, is to roll around and beneath the lips of the blastopore. Then, after having moved upward and dorsally on the inside of the egg, it becomes the notochord and mesoderm (chorda-mesoderm).

3. The zone of prospective endoderm is composed, in large part, of the large yolk-rich cells of the vegetal hemisphere; but it includes-also some smaller and more active cells which border the prospective chorda-mesoderm. This zone could be designated the "zone of invagination," for during gastrulation it sinks and glides into the interior of the egg and becomes endoderm. In effect, it is overgrown by the descent of the lips of the blastopore. It is within this zone, a little below its dorsal margin, that the first slitlike blastopore appears. The position of this first invagination is indicated by a small arrow on the fate map.

Each of the three primary zones may be further subdivided:

1. During the neurulation which follows gastrulation ation, approximately the dorsal half of the prospective ectoderm folds inward and becomes the brain and spinal cord. This area is the prospective neural plate. The ventral half of the prospective ectoderm is the prospective epidermis.

2. During neurulation, also, the cells of the prospective chorda-mesoderm become divided into a central notochordal rod and several regions of mesoderm, namely, prechordal mesoderm, axial mesoderm (epimere), intermediate mesoderm (mesomere), and lateral mesoderm (hypomere). These subareas are shown on the fate map and will be defined later.

3. That .part of the prospective endoderm which first enters the egg during gastrulation gives rise to the lining of the foregut, mainly to the pharynx (as distinguished from the ectodermal stomodaeum). From it, the mouth and gill clefts form. The rest of the prospective endoderm becomes the yolk-laden midgut from which the intestine is formed. In fact, the large yolk-filled cells of the vegetal pole come to lie on the floor of the intestine and contribute to the nutrition of the embryo.

GASTRULATION

The mass movements of gastrulation actually begin in the late blastula when the roof of the blastocoel thins, expands, and presses downward around the equator. The descending margins of the roof appear to force the yolk cells of the floor of the blastocoel upward into the blastocoel. But this certainly is not the mechanism which is involved, for these mass movements take place even in isolated pieces (explants). They are therefore autonomous.

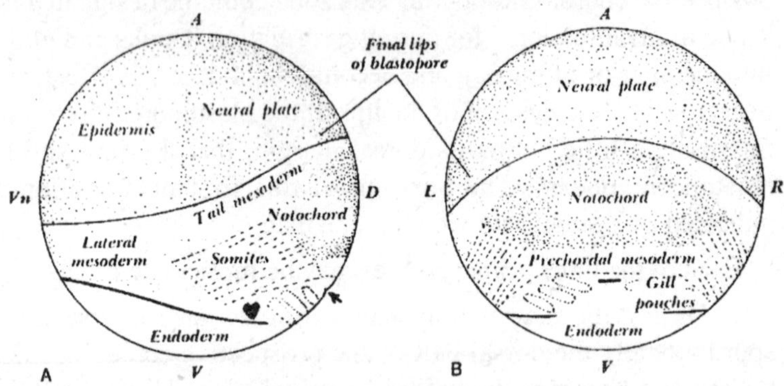

Figure 4.7 : "Fate map" of an amphibian blastula (salamander) at the beginning of gastrulation. A. View from the left side. B. View from the dorsal side. The short arrow (short dark line in B) marks the location of the beginning invagination of endoderm. The lower heavy line indicates the initial lateral and ventral lips of the mesodermal blastopore. It is along this line that prospective mesoderm splits away from prospective endoderm. The upper line marks the lips of the final blastopore after involution is complete.

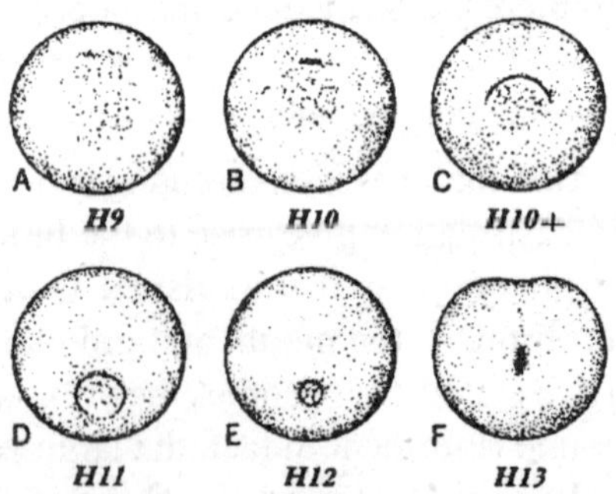

Figure 4.8 : Gastrulation in the amphibian egg as seen from the vicinity of the vegetal pole. A and B. Gastrulation begins by an invagination of prospective endoderm on the dorsal side about halfway between the vegetal pole and the equator. C to E. Gastrulation continues by the involution of prospective chorda-mesoderm at the dorsal, lateral, and finally at the ventral lips of the blastopore. F. Late gastrula, showing the closure of the blastopore by the apposition of its lateral lips. Harrison's stages 9, 10, 10+, 11, 12, and 13.

Invagination of the Endoderm

The account which follows applies primarily to the eggs of salamanders. Frogs eggs perform in much the same manner, although they differ in certain details.

The superficial aspects of gastrulation are readily described. A shallow, transverse, and slightly pigmented groove appears on the dorsal surface of the egg. It is located in the region of prospective endoderm, about halfway from the equator to the vegetal pole. The groove narrows, deepens (invaginates), and then widens laterally into a crescent concave toward the vegetal pole. This crescent is the initial or *endodermal* accomplished? Stained sections through the early blastopore show that the cells invaginate by changing their shapes.

How is this initial invagination become flaskshaped by the contraction of the cortex at their outer surface and the withdrawal of most of their substance inward. They will do this in explants even when the surrounding tissue has been cut away. The exposed tips of the flask-shaped cells are pigmented. Hence the furrow is dark.

The initial furrow of invagination deepens as the flask-shaped cells sink farther inside the egg. At the same time, the prospective endoderm cells which border the blastopore move toward the furrow and follow the flask-shaped cells in. Once inside the egg, the cells regain their cuboidal shape and expand upward toward

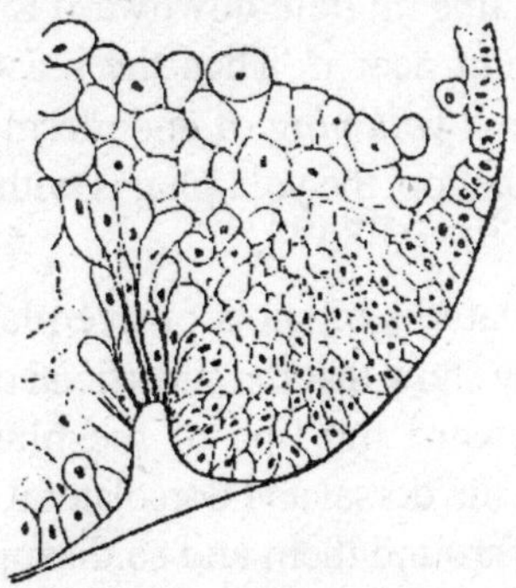

Figure 4.9 : Median section through the beginning blastopore of an amphibian egg.

the animal pole. Thus is formed the beginning of the *archenteron* (primitive gut).

For a brief time, the early gastrula is a twolayered structure consisting of an outer and an inner layer. The inner layer is definitely endoderm; but the outer layer is prospective chorda-mesoderm and endoderm, as well as ectoderm. The terms *epiblast* and *hypoblast* are sometimes applied to these two transitional layers.

The invagination of endoderm continues during the involution of the chorda-mesoderm, which is to be described next. The prospective endoderm of the vegetal area glides beneath the descending lips of the blastopore. Most of it disappears from view beneath the dorsal and dorsolateral lips and becomes the floor of the archenteron. The lateral margins of the endoderm split away from the mesoderm and glide upward toward the animal pole. They also move dorsally toward the midline. Thus the endoderm, after invagination, forms a sort of trough which is open dorsally.

The early splitting away of the endoderm from the mesoderm is less obvious in the frog than it is in the salamander, for the cells of the two layers are difficult to distinguish. Later they separate, apparently by delamination.

Involution of the Chorda-Mesoderm

The crescent-shaped blastopore widens to a semicircle, then to the shape of a horseshoe, and finally it closes to a complete circle. As it does so, its lips migrate downward toward the vegetal pole or rather to a point near it. Thus the blastopore comes to be a small circle, with *a yolk plug* of endoderm in its center. Toward the close of gastrulation, the yolk plug is withdrawn into the interior of the egg.

Careful observations of spots of dye placed on the surface of the blastula clearly show that the superficial cells stream downward and converge toward the lips of the blastopore. They move especially toward the dorsal and dorsolateral lips. When they reach the lips, they roll around them and so disappear from sight. Once inside the egg, they migrate upward (toward the animal pole), keeping in close contact with the inner surface of the ectoderm: Their fate is to become notochord and mesoderm. Note carefully that the chorda-mesoderm cells enter the interior of the egg by *involution.* Instead of becoming flask-shaped with their broad ends inward, as did the invaginating endoderm, they become temporarily wedge-shaped with their broad ends directed outward.

The actual beginning of the movements of the prospective chorda-mesoderm is internal and is not visible from the outside. Certain cells which are situated around the borders of the blastocoel split away from the adjacent endoderm cells and wander upward toward the animal pole. As they do so, they keep in close contact with the under surface of the roof of the blastocoel. The splitting away begins on the dorsal side and spreads ventrally, although it does not involve the immediate middorsal area. The angioblasts are followed by an internal ring (incomplete dorsally) of upward-wandering mesoderm cells. The involution of the chorda-mesoderm, which is seen from the outside, follows directly in the wake of these inner cells.

In normal development the involution of chorda-mesoderm appears to be the direct successor of endodermal invagination. Observations on abnormal development, however, show that this is not the case. The two processes are independent. When, for some reason, the invagination of endoderm is retarded, it sometimes happens that two grooves appear: an endodermal groove below, and a chordamesodermal groove above it (nearer the equator). Each groove has its own dorsal lip. The lower endodermal groove develops on the dorsal side only. It does not spread laterally. The mesodermal groove, on the other hand, although it begins on the dorsal side, spreads laterally until it forms a complete circular blastopore.

Having now entered the egg by involution, the chorda-mesoderm streams upward, mainly on the dorsal side. For a time, it forms the roof of the archenteron. It would form the side walls of the archenteron, also, if it were not for the fact that the upward cupping of the sides of the endoderm separates it from that cavity.

Closure of the Blastopore

The yolk plug, which has been protruding between the lips of the small circular blastopore, finally withdraws into the gastrula. Then the blastopore closes. Its lateral lips come together in the midline, and as a result the blastopore becomes a vertical slit. The closed blastopore of an amphibian is comparable to the last remnant of the "primitive streak" of bird and mammal embryos, and it is often referred to by that name. The closure marks the end of the invagination of the endoderm, but the expansion of ectoderm and the involution of chorda-mesoderm continue for a time.

As a consequence of the shift of the yolkladen endoderm toward the ventral side, the center of gravity of the gastrula is changed. The ventral side is now heaviest. As a result, the egg rotates until its dorsal side is uppermost. The animal pole area is now anterior, and the region of the blastopore is posterior.

Transplantation Experiments on Early Gastrulas

In 1918 Spemann began an important series of experiments in which he transplanted small discs of cells from one region of an early gastrula to another region of another gastrula. In his early experiments, he used different species of salamanders as donors and hosts in order that he might later distinguish donor cells from host cells. Later, the method of staining the donor embryo with Nile blue sulfate was adopted. What happened depended on where the discs came from and where they were planted.

In Spemann's original work, he found that a disc transplanted from one part of the prospective ectoderm to another part of the same zone developed according to its new location. Thus, a disc of prospective epidermis which was transplanted into the area of the future neural plate developed as an integral part of the neural plate. Conversely, a disc of prospective neural plate, when planted into the region of prospective epidermis, became epidermis. A disc of prospective ectoderm, when transplanted to a region of prospective chord a- mesoderm, may become notochord and mesoderm.

We conclude, therefore, that at the start of gastrulation the cells of the animal hemisphere (prospective ectoderm) are either undiffer entiated and undetermined as to their fate (uncommitted) or else they are labile and capable of reversing their differentiation when transplanted to changed surroundings.

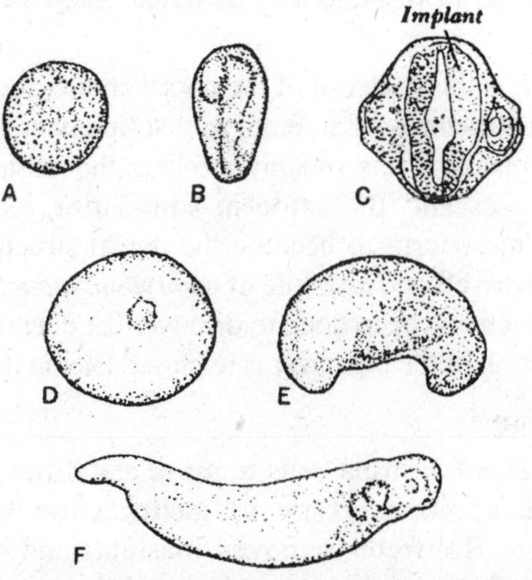

Figure 4.10 : Spemann's classic experiment, 1921, in which he exchanged small discs of cells between two species of salamanders. A to C. Discs of prospective epidermis of Triton cristatus were implanted in the region of the prospective neural plate of Triton taeniatus. They developed according to their new location into brain and retina. D to F. The converse experiment in which discs of prospective neural plate were implanted in the region of prospective epidermis. The discs became epidermis.

What determines whether prospective ectoderm will become epidermis or neural tissue? Transplantation experiments reported in 1924 by Spemann and Hilda Mangold leave no doubt as to the answer. The fate is decided by the relation of the ectoderm to adjacent chordamesoderm. If a disc of dorsal chorda-mesoderm is transplanted to the ventral side of an egg, or if it is placed in the blastocoel so that it comes into contact with prospective ectoderm, it brings about the differentiation of axial structures of an embryo. The disc itself becomes notochord and axial mesoderm, and it induces the adjacent ectoderm to become a neural plate. The lines are not sharp, however, between the implant and the host tissues. Some cells of the implant may become neural tissue, and some cells of the host may form mesoderm and even notochord. The important point is that host and implant tissues together constitute one self-regulating "embryonic field" (in the sense in which Spemann used the word), and they differentiate as an organized whole.

So important is this material of the dorsal chorda-mesoderm in organizing the structures of an embryo that Spemann tentatively called it "the organizer." It is, roughly speaking, the substance which was the gray crescent. Its action in stimulating the adjacent ectoderm and mesoderm to become the dorsal structures of an embryo is the now-classic example of *embryonic induction.* Some of the work which has been done to discover the chemical nature and mode of action of the organizer is reviewed later in this chapter.

Exogastrulation

The capacities of gastrula cells to move and differentiate are shown in the abnormal type of gastrulation known as exogastrulation. Holtfreter removed blastulas and beginning gastrulas from their membranes and placed them in a slightly hypertonic solution. The prospective endoderm at first formed an endodermal blastopore. Then the prospective chorda-mesoderm, instead of rolling inward (involution), rolled outward. The endoderm, which had begun to sink inward, everted. Thus, both the endoderm and the chorda-mesoderm turned inside out. They retained no contact with the prospective ectoderm.

Much has been learned from these exogastrulas:

1. The prospective endoderm, which glided outward instead of inward, differentiated into the same histological structures (glands and epithelia) which it would have formed if it had invaginated normally.

2. The prospective chorda-mesoderm went through the same mass movements in exogastrulation that it would normally have gone through, except that in this case the movements were outward instead of inward. First, the cells converged toward the blastoporal lips, especially the dorsal lip, in a quite normal fashion. Then they narrowed at the blastopore, as though they were passing through a ring. Following this they stretched and spread outwardly, much

as they would do inside the egg. But they were outside the egg, and they became enfolded within the endoderm instead of folding around the endoderm. The chordamesoderm then differentiated into the notochord and mesodermal structures.

3. The prospective ectoderm expanded, but it did not differentiate. Instead, it remained as a primitive epithelium.

There is much to comment on: the independence of the endodermal and the chordamesodermal blastopores; the apparent selforganizing capacity of the endoderm and chorda-mesoderm and the interrelations between them; the complete dependence of the ectoderm on the other germ layers for its differentiation.

THE GASTRULA

At the time the blastopore closes to a slit, the amphibian gastrula consists of three layers of cells: ectoderm, chorda-mesoderm, and endoderm. It is a triploblastic structure. The outer layer is ectoderm except at the posterior end where some one-fifth of the apparent ectoderm is still destined to undergo involution and become notochord and mesoderm. The chorda-mesoderm forms the roof of the archenteron. Its free lateral margins have pushed ventrally at the sides, between the ectoderm and endoderm. The endoderm underlaps the lateral chorda-mesoderm internally and forms the sidewalls and floor of the cavity of the archenteron. This description applies to salamanders. In the frog, the relations of the chorda-mesoderm and endoderm are not easy to demonstrate.

The anterior portion of the archenteron is broad and thin-walled. It consists of the endodermal cells which first invaginated. It be comes the foregut. Near its anterior end it adheres closely to the ventral ectoderm. This is the location of the oral plate which later breaks through and becomes the mouth opening. Elsewhere, except at the gill clefts and the anus, the ectoderm and the endoderm abhor contact. The major portion of the endoderm, however, consists of the large yolk-laden cells of the *midgut,* that is, of the intestine. Later the cells of the ventral blastoporal lip give rise to the *hindgut,* from which the cloaca is formed.

Transplantation Experiments on Late Gastrulas

We noted that when Spemann transplanted discs of prospective ectoderm of early gastrulas to new locations they differentiated *according to their new location.* When he did the same thing with discs of ectoderm of late gastrulas they differentiated *in accord with their origin.* Something had taken place between the beginning and end of gastrulation. The cells had undergone *determination.*

What is determination? It is a change of some sort which a cell or region of cells undergoes, by which it becomes specified to develop in a certain way. Previous to determination, the region is "indifferent" to its fate and subject to the inductive influences of its environment. Following determination, it is committed to its fate. It is no longer subject to its surroundings. Since the change is not at first visible, it has been called invisible or chemical differentiation. After determination, the gastrula is a mosaic of self-differentiating regions.

It must not be supposed that determination is a sudden process which takes place all at once. On the contrary, it may take place by stages. First, the cells acquire a general predisposition ("bias"), or competence, to respond to further stimulation. This has been called "labile determination." Then later, as a result of continuing stimulation or of a second inductive influence, the determination becomes irreversible.

This may be illustrated by some experiments of Okada on the determination of the endoderm. If a fragment of prospective endoderm from any part of a late gastrula (or early neurula) is removed and enfolded in an envelop of ectoderm (of an early gastrula), the endoderm becomes nothing more than a shriveled mass of yolk-laden cells. But if fragments of mesoderm are included with the endoderm, the latter differentiates into recognizable tissues of the gut. What it becomes depends upon where the endoderm came from and also where the mesoderm came from. The endoderm has a predisposition of its own, but it requires the influence of the mesoderm in order to realize its predisposition; moreover, the mesoderm may modify its fate.

In Okada's experiments, the fate of the endoderm was altered according to whether the mesoderm came from a more anterior or more posterior location. If the mesoderm was head mesenchyme, the fate of the endoderm was shifted to a more, forward organ. What normally would have been stomach endoderm now became endoderm of the gill region. If, on the contrary, the mesoderm was from the flank, the fate of the endoderm was shifted backward. Prospective gill endoderm became intestinal endoderm. The influence of mesoderm and endoderm is reciprocal, for the fate of the mesoderm is also shifted. The result is that mesoderm and endoderm, differentiate harmoniously into the several organs of the alimentary tract.

NEURULATION

Neurulation is the process by which a neural plate forms and then folds or otherwise transforms into a neural tube. During neurulation, also, the chorda-mesoderm subdivides into the notochord and several regions of mesoderm. The mesoderm pushes anteriorly and laterally between the ectoderm and endoderm until it almost completely surrounds the embryo. At the same time, the free dorsolateral margins of the endoderm move dorsally and close in beneath the notochord. (In the frog, the margins of the endoderm reach the notochord earlier, about midgastrulation.) Other changes also take place during neurulation, so that by the time the process nears completion a "young embryo," recognizable as such, may be said to have taken form.

Neural Plate and Neural Tube

The *neural plate* becomes visible about the time the blastopore closes to a slit. It is a racket-shaped area of dorsal ectoderm, broadest at its anterior end, and narrowing posteriorly toward the blastopore. It is somewhat thicker than the surrounding epidermis and is usually pigmented.

The neural plate shows a shallow, central longitudinal groove, the *neural groove.* This extends from the center of the broad forward area of the plate back to the dorsal lip of the blastopore. The plate thickens and narrows because its cells become columnar.

At the same time the adjoining epidermis becomes thinner and spreads. Soon the margins of the neural plate rise up as the *neural folds,* and move toward the middorsal line. They come together, fuse, and so form the *neural tube.* Hence it is that the middorsal lines of the epidermis and neural tube are lines of suture. The cavity of the neural tube is known as the *neurocoel.*

The fusion of the neural folds begins in the region of the future midbrain and progresses forward and backward. An opening, the *anterior neuropore,* remains for a brief time at the anterior end. At the posterior end, the neural folds terminate at the lateral lips

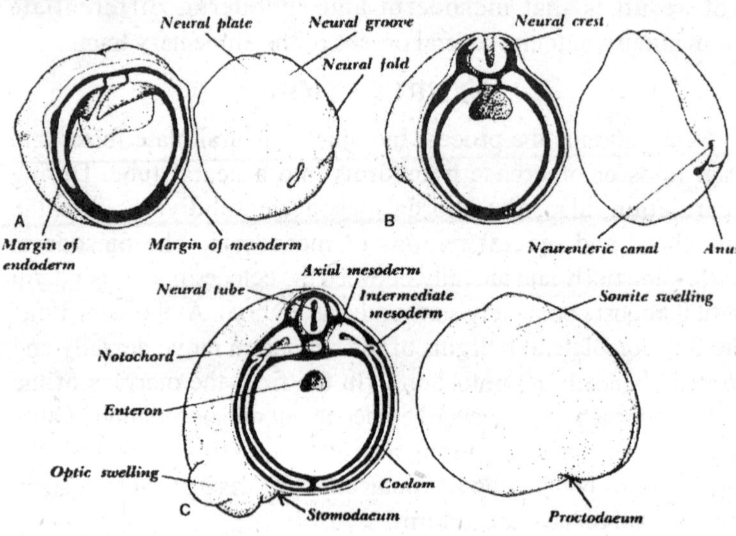

Figure 4.11 : Diagram of neurulation in salamander development (highly schematic). The germ layers are in reality closely packed together.

of the blastopore. When ultimately they come together, they enclose the dorsal opening of the slitlike blastopore. Thus, for a brief time, there is potentially a passageway between the cavity of the neural tube (neurocoel) and the cavity of the gut (enteric cavity, which is known as the *neurenteric canal.*

Neural Crest

Particular note must be taken of the cells along the margins of the neural plate. They form what is known as the *neural crest.* Unlike the cells of the neural plate proper, they early lose their epithelial character, become loose, and migrate individually. They give rise to various tissues, notably nerve ganglia, pigment cells, and certain cartilages of the head.

The Chorda-Mesoderm

The subdivision of the chorda-mesoderm into notochord, axial mesoderm, intermediate mesoderm, and lateral mesoderm will be referred to when we describe the neurula. Differences between these tissues are not easy to recognize in cross sections of young frog embryos, for the cells are closely packed together and are full of yolk granules. Yet, although they look alike, they are different, for they engage in different morphogenic movements. By the time the neural folds come together, they have acquired the capacities to differentiate and to induce ectoderm and endoderm to differentiate into the various parts of the embryo.

The involution of chorda-mesoderm continues throughout the period of neurulation. At the beginning of neurulation roughly one-fourth of the open neural plate is still destined to roll around the lips of the slit-shaped blastopore and then move forward on the inside of the egg as a part of the archenteric roof. The material of the future tail bud is a band across the neural plate, somewhat forward of its posterior end. The posterior end of the neural plate becomes the underside of the tail bud just posterior to the anus.

The Endoderm

We described the endoderm as a trough which is open dorsally. During neurulation, its free lateral margins move upward to the midline beneath the notochord. Here they fuse and form a new or secondary roof over the gut. Hence the gut is no longer an archenteron (primitive gut) but an enteron. In the frog, the upward pushing of the endoderm margins is precocious so that, as seen in sections, the endoderm seems to split away (delaminate) from the mesoderm.

ANALYSIS OF PRIMARY INDUCTION

The determination of the neural plate is the result of influences arising in the underlying chorda-mesoderm. It is a classic example of *embryonic induction.* How is this accomplished? What is its mechanism? A great deal of experimentation has been carried on in seeking an answer to this question.

It has been found that induction is a process which is limited in both space and time. Only prospective ectoderm is competent to respond to the inducing stimulus of the chorda-mesoderm and to give rise to neural tissue. Moreover, it is only for a definite period during gastrulation that it will so respond. As gastrulation progresses, the competence wanes. Then, soon after neurulation has begun, it ceases entirely. Neurula ectoderm has new competencies; for example, its epidermis will respond to the stimulus of an optic vesicle by forming a lens.

For a time it was thought that the inducing agent acts only as a releasing stimulus, much as pulling the trigger of a gun releases energies pent up in the cartridge. According to this interpretation, the nature of what is induced is determined by the nature of the material which responds. This view was based on the discovery that in salamanders many different materials are able to induce, not only chorda-mesoderm, but also brain tissue, muscle segments, and even adult tissues, both living and dead. Furthermore, various chemical substances were found which bring about the differentiation of ectoderm into nervous tissue. But this effect could be explained in many cases as an indirect effect: the chemicals injure the living tissue so that the tissue releases substances with inductive powers.

This view that the inducing agent acts as a stimulus only has in recent years been changed by the discovery by Spemann, Yamada, and others that different agents have different inductive effects. What is induced is determined, at least in part, by the nature of the inducing agent. (1) Thus the dorsal lip of the blastopore, at the beginning of gastrulation, induces ectoderm to form forebrain, eyes, and nose. It has been called an *archencephalic inductor.* (2) The dorsal lip at a somewhat later stage (the cells of the initial dorsal lip having entered within the gastrula) induces the production of midbrain, hindbrain, and inner ears (otocysts). It is termed *a deuterencephalic inductor.* (3) Still later, when gastrulation is nearing completion, the now dorsal lip stimulates the ectoderm to become spinal cord and even notochord and somites of the tail. It is spoken of as *a spinocaudal inductor.* (4) Finally, some inducing agents have been found which cause early gastrula ectoderm to become mesodermal and endodermal tissue.

It will be noted that in each of these cases the inductor determines some *region* of the embryo, not particular organs. Thus, the same agent will cause a variety of organs to be produced-ectodermal, mesodermal, and even endodermal; but they all belong to the same region of the embryo. (There are exceptions, and certain unnatural agents may induce the production of tissues which are chaotically disorganized.)

For a long time, it seemed that the inducing influence passes from the inductor to the induced only when there is actual contact between the two. But it was found by Twitty and Niu that in salamanders if a bit of embryonic tissue which is capable of acting as an inducing agent is explanted into a small drop of suitable saline solution (on a hanging-drop slide) and grown there for a week or more, the solution becomes "conditioned." It acquires the capacity to induce. If now a few cells of ectoderm are placed in the solution for 24 hours or more (the original tissue having first been removed), they will transform into nerve cells, mesodermal tissues, etc. Thus it seems evident that the inducing substance is soluble.

Much of this work on induction has been facilitated by the technique of inserting the material to be tested into a sandwich of ectoderm taken from the animal hemisphere of a beginning gastrula. The cut margins of the ectoderm heal together and form a vesicle with the test object inside. If the test object lacks inducing power, then the ectoderm becomes a wrinkled epithelium which soon degenerates. If, on the other hand, it has the capacity to induce, then the ectoderm responds by differentiating into recognizable tissues of an embryo.

This sandwich method has been employed in studying the inductive action on salamander ectoderm of adult tissues of guinea pigs and rats. Of course, tissues of an adult mammal are not the normal inductors of amphibian development, but they have served as models to point the way to principles which possibly apply to normal development. Hayashi found, for example, that liver tissue has predominantly archencephalic induction properties (forebrain, eyes, nose), while kidney tissue induces, for the most part, deuterencephalic and spinocaudal structures (midbrain, hindbrain, ears, spinal cord, notochord, and somites of the tail). Similar experiments with bone marrow have shown that it possesses the capacity to induce gastrula ectoderm to become mesodermal structures (limb buds, notochord, pronephric tubules, and mesenchyme), and even endodermal structures (pharynx, esophagus, lung buds, stomach, and intestines) but not neural structures.

As a result of observations such as these, Nieuwkoop has proposed the view that two substances are involved in induction. Toivonen refers to them as (1) a "neuralizing factor" which is concentrated toward the dorsal side and favors the development of the organs of the dorsal side, and (2) a "mesodermalizing factor" which increases in concentration toward the posterior end and which tends toward the production of mesoderm. According to this interpretation, the neuralizing factor, if present alone (as in liver), induces archencephalic structures. The neuralizing factor, along with a fair amount of mesodermalizing factor, favors deuterencephalic structures. If the mesodermalizing factor is present in still greater proportion (as in kidney), the result is spinocaudal organs. If, finally, the mesodermalizing factor strongly, predominates (as it does in bone marrow), only mesodermal and endodermal structures are produced.

Of the two factors, the neuralizing factor is the more stable. It is not destroyed by heat, alcohol, and various chemical treatments. The mesodermalizing factor, on the other hand, is thermolabile. Toivonen found, for example, that when kidney tissue is boiled, its deuterencephalic and spinocaudal induction capacities are reduced, but its archencephalic induction powers largely remain. This two-factor hypothesis has been put to the test by placing both a pellet of guinea-pig liver and a pellet of guinea-pig bone marrow in the blastocoel of an early amphibian gastrula. Now, a pellet of bone marrow by itself will induce mesodermal structures only. But the two tissues placed together within the blastocoel induce structures belonging to all levels of the embryo. What is induced depends upon the relative amounts of the two agents which are present.

The work reported above was performed on salamander (urodele) material. The ectoderm of frog and toad gastrulas is not responsive to the same wide variety of inducing agents which affect salamander ectoderm. It indeed responds to living chorda-mesoderm cells of frog or salamander eggs by forming neural tissue; but, generally speaking, it is not influenced by dead or unnatural agents. An explanation for this discrepancy has not yet been found.

THE NEURULA

During neurulation, the three germ layers reach their final positions with respect to one another, and their fates begin to be determined. These are matters of importance, for the development of unified organs depends upon the normal interaction between germ layer and germ layer.

The approximate location of certain organ rudiments in an early neurula of a salamander. Note that the neural plate is divisible into forebrain, midbrain, and hindbrain. The forebrain and midbrain overlie that part of the chorda-mesoderm which is known as *prechordal mesoderm.* The central portion of the latter is still a part of the roof of the archenteron and is termed the *prechordal plate.* Its lateral portion, here labeled "mandibular mesoderm," is underlaid by endoderm. It receives contributions of cells from the neural crest and gives rise to the upper and lower jaws. The prechordal plate becomes separated from the roof of the pharynx by the closing in of endoderm beneath it. It then separates to the right and left and gives rise to the extrinsic muscles of the eyeballs.

The most anterior region of the neural plate is the *optic area.* As a result of inductive action by the prechordal plate which lies beneath it, it acquires the capacity to become retinas and optic nerves. The fact that it forms two eyes depends upon the prechordal plate separating to the right and left. If, by reason of retarded development, this separation fails to occur, a single median eye is formed, a condition known as *cyclopia.*

Anterior and lateral to the optic areas are the *olfactory areas* which give rise to the nasal pits. In cyclopian embryos, the nasal pit is single and dorsal to the median eye.

The central axis of the hindbrain overlies the notochord. Its flanks overlie the head portion of the axial mesoderm. Inductive interactions control the differentiations of this part of the head. The *auditory area* of the epidermis, for example, is related both to underlying axial mesoderm and to the forward part of the hindbrain. It gives rise to the auditory vesicles (otocysts), from which the labyrinth of the inner ear is derived.

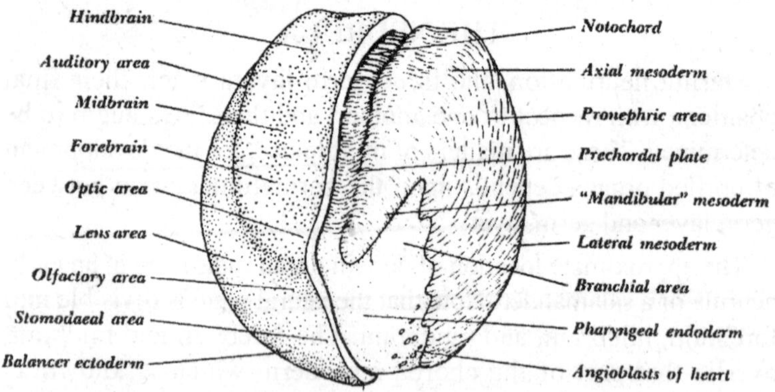

Figure 4.12 : Diagram of an early neurula of a salamander.

The epidermis ventral to the forward tip of the neural plate is free of mesoderm at the neural plate stage and has immediate contact with the forward wall of the foregut (pharynx). The epidermis responds by developing the *stomodaeum,* the ectodermal-lined part of the oral cavity. Here is formed the *oralplate,* which later breaks through.

Note that the mesoderm has not yet entered the region immediately ventral to the mandibular mesoderm. This is where the first pharyngeal pouch (endodermal) comes into contact with the epidermis at the side of the head. It forms a plate, but it does not break through in amphibians. The other pharyngeal pouches push through the mesoderm, make contact with the epidermis, and give rise to gill openings.

Loose mesenchymal cells having pushed forward from the margin of the lateral mesoderm. These are *angioblasts,* which are destined to become the endothelial linings of the heart (endocardium) and blood vessels. The muscles of the heart (myocardium) will come from lateral mesoderm which moves ventrally and enfolds the endocardium.

Posterior to the head region the chordamesoderm is divisible into notochord, axial mesoderm (from which the body segments, or somites, are derived), intermediate mesoderm, and lateral mesoderm. The forward portion of the intermediate mesoderm gives rise to the pronephric tubules, the first excretory organs of the embryo. The lateral mesoderm becomes the mesoderm of the visceral and body walls, with the body cavity between. The anterior limb buds (not labeled in the figure) come from the lateral mesoderm of the body wall just ventral to the pronephric area.

CHANGES IN CELL PROPERTIES DURING GASTRULATION AND NEURULATION

The onset of gastrulation is associated with important changes in the chemistry of the cells: (1) basic proteins increase within the nucleus; (2) the synthesis of ribosomal RNA, absent during cleavage, is resumed; (3) nucleoli, not present during cleavage, reappear within the nuclei; (4) messenger RNA, entering the cytoplasm or becoming unmasked, joins with the ribosomes to form polyribosomes; and (5) the ribosomes become increasingly attached to the endoplasmic reticulum.

These events are presumably related. The proteins and the ribosomal RNA unite in the production of the substance of the nucleoli. The nucleoli in turn are the stuff of which ribosomes are made. The polyribosomes engage in the synthesis of the new proteins characteristic of the regions of the differentiating embryo. Their attachment to the endoplasmic reticulum signifies that proteins are about to be secreted.

The evidence for these statements comes from biochemical studies of several sorts. In some studies the cells are labeled with radioactive precursors of RNA and protein, and then the location of the label is ascertained by means of radioautographs. In other studies, the new proteins are detected by immunological methods.

A third technique involves treating the cells with substances which inhibit synthetic processes. It will be recalled that actinomycin D is an antibiotic which specifically inhibits the production of new RNA at gene (DNA) templates; that is, it prevents transcription. The old ribosomes and mRNA carried over from the oocyte are sufficient for the needs of cleavage and blastula formation. But new mRNA and new types of protein are required for gastrulation, neurulation, and the differentiations which then get under way.

Another observation which points in the same direction concerns interspecies hybrids. These develop quite normally through cleavage but fail to gastrulate. Again the explanation seems to be that the old mRNA already present in the egg cytoplasm is sufficient for the needs of cleavage, but the unfamiliar genes which are brought in by the foreign sperm are unable to cooperate with the egg's cytoplasm in the production of the new mRNA needed for differentiation. As a result, the proteins needed for further development are not produced, and death results. Strangely enough, it has been found that if the blocked tissue is grafted into a normal host, "revitalization" occurs. Possibly the new RNA which is lacking in the graft is supplied by the neighboring host cells.

The ribosomes are not distributed evenly throughout the cytoplasm of the egg. They are most abundant around the animal pole and on the dorsal side. Any treatment which modifies the arrangement of the ribosomes by increasing or decreasing the gradient of their distribution produces characteristic abnormalities. For example, a strong centrifugal force can produce an accumulation of ribosomes on one side of the egg and so give rise to a secondary embryonic axis. Chemical treatments which reduce the steepness of the gradient can result in microcephaly (underdevelopment of the head).

During the course of neurulation, the processes of differentiation enter a new phase. We have already noted that gastrulas and early neurulas are sensitive to actinomycin D. But later neurulas and the tail-bud stages which follow are less sensitive. Why is this so? The probable explanation is that at these more advanced stages sufficient new RNA has already been produced to provide for the production of the proteins needed in differentiation. On the other hand, those drugs, such as puromycin, which interfere with translation, that is, with the new production of protein by RNA, bring differentiation to an immediate halt. It is during the period of translation when the cells have lost much of their sensitivity to actinomycin that differentiations first become visible.

The mass movements and differentiations which take place at the time of gastrulation and neurulation no doubt require energy. A progressive increase in respiration (in the ultilization of oxygen) does indeed accompany these processes. But just how much of this increase is due to a general speeding up of life processes, and how much is related specifically to morphogenetic activities, cannot be determined with certainty. The increased demand for energy is accompanied, as might be expected, by an increase in the number of mitochondria, the "powerhouses of the cell." Also, the outer layer of the yolk granules is dissolved, glycogen is consumed, and water enters the cells. As a result the volume of protoplasm is increased. These processes take place first and most notably in those cells which are engaged, or are about to engage, in morphogenetic movements, namely, in the cells of the dorsal blastoporal lip and later in those of the neural plate. But this fact in itself does not prove that the increased energy is being used to support morphogenetic movements.

THE BEHAVIOR OF FRAGMENTS OF EMBRYOS AND OF DISSOCIATED CELLS

Blastula cells are loosely bound together. When a fragment of a blastula is placed in a calcium- and magnesium-free salt solution, the bonds between the cells weaken and the cells fall apart. If cells which have been dissociated in this manner are then transferred to an abundance of a suitable physiological salt solution, they may live for days nourished by the yolk granules in their cytoplasms. But, generally speaking, they do not differentiate. Some adhere to the bottom of the dish or move about in amoeboid fashion; but this is as far as they go.

When the dissociated cells of a blastula come into contact with one another, they adhere and draw together into tight balls. After a day or two, some of the balls may develop cilia and roll around. But only if the mass is of sufficient size do some of the cells in the center of the balls show a tendency to differentiate.

The behavioral properties of cells change during gastrulation and neurulation. Cells which form epithelial layers adhere together with ever-increasing strength, as any one who dissects living embryos will discover. To bring about dissociation it is now necessary to use powerful methods, such as exposing the fragments to an alkaline solution or to a weak solution containing trypsin. If, after dissociating, the cells are promptly returned to a suitable physiological salt solution, they appear to be uninjured. After sinking to the bottom of the dish, some types undergo differentiation. For example, future nerve cells produce one or more pseudopod-like outgrowths, the forerunners of axons; future notochordal cells develop a fringe of clear protoplasm around their peripheries; and future muscle cells produce lobes at opposite poles and become spindleshaped.

When gastrula or neurula cells of different sorts come into contact with one another, they tend to adhere. Then they crawl around on each other and rearrange themselves in characteristic manners. Holtfreter has described the results and has noted that they are similar to normal processes of development. First he devised a salt solution-which now bears his name-in which cells or fragments will live for days and behave quite normally. To bring about dissociation, he added KOH until the pH became about 9.8. Then he returned the cells to his physiological salt solution at pH 8.0. The cells did not attract one another. But when they came into contact they adhered like soap bubbles. Holtfreter called the principle "affinity," although "adhesiveness" would seem to be an adequately descriptive term. A few of Holtfreter's results are as follows:

When dissociated prospective ectoderm cells of a gastrula reaggregate, they form a cyst. The wall of the cyst thins and becomes wrinkled. This process may be compared to the expansion by which epidermis spreads over the outside of an embryo. Prospective endoderm cells round up into a compact mass.

Then, about the time that the margins of the endoderm of a gastrula are migrating dorsally and closing in beneath the notochord, some of the endoderm cells spread out on the glass bottom of the containing dish and form a layer one cell thick. The exposed surface corresponds to the exposed surface of an intestinal epithelium.

When prospective ectoderm and endoderm cells are intermingled, the endoderm draws toward the interior, and the ectoderm spreads out on the surface as a cap. This indicates, according to Steinberg's interpretation, that the adhesion of endoderm for endoderm is stronger than of ectoderm for ectoderm and that the sum of their tendency to adhere to their own kind is greater than the tendency of endoderm to adhere to ectoderm. About the time that gastrulation takes place, the endoderm and ectoderm separate, and the exposed surfaces of both become nonadhesive. This may explain why the lips of the blastopore do not adhere to the yolk plug.

The most adhesive and at the same time the most independent of the three germ layers is the mesoderm. Fragments of the prospective chorda-mesoderm from an early gastrula tend to go through the mass movements of gastrulation. Those cells which undergo the motions of involution differentiate as notochord and mesoderm. Those which fail to do so, even though they are prospective chordamesoderm, become ectodermal tissues, i.e., epidermis and neural tissue.

Ectodermal and mesodermal cells which are mingled together draw into a compact cluster. Then they segregate, and the mesoderm migrates inward. Soon, however, the mesodermal cells pinch away from the ectodermal cells, much as they do during normal gastrulation, but they remain connected by a narrow waist. Later they come together again, the ectoderm on the surface, the mesoderm as a compact mass within. The mesoderm then self-differentiates into notochord, somites, occasional pronephric tubules, and some free mesenchyme. The ectoderm, under the inductive influence of the mesoderm, differentiates into neural plate and epidermis. Mesoderm plus endoderm behaves somewhat like mesoderm plus ectoderm. First the mesodermal cells move to the interior of the mass, where the mesoderm differentiates into notochord and somites. The endoderm differentiates with its epithelial surface facing outward.

What happens when ectoderm, endoderm, and mesoderm are explanted together? Both ectoderm and endoderm tend to enclose mesoderm, but ectoderm tends to enclose endoderm. The problem is solved, as in the embryo, by ectoderm spreading on the outer surface, mesoderm becoming an intermediate layer, and endoderm forming a hollow tube within. The epithelial surfaces of the ectoderm and endoderm become nonadhesive. Their surfaces in contact with mesoderm, however, are strongly adhesive. Indeed, the adhesion of ectoderm and endoderm with mesoderm may be stronger than the adhesion of mesoderm with mesoderm, for cavities appear in the mesoderm which may be compared to the coelom of the embryo.

New factors appear during neurulation. For example, neural tissue becomes distinct from epidermis. When the ectoderm of a neurula is disaggregated and then reassembled, the future neural cells move inward and become a compact internal mass. The epidermal cells spread on the surface. The boundary between the two types is clean cut. Indeed, a space forms between them. Then a cavity appears in the neural mass by cavitation. Regional differentiation of the neural tissue does not take place, presumably because the inductive influence of the chorda-mesoderm is lacking. But if mesenchyme is present, or even if mesectoderm from the neural folds is present, the neural tissue may undergo some differentiation. For example, an optic vesicle may form and cave in to form an optic cup.

5

Young Embryo

This chapter is written with a young amphibian embryo in mind, yet much of what is stated applies in a general way to the embryos of other air-breathing vertebrates. The "young amphibian embryo" begins at approximately the late neurula or tail-bud stage of a frog or salamander. It may be compared in many respects to a 13- to 18-somite chick (33 to 38 hours of incubation), or to a 2.5-mm mammal (15-day pig or 22- to 26-day human).

Although the earliest stages of vertebrate development are vastly modified by the amount of yolk which may be present in the egg and by the presence or absence of fetal membranes, yet, by the time neurulation gets under way, the embryos of all vertebrates, especially air-breathing vertebrates, are astonishingly similar. This is true whether the embryo's outer habitat is water (as in amphibians), air (as in reptiles and birds), or the maternal uterus (as in mammals). The late neurula stage has been the most conservative stage in the evolution of the vertebrates.

Of course any stage in embryonic development is an embryo. We are using the word in a narrow, and probably improper, sense to refer to those stages in which the form of the new individual is becoming apparent. As thus defined, the young embryo is quite straight and, for the most part, symmetrical. We visualize it in a standard position, namely, with the head forward and the back upward. Anterior (cephalad), therefore, means toward the head, and posterior (caudad) means toward the tail. Dorsal (dorsad) is

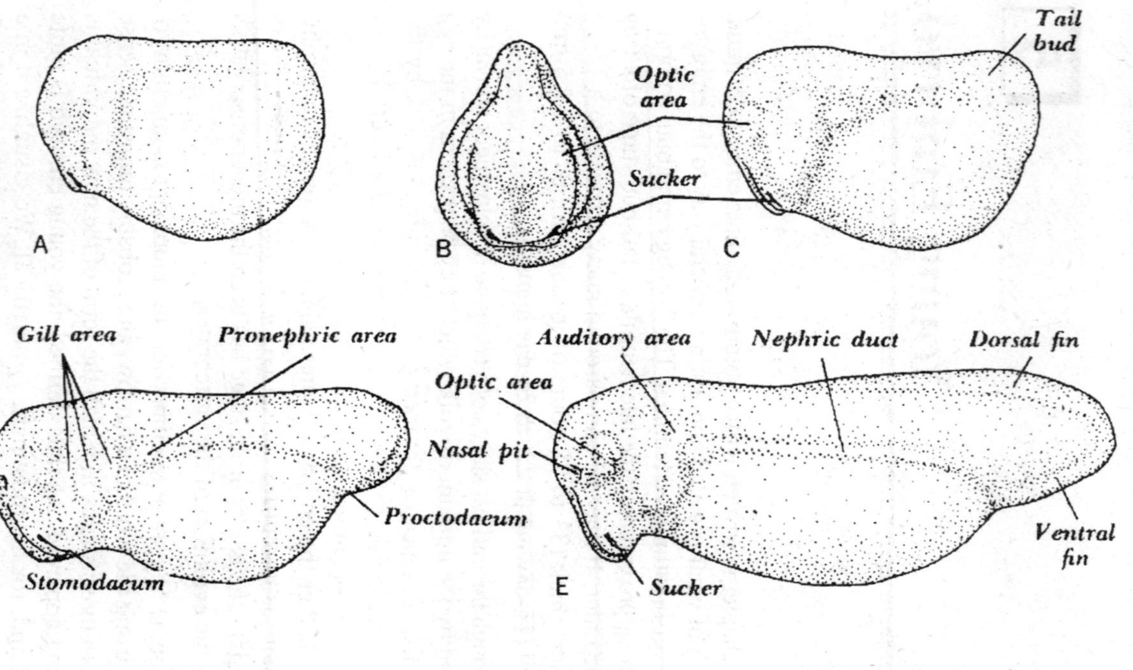

Figure 5.1 : Young embryos of the leopard frog Rana pipiens. A to E. Shumway's stages 15, 16, 17, 18, and 18+. Approximately x 12.

upward, and ventral (ventrad) is downward. (Unfortunately, the terms anterior and posterior are used otherwise in human anatomy. They are used as synonyms of ventral and dorsal.) Right and left always refer to the embryo's right and left.

TABLE 5.1 : "NORMAL STAGES" IN THE DEVELOPMENT OF RANA PIPIENS

Stage 1. Unfertilized egg.

Stage 2. Fcrtilized egg showing gray crescent. (1 hour).

Stage 3. Two-cell stage. (3.5 hours.)

Stage 4. Four-cell stage. (4.5 hours.)

Stage 5. Eight-cell stage. (5.7 hours.)

Stage 6. Sixteen-cell stage. (6.5 hours.)

Stage 7. Thirty-two cell stage. (7.5 hours.)

Stage 8. Midcleavage. (16 hours.)

Stage 9. Late cleavage. (21 hours.)

Stage 10. Dorsal lip of blastopore appearing. (26 hours.)

Stage 11. Midgastrula; semicircular blastopore. (34 hours.)

Stage 12. Late gastrula; circular blastopore, onefifth the diameter of the egg. (42 hours.)

Stage 13. Early neurula; broad neural plate; shallow neural groove. The blastopore is in the process of closing. (50 hours.)

Stage 14. Midneurula. The neural folds have moved about halfway toward the midline. (62 hours.)

Stage 15. Late neurula. The neural folds are in contact one-half to three-fourths of their length. The rotation of the embryo (a result of the development of cilia by the epidermis) begins.(67 hours.)

Stage 16. 2.5 mm long. The neural folds have closed. The. swellings of the optic vesicle, mandibular arch, and gill areas are seen. (72 hours.)

Stage 17. 3 mm. The tail bud is beginning to grow out. (84 hours.)

Stage 18. 4 mm. Lateral bending, due to unilateral muscle contraction, is seen for the first time. At this time the tail bud is about one-fifth the length of the embryo. (96 hours.)

Stage 19. 5 mm. The heart begins to beat. The tail is approximately one-third the length of the whole embryo. (118 hours.)

Stage 20. 6 mm. Circulation of blood can be seen in the external gills as soon as they appear. The tail is approaching one-half the total length. During this stage the embryo hatches unless, by reason of crowding or temperature, it has already done so. (140 hours.)

Stage 21. 7 mm. The external gills have now fully grown out; the mouth is open. The corneas of the eyes are becoming transparent. Occasional spontaneous swimming takes place. (162 hours.)

Stage 22. 8 mm. The opercular folds are clearly seen. The first circulatory loops are visible in the tail fins. (192 hours.)

Stage 23. 9 mm. Teeth beginning to appear. (216 hours.)

Stage 24. 10 mm. The operculum has covered the gill on the right. (240 hours.)

Stage 25. 11 mm. The opercular folds are complete (except for the spiracle on the left side). Soon the hind limb buds will appear. (284 hours.)

Medial means near the midplane, and lateral means away from it. Proximal (referring to appendages) is toward the body, and distal is away from it. When an embryo, in the case of birds and mammals, becomes flexed like a hibernating squirrel, it may come about that the anterior and posterior ends come close together. This need cause no difficulty in terminology if the embryo is thought of as straightened out.

"Stages" in the Development of the Frog

For those who use the egg of the leopard frog, *Rana pipiens*, in the laboratory, Table 5.1, based on a paper by Shumway, will prove useful. The approximate age in hours (at 18°C) is indicated in parentheses. However, the stage in development varies, not only with temperature, but with crowding and the amount of oxygen in the water.

The young embryo may be described as tubular and consisting of six longitudinal elements:

1. The outer epidermal covering
2. The dorsal neural tube
3. The notochordal rod
4. The endodermal canal
5. The right mesodermal plate
6. The left mesodermal plate

Between these elements there are loose wandering cells known as mesenchyme. Although the mesenchyme is mostly of mesodermal origin, yet the other germ layers, especially the ectoderm, contribute to it. It gives rise to supportive tissues, to muscles, to the blood vessels, and to the blood.

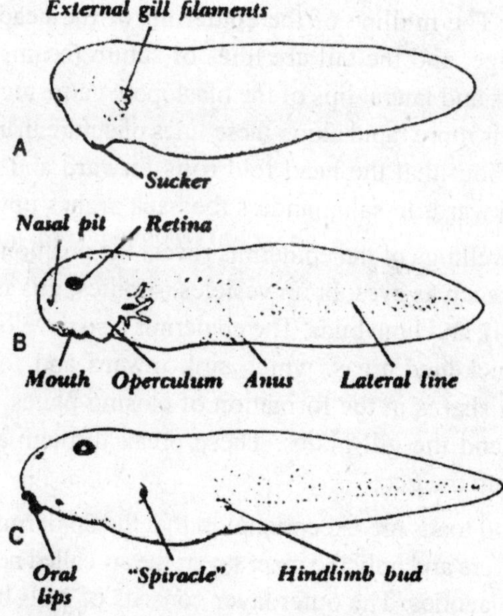

Figure 5.2 : Tadpoles of the leopard frog. A to C. Shumway's stages 20, 22, and 25. × 9, × 6½, and × 5½, respectively.

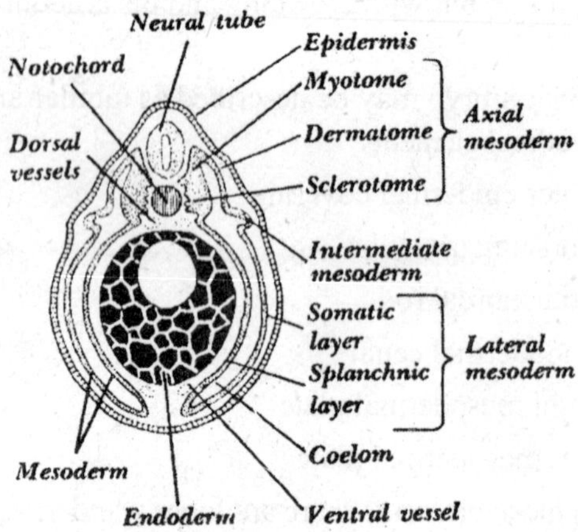

Figure 5.3 : Diagrammatic cross section of a young embryo. The labels indicate the longitudinal elements and the subdivisions of the mesoderm.

THE EPIDERMIS

The ectoderm of the outer surface of the young embryo is the epidermis. The midline of the epidermis of the head, the dorsal sagittal ridge, and the tail are lines of suture (seams) where the neural folds and lateral lips of the blastopore came together. Since elongation is more rapid along these lines of suture than elsewhere, it comes about that the head fold rolls forward and the tail bud grows backward. In salamanders the back arches upward.

Local swellings of the epidermis reveal the positions of internal structures, such as eyes, brain vesicles, somites, gill area, kidneys (pronephroi), and limb buds. The epidermis also develops placodes, or local thickened areas, which sink inward and form sensory vesicles. It shares in the formation of closing plates, such as the oral plate and the gill plates. These break through and become openings into the gut.

Frogs and toads are exceptional in that the epidermis is divided into two layers and only the inner layer, the so-called nervous layer, develops placodes. The outer layer consists of cells bearing dark pigment and, interspersed among them, glandular cells which secrete mucus.

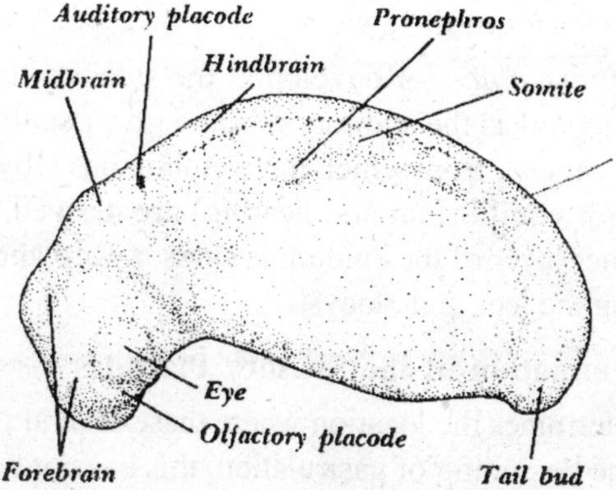

Figure 5.4 : Salamander embryo* (Ambystoma) *from the left, showing the regions of the epidermis. Harrison's stage 28. Approximately × 9½.

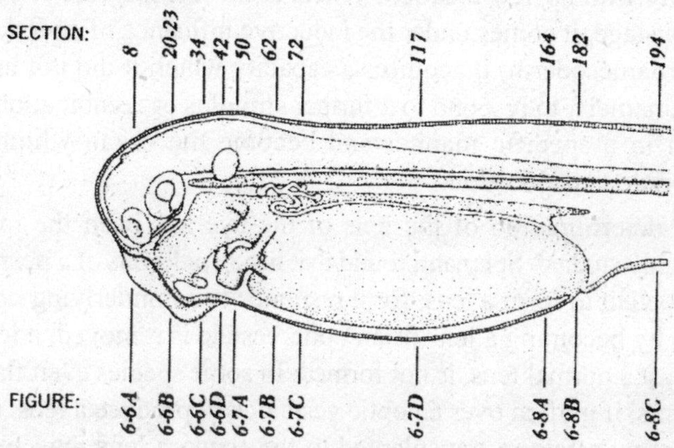

Figure 5.5 : Lateral dissection of a 6-mm leopard frog embryo. Shumway's stage 20. Note the three pronephric tubules and the primary nephric duct. × 15.

Sensory Placodes

The most anterior of the sensory placodes are the *olfactory placodes* near the anterior tip of the embryo close to the forebrain. These become the olfactory pits and ultimately give rise to the olfactory membranes of the nasal cavities.

The *lens placodes* are next in order. They form where the developing optic vesicles come into contact with the epidermis. Soon they cup inward, and after pinching away from the epidermis, become the lenses of the eyes.

The *auditory placodes* develop at the sides of the hindbrain. They sink inward as the auditory pits and give rise to the otocysts (auditory vesicles), from which the membranous labyrinths of the inner ear (for equilibrium and hearing) are derived. In the frog, only the inner layer of the epidermis sinks inward and is involved in producing the lens and otocyst.

The Determination of the Sensory Placodes

What determines the location where these several placodes will arise? At the beginning of gastrulation, this has not been decided. The prospective epidermis is still undifferentiated. If the region of a placode is transplanted to a new location, it will develop in harmony with its new location. When, at the late gastrula or early neurula stage, it comes under the inductive influence of endoderm or chordamesoderm, it acquires a capacity which it did not have before, namely, to respond to a further stimulus or combination of stimuli in a specific manner and become the organ which is appropriate to its location.

The determination of the lens of the eye has been the most thoroughly studied. Spemann found that head epidermis of a neurula is competent to form a lens, for it responds to an underlying optic vesicle by becoming a lens. If an optic vesicle is removed, a lens, or at least a normal lens, is not formed. In some species even flank epidermis, if grafted over an optic vesicle, will produce a lens. Or, if an optic vesicle in transplanted to the flank, a lens may form from the epidermis of the flank. Note, however, that in all cases it is the epidermis of a *neurula* which is competent to respond. Prospective epidermis of a gastrula responds to a similar contact with an optic vesicle by producing neural tissue.

Similar principles apply to the otocyst. During neurulation, the epidermis of the side of the head responds to an induction arising in head mesenchyme by becoming competent to form an otocyst. But this is not its final determination. Later, in the tail-bud stage, the location of the otocyst is made definite and precise as a response to a second inductive stimulus which originates in the hindbrain. A similar double induction seems to account for the determination of the olfactory placodes. First, the epidermis of the neurula is influenced by an induction arising in endoderm of the forward wall of the pharynx. (Mesoderm has not yet entered this area). Then later, it is acted upon by an induction of forebrain origin.

Jacobson has restudied the determination of the sensory placodes. After extensive explantation and transplantation experiments he concludes that determination is a continuing process which begins in gastrulation when the epidermis first comes into contact with endoderm and mesoderm. It continues as mesoderm pushes out from beneath the neural plate. Finally, it becomes complete through the inductive action of the neural plate itself. Although any one of these several influences may call forth the production of placodes, yet it takes all of them, acting in proper sequence, to bring about the normal differentiation and positioning of the nose, lens, and ear. Strangely enough, the placodes themselves do not influence each other. They may develop in contact with one another, even out of sequence.

Stomodaeum, Hypophysis, and Branchial Furrows

The *stomodaeum is* a shallow ectodermal depression on the underside of the head fold where the endoderm of the floor of the foregut comes into contact with epidermis. The *oral plate* which is thus formed breaks through and becomes the oral opening of the embryo. The ectodermal stomodaeum, at first shallow, becomes deeper as a result of the thickening of the mesoderm on each side of it.

Balinsky and others have shown that the formation of the stomodaeum is a response of the epidermis on the underside of the head to contact with the endoderm of the foregut. During later gastrulation, much of the epidermis of the head acquires the competence to so respond. Other epidermis does not, or acquires it to a less extent. If no contact is made between epidermis and endoderm, no stomodaeum is formed. But once contact is made, a stomodaeum will form even though the endoderm is afterward removed.

Epidermal cells of the forward wall of the stomodaeum form a median thickening which sinks inward. This is the *hypophyseal rudiment.* In birds and mammals it is hollow, but in amphibians it is a solid cord of cells. It migrates upward, through the head mesenchyme, until it comes into contact with the infundibulum on the underside of the forebrain. Ultimately it becomes the anterior lobe of the hypophysis (pituitary body). (It gives rise to a part of the posterior lobe as well.)

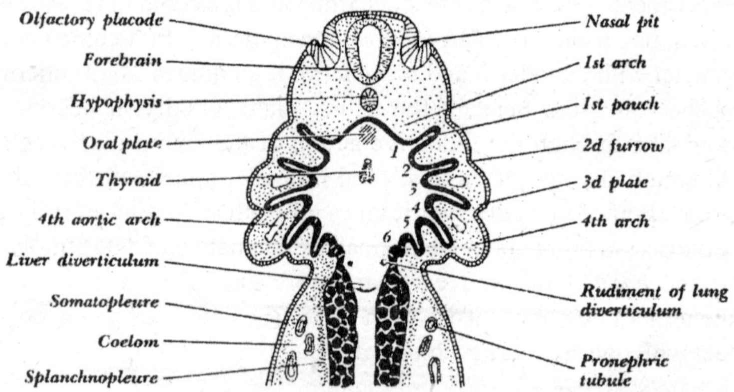

Figure 5.6 : Schematic frontal section through the head of a frog embryo. The oral plate, thyroid, and liver diverticulum are shown beyond the plane of the section. The asterisks mark the location of the future lung evaginations.

A series of ectodermal furrows develops on each side of the head, lateral to the foregut . We shall call them *branchial furrows.* They originate in a manner similar to that by which the stomodaeum is formed; that is, the endoderm of a pharyngeal pouch pushes laterally through the head mesenchyme and comes into contact with epidermis at the side of the head. The *branchial plates* (gill plates) which are thus formed consist of epidermis and endoderm with a very little mesoderm between. In the frog, the gill plates break through (except the first pair) and become open *branchial clefts* (gill slits).

The tissue at the sides of the head, anterior and posterior to each branchial plate or cleft, is known as a *branchial arch.* The first pair of branchial arches are also termed the *mandibular arches.* They are lateral to the stomodaeum and later become the upper and lower jaws. Posterior to the mandibular arches are the first branchial plates. These plates close the *hyomandibular clefts.* In the shark, they break through and the resulting openings are known as the spiracles. In amphibians and other air-breathing vertebrates they do not break through (or if they do they close again), but instead they become the ear drums (tympanic membranes).

The second branchial arches are the *hyoid arches.* These support the tongue. Then come the second branchial plates, and so on, until finally we come to the sixth branchial arches.

The several branchial furrows do not develop simultaneously. In the frog, the first (or hyomandibular) furrows appear at about stage 15 or 16. They separate the mandibular arches anteriorly from a swelling on each side of the head which we shall call the *gill areas*

The fifth branchial furrows also appear at about the same time at the posterior margin of the gill areas. They mark off the gill areas from the trunk. Later, at about stage 18, two vertical grooves are seen crossing each gill area. These are the second and third branchial furrows. The fourth furrow develops later. (Utimately, there is a fifth furrow and, so it is said, a rudimentary sixth.)

(Note: Many authors use the term "visceral" for the several structures which we have termed "branchial." They reserve the latter word for the clefts and arches which actually develop gills. Primitively all the arches bore gills. It is customary to refer to the homologous structures of mammal embryos as "gill arches and clefts" in spite of the fact that the mammal embryos have no gills and the clefts do not break through to the outside.)

Processes of one sort or another grow out from the gill arches. In salamanders, the first branchial arches give rise to tentacle-like outgrowths known as *balancers,* which serve to support the larva as it rests on the substrate. After the limbs appear, they degenerate. In the frog, the ventral surface of each mandibular arch produces a sucker. These also are temporary structures. By them the newly hatched tadpole attaches to objects in the pond. Balancers and suckers may possibly be homologous organs, for in a remarkable experiment performed by Schotte prospective ectoderm of a frog gastrula was substituted for the prospective head epidermis of a salamander gastrula. The larva which resulted was a salamander larva with a frog mask over its face. The head mesenchyme of the salamander had induced the epidermis of a frog to produce frog structures in the manner in which normally the mesenchyme induces its own epidermis to form the facial features of a salamander. Suckers were induced by mesenchyme of the mandibular arches of a salamander.

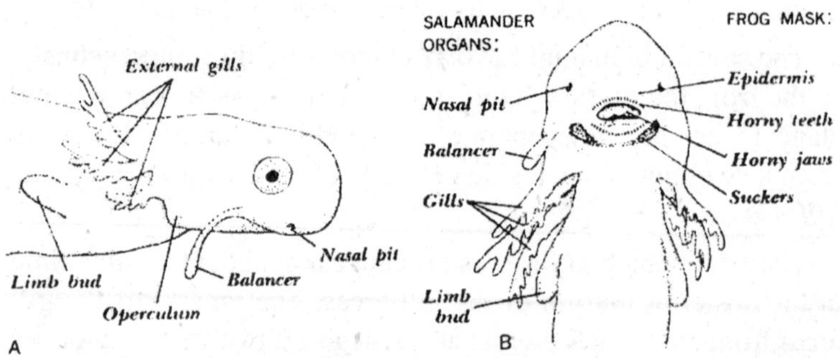

Figure 5.7 : A. Head of a salamander larva. Harrison's stage 40. B. Salamander larva with a frog mask, the result of grafting a patch of prospective epidermis from a beginning frog gastrula to the region of the prospective mouth of a beginning gastrula of a salamander.

This experiment points up the important distinction which must be made between *species characters* and *organ characters.* The ectoderm of the frog responded to the inductive stimulus of the mesoderm of the salamander by forming *organs* of a character appropriate to their location in the host. But the *species* character of the organs, indeed their individual character, was determined by the protoplasm of the donor. The epigenetic factors which determine organ characteristics have remained remarkably stable during the course of evolution, while the genetic factors which control species and individual characteristics have evolved.

The hyoid arches of amphibians give rise to opercular folds which grow backward and cover the open gill clefts. The third, fourth, and fifth branchial arches of salamanders produce external gill filaments which serve as respiratory organs. In frogs, the third and fourth branchial arches produce external gills which are soon overgrown by opercular folds. Finally only a small opening remains to the outside, namely, the "spiracle," situated on the left side of the body. By this time the external gill filaments have been replaced by internal gill filaments derived from the endoderm of the pharyngeal pouches.

THE NEURAL TUBE

Almost from its beginning, the neural tube is divisible into four regions: forebrain, midbrain, hindbrain, and spinal cord. It is conventional to further subdivide the forebrain and hindbrain as shown in the outline at the foot of this page.

Telencephalon

The first division of the forebrain is the *telencephalon*. Its anterior extremity is close to the olfactory epithelia. In relation to this, indeed partly in response to it, the forebrain develops nerve centers dominated by the nerves of smell. The sidewalls of the telencephalon give rise to lateral swellings which become centers of higher sensory correlation, the paired cerebral hemispheres.

Diencephalon

The second part of the forebrain is the *diencephalon*. Early in the development of the neural tube, its sidewalls bulge laterally and form the *optic vesicles*. These then cave in and become optic cups, from which the retinas of the eyes are developed. Beneath, and somewhat posterior to the optic vesicles, the floor of the diencephalon pushes downward as the so-called *embryonic infundibulum*. It comes into contact with the hypophyseal rudiment, and together they produce the pituitary body, or *hypophysis*. The hypophyseal rudiment becomes the embryonic anterior lobe. The embryonic infundibulum becomes most of the posterior lobe. It also becomes the stalk (infundibulum proper) which attaches the pituitary body to the brain. The sidewalls of the diencephalon thicken and develop the important nerve centers of the *thalamus* and *hypothalamus*. From the roof of the diencephalon, a small outgrowth pushes upward known as the *epiphysis*.

Mesencephalon

The midbrain, or *mesencephalon*, located posterior to the eyes, is dominated by the centers of reflexes based on vision. In those animals in which reflexes based on sight are highly organized-this is true of amphibians and birds-the dorsal side of the midbrain becomes large and forms *two optic lobes.* The ventral side of the mesencephalon develops the nerve centers of two pairs of nerves which supply muscles that move the eyeballs.

The neural tube bends downward in the midbrain region. This is the *cranial flexure. Pos*terior to the midbrain, the neural tube narrows to the *isthmus*. This marks the boundary between midbrain and hindbrain.

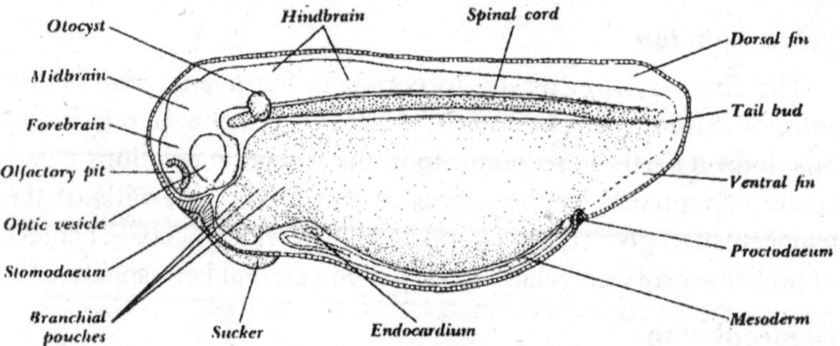

Figure 5.8 : Neural tube and gut of a 3½-mm embryo of the leopard frog* Rana pipiens *Shumway's stage 18. × 24.

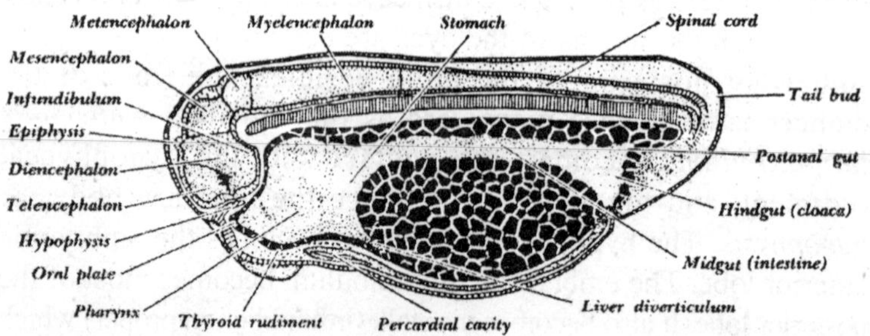

Figure 5.9 : Median view of the right half of a 3½-mm leopard frog embryo.

The anterior part of the hindbrain, namely, the *metencephalon,* is situated just anterior to the otocysts, the sensory organs of equilibrium. Hence it is appropriate that the metencephalon give rise to the *cerebellum* in which are located the nerve centers for balance. The cerebellum is small in amphibians but large in birds and mammals, which depend greatly on balance.

Posterior to the metencephalon is the *myelencephalon.* Most of its roof becomes broad, thin, and completely lacking in nervous tissue. Its thick sidewalls and floor form the *medulla oblongata.* Since the entire hindbrain lies dorsal to the pharynx, it is understandable that it contains the nerve centers for the sensory and motor nerves which supply the branchial arches.

Spinal Cord

The hindbrain tapers gradually to the spinal cord. The nerves to the body wall, limb buds, and most of the nerves to the viscera originate from the cord.

Experiments on the Neural Plate

When and how is the pattern of the neural plate determined? When is it decided what each of its regions will become? At the beginning of gastrulation, as we have already seen, the prospective neural plate and the prospective epidermis are not yet fully committed in their capacities for development. But when, as a result of gastrulation, the prospective neural plate comes into contact with the chordamesoderm of the archenteric roof, it undergoes its initial determination; that is, it acquires the capacity, if transplanted or explanted, to become nervous tissue. But it is still labile and dependent on underlying notochord and mesoderm for the pattern of its further differentiation.

Many years ago, Spemann discovered that if a square is cut from the anterior part of the neural plate, rotated 180° and replaced, the material which would have become midbrain, becomes forebrain and eyes, while the material which would have become forebrain becomes midbrain. The result is entirely different if the underlying archenteric roof (chords-mesoderm) is taken up along with the square of neural tissue and both tissues are rotated and reimplanted together. In this case, eyes form posterior to the otocyst, or if the eye-inducing mesoderm has been divided in the operation, four eyes may form, two in front and two behind. The same results are obtained also when only the chorda-mesoderm is rotated and the neural tissue is not rotated.

It is clear from these experiments that the differentiation of the pattern of the neural plate takes place progressively during neurulation and is dependent on inductive influences emanating from the chorda-mesoderm beneath it. The eye, for example, depends on the prechordal mesoderm. If this is removed before the open-neural-plate stage, no eye is formed. If, as a result of chemical or other inhibition, the prechordal mesoderm remains in its original position anterior to the notochord and fails to divide to the right and left, a single median eye will result. This condition is *cyclopia*. If, however, as normally takes place, the prechordal mesoderm separates half to one side and half to the other, then two eyes are produced.

The differentiation of the cross section of the neural tube is dependent on the notochord and mesoderm. Holtfreter found that an isolated piece of neural plate (with no mesoderm) will round up and differentiate nerve cells, but it does so inside-out; that is, the nuclei of the nerve cells are now crowded next to the outside of the piece, and solid white matter (axons) forms within. However, if the isolated piece is surrounded by mesenchyme, the arrangement of nervous tissue is more normal. White matter is now on the outside, as it should be, and the nuclei crowd around a central lumen. But even so, the central lumen is circular. If, however, the piece is in contact on one side with the notochord, then the lumen is slitlike in cross section, as it is in normal development, with one end of the slit directed toward the notochord. If the piece is in contact with muscle cells, there is an increase in the white matter on the side next to the muscle cells. Many details of the patterning of the nervous system, however, remain to be discovered.

THE NEURAL CREST

When the neural folds rise up and close inward toward the middorsal line, certain cells at the margins of the neural plate known as mesectoderm break loose from adjacent epidermis and form *neural crests* along the top of the neural tube. These cells have varied and important fates. Instead of remaining astride the midline, they migrate in loose streams to the sides of the embryo. One stream passes in front of the eye and ultimately gives rise to some of the cartilages of the skull. A second stream descends behind each eye and becomes the cartilage of the first (mandibular) arch. Other streams farther back enter the remaining arches and give rise to branchial cartilages.

The cranial ganglia of the head are formed in part from neural-crest cells; but they also receive contributions from adjacent epidermal placodes related to the branchial arches. Furthermore, much of the mesenchyme of the head, from which the dermis and subcutaneous tissue is formed, is of neural-crest origin. This includes the papillae of the teeth.

In the trunk, the neural-crest cells wander in amoeboid fashion to the sides of the embryo and form loose longitudinal strands. The strands which lie between the neural tube and the somites become subdivided into a series of segments, the *spinal ganglia.* This segmentation, however, is secondary to the segmentation of the mesodermal somites, for if a somite is removed, a discrete ganglion is not formed. Other strands of crest cells form along the aorta and in tissue ventral to it. Here they give rise to the ganglia of the autonomic nervous system and to the medulla of the adrenal glands. Still other neural-crest cells migrate individually, multiply, and become pigment cells (melanophores). They appear to repel one another, but finally they settle in certain regions as though they were attracted by these regions.

A few neural-crest cells remain in the middorsal line where they give rise to the mesenchymal core of the dorsal fin fold. If neuralcrest cells are transplanted to the flank of an embryo, they often induce the formation of a fin fold in their new location. A fin fold on the underside of the tail bud arises in a similar way, induced in this case by neural-crest-like cells which are derived from the most posterior part of the neural folds. The initial determination of the neural-crest cells, like that of the neural plate, is the result of embryonic induction by underlying chorda-mesoderm.

THE NOTOCHORD

The notochord extends along the midline of the embryo beneath the hindbrain and spinal cord. Because of the cranial flexure and also because of the elongation of the notochord itself the anterior end of the notochord comes close to the infundibulum on the underside of the forebrain. In amphibian larvae and in some of the lower fish the notochord functions as a skeletal rod. As such, it consists of a core of pithlike cells containing gelatinous vacuoles. A sheath and membrane develop around the cord, apparently having been produced by the notochord itself. In most vertebrates, however, the notochord is surrounded and then more or less completely replaced by skeletal elements derived from mesoderm.

If the notochord is experimentally removed or prevented from forming, the embryo fails to elongate properly and the somites of opposite sides may be united across the midline.

THE ENDODERMAL CANAL

The endodermal canal, or gut, begins at the oral plate and ends posteriorly at the anal plate. Actually it begins a bit forward of the oral plate in a shallow temporary recess termed Seessel's pocket. The gut ends behind the anal plate in a temporary extension of the gut known as the postanal or *tail gut.* In the amphibian, the endodermal canal is commonly described as consisting of three regions: foregut, midgut, and hindgut. (These terms must not be confused with the same terms used in invertebrate zoology, where "foregut" refers to the stomodaeum, and "hindgut" to the proctodaeum.)

The *foregut* is that portion of the endodermal canal which is anterior to the main yolk mass. It gives rise to the pharynx, esophagus, stomach, liver, pancreas, and the forepart of the duodenum. Its walls are at first one cell thick. The *midgut is* the future intestine. Its sides and floor are the yolk-rich cells of what was the vegetal area. In salamanders the center of its roof is a suture (seam) formed during neurulation at the place where the lateral margins of endoderm closed in beneath the notochord). The *hindgut* is that portion of the endodermal canal which is posterior to the main yolk mass and ventral to the tail bud. It gives rise to the cloaca and the temporary postanal gut. These definitions apply to amphibians. They must be modified when applied to birds and mammals, which have a yolk sac.

The Pharynx

The oral plate (pharyngeal membrane) forms on the underside of the pharynx near its anterior end where a downpocket of endoderm comes into contact with the ectoderm of the stomodaeum. Later the plate breaks down and disappears so that no clear evidence remains as to where ectoderm ends and endoderm begins.

Behind the oral plate the pharynx is broad, but it narrows toward its posterior end. We have already described how, from each side of the pharynx, a series of five pharyngeal pouches push through the mesenchyme until they make contact with the epidermis at the sides of the head. The gill plates which are thus formed later break through (except the first pair) and become open gill clefts (branchial clefts).

A median ventral downpocketing from the floor of the pharynx between the second pair of pharyngeal pouches is the primordium of the *thyroid gland*. Later, after the embryo has hatched, the floor of the pharynx posterior to the thyroid forms a midventral longitudinal groove known as the *laryngotracheal groove.* From its posterior end *lung buds* push laterally and grow backward. It has long been debated whether or not the lung buds represent a posterior pair of pharyngeal pouches.

Esophagus, Stomach, and Liver Diverticulum

In addition to the pharynx, the foregut gives rise to the esophagus, stomach, liver, and parts of the pancreas and duodenum. At first these organs are represented by narrow transverse bands of endoderm posterior to the pharynx; but later, as the embryo grows in length, the bands constrict, elongate, and take the form of the several organs.

The *liver diverticulum* is formed very early in development as a deep downpocketing of the foregut just anterior to the yolk of the midgut. Later, its anterior wall forms cords of cells which grow forward and ramify among the endothelial cells of the future ventral blood vessels. Together, the endodermal cords and the endothelia of the blood vessels become the liver. Farther back, the posterior extremity of the liver diverticulum becomes the *gall bladder*. (A strange feature of frog development is that the liver diverticulum perforates the ventral endoderm and unites with the remnant of the blastocoel.)

The Intestine

The yolk-rich cells of the amphibian midgut become the intestine. As the digestion of the store of yolk proceeds, these cells organize as an intestinal epithelium. From the beginning its lumen is narrow. In some amphibians it becomes completely closed, and the final lumen is a new cleft which opens through the center of the mass of yolk cells.

The Cloaca

The hindgut lies between the yolk mass of the midgut and the lips of the closed blastopore. It forms the *cloaca*. As the tail bud grows backward, the dorsal wall of the cloaca is drawn out with it. This is the temporary tailgut (postanal gut). It has been said to represent the neurenteric canal, but actually it is more dorsal in position. The primary nephric ducts from the pronephros grow backward at the sides of the embryo until they reach and then open into the cloaca. Thus, by definition, the cloaca is the common passageway for the wastes from both the alimentary canal and the excretory organs. Later it serves the reproductive organs as well.

The anus appears to be a new formation. The ventral opening of the slitlike blastopore closes, but the ectoderm and endoderm remain in contact and constitute an *anal plate* (cloacal membrane). The narrow groove which appears in the ectoderm is the *proctodaeum*. After hatching, the anal plate breaks down, so that the anus (like the mouth) is a new opening to the outside.

Far along in the course of development, namely, about the time of metamorphosis, a pocket pushes forward from the anterior wall of the cloaca and becomes the urinary bladder.

Experimental Observations

When and how does the endodermal canal become organized into its several regions? What are the steps in its determination?

It will be recalled that if the prospective chordamesoderm of the dorsal lip (organizer) of a gastrula is implanted to the ventral side of another gastrula, a secondary embryonic axis results. This axis may include a pharynx with pouches and even a secondary intestinal lumen. The endoderm, therefore, like the ectoderm, is dependent on chorda-mesoderm for its initial organization. By the time gastrulation is complete, the gut has already undergone anteroposterior determination, although it is still subject to inductive influences of the chorda-mesoderm. For a time it remains dorsoventrally undetermined. Thus if the entire endoderm of an early neurula is removed and replaced upside down (i.e., inverted dorsoventrally) within the outer ectodermal-mesodermal shell, a fairly normal embryo may develop; but, if it is reversed end for end (anteroposteriorly), abnormality results.

After neurulation is complete, the parts of the endoderm, if transplanted or explanted, develop according to their original prospective fates and are no longer dependent on their surroundings. The determination of the gut has been accomplished.

THE MESODERM

When discussing neurulation it was noted that the right and left sheets of mesoderm are divisible into several regions.:

1. The mesenchyme of the head
2. The dorsal or axial mesoderm (epimere)
3. The intermediate mesoderm (mesomere)
4. The lateral mesoderm (hypomere)

In addition to these there are loose cells (angioblasts) which, during gastrulation, migrate ahead of the mesoderm proper. They ultimately give rise to blood islands (essentially a single island in amphibians), blood vessels, blood cells, and possibly to the germ cells as well.

Mesenchyme of the Head

The mesoderm anterior to the notochord (prechordal mesoderm) and the axial mesoderm anterior to the otocysts break down into loose cells (mesenchyme) which wander forward in the head and fill the spaces between the other tissues. This mesenchyme receives important contributions from the neural crest (mesectoderm) and from the epidermal placodes of the cranial nerves. As we have seen, the mesoderm has much to do with the determination of the structures of the head. Ultimately it gives rise to the head skeleton and to the muscles of the eye.

The Axial Mesoderm: the Somites

The axial mesoderm (epimeres) consists of longitudinal bands, one on each side of the notochord and neural tube. Beginning in the region of the hindbrain and progressing posteriorly, the bands become divided by transverse clefts into a series of blocklike segments, the *somites*. The last somites which form are always the most posterior. Each somite may develop an inner cavity, the *myocoel,* but these are transitory.

The outer wall of each somite is called the *dermatome*. It is adjacent to the epidermis and ultimately forms much of the inner or connective tissue layer of the skin (the dermis) and the subcutaneous tissues which lie beneath the skin. The dorsal edge of the inner wall of each somite is the *myotome.* At first it is small; but it grows tremendously, and its cells elongate in a longitudinal direction to become the axial muscles of the body. The dermatomes and myotomes push dorsally and ventrally beneath the epidermis and, having received major contributions from the lateral mesoderm, completely surround the embryo. The ventral part of the inner wall of each somite is the *sclerotome.* It breaks down into loose cells which migrate around the notochord and spinal cord and give rise to the supporting tissues (connective tissues, cartilage, and later bone) of the vertebral column.

The Intermediate Mesoderm

The intermediate mesoderm (mesomeres) consists of narrow bands of cells which border the axial mesoderm laterally. It gives rise to the excretory and reproductive organs. In most vertebrates the anterior portion of each band divides into a series of segments known as *nephrotomes.* At first each nephrotome is connected to a somite by a narrow neck, but this connection is transitory. It is usual for the lateral wall (outer layer) of each nephrotome, beginning with the most anterior, to produce a tubule, *a pronephric tubule.* This grows outwardly toward the epidermis and then, turning backward, it joins the tubule immediately behind it. The result is a longitudinal duct, the *primary nephric duct.* The duct, with some possible addition from the intermediate mesoderm farther back, grows posteriorly along the lateral border of the intermediate mesoderm until it comes to the region of the hindgut. It then turns ventrally and enters the hindgut.

The medial end of each pronephric tubule opens into the body cavity by a ciliated funnel known as a *nephrostome.* The median wall of the body cavity adjacent to each nephrostome develops a tuft of blood capillaries known as an *external glomerulus*. Each glomerulus is fed by a short nephric artery directly from the dorsal aorta.

In the case of the frog, the development of the pronephros is somewhat more direct than has just been described. The outer layer of the intermediate mesoderm ventral to somites 2, 3, and 4 thickens and projects ventrally as a "shelf" between the epidermis and the lateral mesoderm. At first the shelf appears to be solid, but then cavities appear which, uniting, become the primary nephric duct and three pronephric tubules. (In salamanders there are generally two pronephric tubules.) The duct grows posteriorly in the manner which already has been described, and the tubules develop ciliated nephrostomes. The tubules become convoluted and are bathed by blood of the posterior cardinal vein. The glomerular tufts in frogs are united on each side into a single body commonly referred to as a *glomus.*

References to some of the experiments which have been performed on the development of the pronephros of amphibians will be made in the last chapter of this book.

The Lateral Mesoderm: the Coelom

The lateral mesoderm, or hypomeres, consists of sheets of cells which cover the flanks of the embryo. The lateral mesoderm never divides into segments. Rather, each sheet splits into two layers: an outer layer next to the ectoderm, known as the somatic layer; and an inner laver next to the endoderm termed the splanchnic layer. The cleft between the two layers is the body cavity, or coelom. Note that it is a cavity *within* the mesoderm, not a cavity between the germ layers. The ectoderm and somatic layer of the hypomere, together with cells derived from the dermatome and myotome, constitute the body wall or *somatopleure.* The splanchnic layer and the endoderm form the visceral wall or *splanchopleure.* Actually, the split between the somatic mesoderm and splanchnic mesoderm is not everywhere evident in young amphibian embryos. Only in the region of the heart and pronephric tubules is it at first easily recognized.

Observe that a mesentery is a double sheet of mesoderm which suspends an organ within the body cavity. It is formed when the splanchnic mesoderm pushes medially both above and below the endoderm of the gut until it almost completely surrounds the gut. The *dorsal mesentery* suspends the esophagus, stomach, and intestine in the body cavity. It carries the blood vessels and nerves which supply these organs. The *ventral mesentery* of the pharynx (it has no dorsal mesentery) wraps itself around the heart tube (the endocardium, presently to be described) and forms the surface and muscular layers of the heart (epimyocardium). Mesenteries are formed above and below the heart; but they disappear, so that the heart becomes free (except at its anterior and posterior ends) within the anterior portion of the body cavity, the portion known as the *pericardial coelom.* The ventral mesentery of the stomach is invaded by the endodermal cords of the hepatic diverticulum, as has already been described. In principle, it is divided by the liver into a dorsal mesentery between the stomach and the liver (gastrohepatic ligament) and a ventral mesentery between the liver and the ventral body wall (ventral hepatic ligament). Across the posterior border of the gastrohepatic ligament, the bile duct (derived from the hepatic diverticulum) travels from the liver to the intestine. The ventral mesentery of the intestine breaks down. The result is that, in the abdominal region, the body cavity of one side opens to the body cavity of the other side beneath the gut.

There is an adhesion on each side, just anterior to the liver, between the splanchnic mesoderm of the heart and the somatic mesoderm of the body wall. These adhesions unite with the ventral mesentery to make a partition, the *septum transuersum,* which partially separates the pericardial coelom in front from the *peritoneal coelom* behind. The transverse septum, however, is only a partial partition, for above it, on each side, communications remain between the pericardial and peritoneal cavities. The lung buds push laterally into these communications so that they (the communications) may be called the *pleural canals,* or recesses. They become cut off from the pericardial cavity in front by a pleuropericardial membrane, but in amphibians they remain widely open to the peritoneal cavity behind.

Experiments on the Mesoderm

The evidence is overwhelming that the chorda-mesoderm takes the lead in the organization of the embryo. Both ectoderm and endoderm obtain their cues from inductive influences emanating from the chorda-mesoderm adjacent to them. But how is the organization of the chorda-mesoderm itself accomplished? For an answer we are thrown back on some form of the gradient theory. The genes of the nucleus can supply the possibilities. But only some spatial factor beyond the gene can determine the time and place.

Experiments were described in the previous chapter which have been interpreted as indicating that at the close of gastrulation the chorda-mesoderm presents two gradients: (1) a dorsoventral gradient in the distribution of a hypothetical "neuralizing factor" (strongest on the dorsal side); and (2) an anteroposterior gradient of a supposed "mesodermalizing factor" (strongest at the posterior end). The biochemical nature of these factors has not certainly been identified. Apparently the head end is relatively free from the mesodermalizing factor. It is possible that the neuralizing factor is a carry-over from the cortical material of the gray crescent and that the mesodermalizing factor has some relation to the time which has elapsed since the material in question gastrulated. Note that the head mesenchyme was the first mesoderm to enter in gastrulation and that the tail mesoderm was the last. However this may be, the initial determination (that is, the commitment of the regions of the chorda-mesoderm to their several fates) may be visualized as taking place in a two-dimensional grid. By the time neurulation has begun, the main territorial subdivisions or "embryonic fields" have been pretty well staked out, and the chorda-mesoderm has become a mosaic of self-differentiating regions. In this respect a field resembles the original state of the egg itself.

At first the several fields are not sharply delimited. On the contrary, they broadly overlap one another, and each constitutes within itself a "harmonious equipotential system" which is capable of self-regulation. The classic example of such a field is the region of the prospective limb bud, to which topic we next turn our attention. It must not be thought, however, that the relation between the mesoderm and the other germ layers is altogether a one-way relation. The continued patterning of the mesoderm requires the presence of the other tissues whose differentiation it has itself induced.

The Limb Buds

In amphibians, the limb buds first appear as moundlike swellings of the body wall. In salamanders, the buds of the forelimbs become visible at about the tail-bud stage just ventral to the pronephric swelling. This in turn is ventral to the 3d, 4th, and 5th somites. Hindlimb buds arise later in the region of the anus. In frogs, the limb buds are slower to develop. The forelimb buds become enclosed in the gill cavities which are formed when the operculum grows backward over the external gills. At metamorphosis, the right forelimb erupts through the operculum, while the left forelimb emerges through the opercular opening (spiracle). The hindlimbs grow rapidly during metamorphosis.

The forelimb buds of salamanders grow outward and backward, and then twist (pronate) so that the original ventral or flexor surface is turned toward the body. They become paddle-shaped by the flattening of their distal ends, with the future palm of the hand or sole of the foot facing inward. The radial border (preaxial border) becomes ventral; the ulnar border (postaxial) becomes dorsal. Soon flexion is seen at the elbow joint.

The region of the prospective forelimb mesoderm has been identified as early as the beginning gastrula in the future lateral mesoderm. Later, namely, at the tail-bud stage, loose mesenchyme cells split away from the outer surface of the somatic layer of mesoderm. They multiply to form the swelling which is the limb bud. In shark embryos, the fin buds receive contributions from the nearby axial mesoderm, but this process has not been observed in amphibians.

Experiments on Limb Buds

How are the limbs determined? Harrison (1918) reported that in salamander embryos the capacity to form a forelimb resides in a disc of somatic mesoderm situated ventral to the 3d to 5th somites. Wherever this disc may be transplanted, whether beneath its own ectoderm, or covered over by strange ectoderm, it will form a limb. Actually, the capacity to form a limb. extends beyond Harrison's disc, for if the disc is removed, cells from the bordering somatic mesoderm move in, the wound heals, and a limb is reorganized. Indeed, it is necessary to remove a disc of mesoderm about five somites in diameter to avoid such reorganization. But this is not the entire story: A large part of the somatic mesoderm of the flank is competent to form a limb bud, provided it is sufficiently stimulated. Balinsky found that if an otocyst or an olfactory vesicle is implanted in the lateral mesoderm of a neurula anywhere between the fore- and hindlimb buds, it may stimulate the development of a supernumerary appendage. In short, the limb area is a field in which three degrees of capacity to form a limb grade into one another: (1) The smaller disc (three somites in diameter, or at least a part of it) is the prospective limb. It becomes a limb, given normal development. (2) A larger disc (five somites in diameter) is potentially a limb and will form a limb if the smaller area is removed. (3) The entire flank mesoderm has the competence to form a limb, but it does so only if it is sufficiently stimulated.

Other experiments performed by Harrison on the amphibian limb bud have further emphasized its field character. It is an "harmonious equipotential system" in Driesch's sense. Any half of the limb disc, whether dorsal, ventral, anterior, or posterior, may be removed, and the half which remains will form a whole limb. The mesoderm of two limb buds may be superposed, one on top the other, and a single limb may result. Remarkably enough, a considerable regulation toward normal size takes place.

The nature and orientation of the limb is not determined all at once. Whether it will be a forelimb or a hindlimb is decided during gastrulation. The anterior-posterior polarity of the limb (AP axis) seems to be carried over from the polarity of the egg. It is not reversible. If a limb disc is removed and then implanted either in the same place or another place, but with reversed polarity, the limb which develops points anteriorly rather than posteriorly. This is true whether the limb disc comes from the same side (homopleural) or from the opposite side (heteropleural). Yet the surrounding tissue is not without its influence, for more often than not, a duplicate limb develops which is oriented harmoniously with the host.

Swett has showed that dorsal-ventral polarity (DV axis) is decided during the period that the tail bud is growing out. Anytime before Harrison's stage 32, a limb disc which is transplanted with its ventral side up will develop a limb having its dorsal side up, as it should be. The first digit will be ventral, and flexion will be downward. But after stage 35, if a limb disc is inverted, the limb which develops is upside down. The first digit then points upward, and flexion is upward. Swett found that the mediolateral axis (ML axis) is not fixed until stage 37. If before this stage the mesoderm of a limb bud is removed and reimplanted with its inner surface outward, a normal limb may nevertheless result. Not until the limb has actually begun to bulge outward is the ML axis settled.

THE HEART AND BLOOD VESSELS

The Primary Dorsal and Ventral Blood Vessels

We noted that during gastrulation certain cells of the prospective chordamesodermi, which border the blastocoel, break away from the adjacent endoderm and wander upward within the blastocoel in front of the involuting mesoderm. These are the *angioblasts,* the forerunners of the linings (endothelia) of the blood vessels and the blood cells. In the neurula, angioblasts are found beneath the pharynx, in the gill arches, and between the endoderm and the splanchnic mesoderm of the intestinal wall. As the splanchnic mesoderm wraps itself around the endoderm of the gut, strands of angioblasts migrate before it, both above the gut and below it.

These strands are the precursors of the *primary dorsal* and *primary ventral blood vessels.*

The primary dorsal blood vessels become (1) the *dorsal aortas;* their extensions forward into the head are (2) the *internal carotid arteries,* and their extension backward into the tail is (3) the *caudal artery*. Above the pharynx, the dorsal aortas are paired, right and left; but from the pharynx backward they unite in the midline and form a single median trunk. Branches of the aorta go to the body wall (somatopleure) and visceral wall (splanchnopleure).

The primary ventral vessels, which are located beneath the gut, have a more varied fate. In the ventral wall of the intestine, they are associated with a more or less unified *blood island,* from which also the first blood cells originate. The island becomes channeled and forms a pair of lateral *vitelline veins* which course forward to the liver. These correspond to the veins of the yolk sac of amniotes (reptiles, birds, and mammals). We have already noted that ventral to the stomach the primitive ventral vessels are invaded by endodermal cords of the liver diverticulum. The combined tissues give rise to the liver. Beneath the posterior part of the pharynx, the ventral vessels fuse together in the midline and become the inner endothelial tube of the heart, the *endocardium.* Farther forward they produce the *ventral aortas*. The splanchnic mesoderm which enfolds the endocardium becomes the *epimyocardium,* from which the muscles of the heart are derived.

A series of six pairs of *aortic arches* of endothelial origin develop within the mesenchyme of the gill arches. They connect the ventral aortas with the dorsal aortas above. The first two pairs (those of the mandibular and hyoid arches), however, are transitory. The third aortic arches remain as the roots of the internal carotid arteries. The fourth, fifth, and sixth arches retain their connections with the dorsal aortas. The third and fourth arches (and in tailed amphibians also the fifth arches) sprout capillary loops into the gill filaments. At the time of metamorphosis the fifth arches disappear, and the sixth arches acquire branches to the lungs, namely, the *pulmonary arteries*.

Thus a complete visceral, or splanchnic, circulation is established early in the development of the embryo. Blood from the capillary plexus in the wall of the intestine is carried forward by the vitelline veins to the liver. It then is pumped through the heart and into the ventral aortas. Next it flows dorsally through the aortic arches and then backward in the dorsal aorta. It finally is distributed by the vitelline branches of the capillaries of the intestine from which it started.

The Cardinal Veins

How does the blood which goes forward to *cardinal veins* (precardinals) brings the blood the head by way of the internal carotid arteries posteriorly from the head. A pair of *posterior* return to the heart? How does the blood which enters the body wall by way of the dorsal and lateral branches of the aorta return? Or again, dorsal aorta to the how does the blood which goes to the tail by the caudal artery get back to the heart? To complete these somatic circulations of the body, the embryo develops within the somatopleure a system of veins known as the cardinal system. *A* pair of *anterior cardinal veins* (postcardinals) carries the blood forward in the body wall from the tail and trunk. These join together lateral to the heart and form the right and left *common cardinal veins* (ducts of Cuvier). The latter cross from the body wall to the sinus venosus of the heart by way of the transverse septum, which thus serves as a bridge between the somatopleure and splanchnopleure. Just before each common cardinal vein crosses its bridge, it is joined by a vein from the ventral side of the gill area (ventral jugular vein) and a vein from the ventral abdominal wall (ventral abdominal vein).

The Heart

The heart (endocardium and epimyocardium) grows in length faster than the pericardial cavity in which it lies. It becomes a counterclockwise spiral. Its chambers, named from behind forward (in the direction of blood flow), are (1) the *sinus venosus,* which receives blood from the liver and from the two common cardinal veins; (2) the *atrium,* located just anterior to the sinus venosus; (3) the *ventricle,* which is bent into a loop beneath the sinus and atrium; and (4) the *truncus,* which discharges forward into the ventral aortas.

By careful observation, the first twitching of the frog heart can be seen at about stage 19, soon after the tail bud has begun to grow out. The circulation of the blood can be seen in the gill filaments as soon as these appear (stage 20).

Experiments on the Heart

Staining experiments have made it possible to identify prospective heart tissue (epimyocardium) as early as the beginning gastrula. It is situated internally in the dorsolateral marginal zone (prospective mesoderm) not far from the endoderm of thc future pharynx.

The heart rudiments move anteriorly (upward) as the leading edge of the lateral mesoderm. They are preceded by the loose cells (angioblasts which are destined to form the endothelial lining (endocardium) of the heart. At the stage of the open neural plate, the heart rudiments lie ventral to the lateral neural folds and beneath the epidermis of the future auditory placodes. During neurulation, the rudiments of the two sides move ventrally between the epidermis and pharyngeal endoderm until at an advanced neurula stage they come together ventral to the posterior part of the pharynx. Here they surround the endothelial cells; and, together, mesoderm and endothelium give rise to the heart.

When and how does the heart-forming material acquire the capacity to become a heart? Is the heart a self-differentiating system, or is it induced by adjacent tissues? Apparently the answer is not simple. Prospective heart substance, in its migration, comes into relation to both endoderm and epidermis. Do these have an inductive influence? Initially, they possibly do not. The work of Ekman, Copenhaver, and Bacon demonstrates that beginning about the stage of the horseshoe-shaped blastopore, the material of the prospective heart, if isolated, will self-differentiate and give rise to pulsating tissue. But it does not form an organized heart. The presence of pharyngeal endoderm is necessary if the latter is to occur. The capacity to self-differentiate histologically as cardiac muscle, therefore, is not the same as the ability to differentiate morphologically into a heart.

At first the primordium of the heart is a field in the same sense that a limb bud is a field. Its boundaries to begin with are not sharply defined. If the prospective heart mesoderm is removed, adjacent mesoderm will move in and produce a heart. Mesoderm of the gill area as late as a tail-bud stage, if substituted for heart mesoderm, is able to produce a heart. Not until a late tail-bud stage is this capacity restricted to the heart material itself. Also, it is not until then that the heart material is independent of pharyngeal endoderm in its surroundings. Jacobson has uncovered a strange relation. If the pharyngeal endoderm of a neurula is removed, no heart forms. But if brain tissue is also removed, a heart does form! It seems that there is an inhibitory influence which emanates from the brain and which confines heart differentiation to the ventral side of the body.

The heart field of an early neurula is an harmonious equipotential system. If one of the lateral rudiments of a heart is removed, the remaining rudiment will form an entire heart. In fact, any half-anterior, posterior, dorsal, or ventral-will similarly organize itself into a whole. Or, again, two heart rudiments, if placed together, will organize into a single whole organ. It is also during neurulation that the axiation of the heart rudiment takes place. The story is similar to the axiation of the limb buds.

First, the anteroposterior axis is determined. If a heart rudiment of an early neurula is removed, revolved 180°, and reimplanted, it develops normally; but later, when the tail bud has appeared, the same operation results in a reversed heart. Yet, even at the early tailbud stage, if the heart rudiment is inverted and implanted with the ventral side up, a normal heart may be produced. Still later, the dorsoventral and mediolateral axes become fixed.

The asymmetry of the heart is a matter of considerable interest. If the two sides of a heart are prevented from uniting in the mid-line, two hearts will form. Under these circumstances, the left heart is always of normal asymmetry. It spirals counterclockwise like a left-handed screw. The right heart frequently shows reversed asymmetry. It spirals clockwise. How is this *situs inversus cardis* brought about? It has been observed that a defect inflicted on the mesoderm of the left side of a gastrula may result in reversed asymmetry. In some way, the mesoderm of the left side seems to dominate the right side. But when the right side is freed from this dominance, or when the left side is weakened, a reversal of asymmetry may take place. It has been suggested that asymmetry is implicit in the cortex of the gray crescent as early as the one-cell stage of development.

THE TAIL BUD

The tail bud merits special attention. It will be recalled that at the beginning of neurulation the material which is to be the tail bud is a band across the neural plate, somewhat forward of its posterior end. The posterior fifth of the neural plate is prospective chorda-mesoderm.

Soon after the end of neurulation, when the neural folds have come together, the tail bud begins to push backward. The result is that the material of the former neural plate becomes bent upon itself. Its dorsal limb becomes the neural tube and notochord. Its ventral limb, extending from the tail bud to the anus, becomes mesoderm and endoderm. It has been shown, by vital staining, that it gives rise to muscles of the tail.

As the tail bud grows backward, the endoderm also is drawn backward as the postanal gut, or *tail gut.* Note that the tail gut is not the same as the neurenteric canal. It is more dorsal in position. Both are temporary structures.

The dorsal and ventral sides of the tail bud are sutures where the neural folds come together. They are also regions of active cell proliferation. Under the influence of neuralcrest cells, they give rise to the caudal fins of the tadpole.

METAMORPHOSIS

There is much of interest in the further development of amphibians, but space permits only a brief reference to the remarkable phenomenon of metamorphosis and to the role which hormones play in the process.

Gudernatsch (1912) noted that when tadpoles are fed desiccated thyroid tissue, they promptly transform into little frogs. Their limbs grow rapidly, their tails are resorbed, and the gill structures disappear. The intestine shortens in adaptation to a more completely carnivorous diet, the skin becomes cornified, and the lungs-already in use-enlarge. The liver begins to produce urea as the principal nitrogenous waste.

B. M. Allen (1918) made the reverse observation; namely, that if the thyroid gland of a frog embryo (tail-bud stage) is surgically removed, the tadpole does not transform into a frog. It feeds and grows until it is many times the size of a normally metamorphosing tadpole, but it does not become a frog. However, if it is fed thyroid, or if it is put in a solution containing thyroxin (the hormone of the thyroid gland, an amino acid containing iodine in its composition), it begins to transform at once.

By similar surgical procedure, it has been found that the embryonic hypophysis also plays a part in metamorphosis. If it is removed, the tadpole remains small, becomes light in color, and does not transform into a frog. Here, then, we have two glands, both of which are necessary if metamorphosis is to take place. But their roles are different. If, for example, both the thyroid and hypophysis are removed, and if then thyroid material is fed, metamorphosis promptly takes place. But if both glands are removed and anterior lobe material (derived from the hypophysis) is grafted into the tadpole, metamorphosis does not take place. Growth is stimulated, but metamorphosis fails. (If pars intermedia, also derived from the hypophysis, is implanted, the tadpole becomes dark owing to the expansion of its melanophores.)

The well-authenticated explanation of these results is that the anterior lobe acts as a "master gland" which produces several hormones, one of which, the so-called thyrotropic hormone, stimulates the thyroid gland to produce and release thyroxin.

Similar results have been obtained with salamanders. In their case, metamorphosis involves a change in texture of the skin, loss of gills and tail fins, and the development of lungs for respiration.

Of special interest is the case of the Mexican salamander known as axolotl, which inhabits lakes near Mexico City. It does not normally metamorphose. Instead it grows, matures, and reproduces while it is yet a larva. (Reproduction by a larva is termed neoteny or paedogenesis.) Why does it not transform? One might guess that the failure is due to a lack of iodine in the water since thyroxin contains iodine in its molecule; but this is not the case. A second guess would be that the thyroid glands of axolotl are deficient in the production of thyroxin. But if the thyroid gland of axoloti is substituted for the thyroid gland of a tiger salamander (which does metamorphose), it proves competent to bring about the metamorphosis of the tiger salamander. The answer to the problem is that axolotl does not metamorphose because its tissues are less responsive to thyroxin than are the tissues of other salamanders. It has been found, however, that if a sufficient amount of thyroid tissue is grafted into an axolotl, it does metamorphose. In this case we see a creature not normally found in nature, namely, a land-adapted axolotl.

It will be noted that during metamorphosis the tissues of a tadpole respond to thyroxin in different ways. Some tissues are stimulated, others are depressed. Eye and limb tissues are stimulated to grow, and will do so even if they have been implanted into the tail and are surrounded by degenerating cells. Tail muscle degenerates even if it is implanted into the trunk next to muscle which does not degenerate. Similar principles apply to the gills. It appears, therefore, that the response of the tissues to the hormone is a direct effect, not one mediated through the surroundings.

6

Induction

As in the chapter on sea urchin development, an attempt will be made here to summarize the various approaches to the problem of differentiation in the amphibian egg. Experimentation has proceeded from the level of tissues and cells to the molecular level. Development of new experimental techniques and approaches depends on technical advances and also on fundamental discoveries in the field of biochemistry. In recent years, the most intensive effort has been at the molecular level. The problems are the same as those encountered in the egg of the sea urchin: the nature and origin of egg polarity; the capabilities of various parts for self-differentiation; the interdependence of different regions upon each other. At the molecular level, the analysis has been mainly concerned with a description of the normal sequence of biochemical events during development of the embryo, most particularly with the synthesis of DNA and RNA and protein during development. The study of transcription and translation of genetic information again provides knowledge of the relationship between geneexpression and differentiation.

Isolation of Blastomers; Evidence of a Regulative System The first experiment on embryonic material of any kind is generally conceded to be that of Wilhelm Roux who studied the effect of killing one of the first two blastomeres of the frog egg. The results of this study were published in 1888. The experiment is of considerable historic interest, even though the conclusions reached by Roux turned out to be in error. Roux was the first biologist to work in the area of causal analysis of development. His underlying motive was to resolve problems of development into fundamental processes which he assumed to be the same fundamental processes underlying inorganic phenomena. This was a strong departure from the ideas of the day, which were mainly concerned with explanations of embryological phenomena in terms of comparative anatomy or evolutionary data. Prior to Roux, an embryonic structure could be considered to appear because it was part of the phylogenetic history of the species to which the embryo belonged. Roux formally put forth the idea that the proper study of the cause and effect during embryonic development was the embryo itself. He founded a new discipline of causal, analytical embryology which he called developmental mechanics. He is frequently called the "father of experimental embryology."

The experiment reported in 1888 was simple in design and was intended to decide the issue of independent versus interdependent (mosaic versus regulative, respectively) development as the underlying principle of differentiation in the frog egg. The experiment was performed at the two-cell stage and consisted of injuring one of the first two blastomeres after the first cleavage. Since the surviving cell gave rise to half an embryo, Roux felt that each cell developed independently of its neighbour and that development of the whole embryo represented the summation of the development of each part. These conclusions were later, shown to be erroneous for the frog egg. If the first two blastorneres were isolated from each other (instead of leaving an injured cell in contact with a live one), each blastomere was found to develop into a complete tadpole and frog, on most occasions. Even though Roux's experiment was shown to be of faulty design, the foundations were laid for the new experimental approach to the study of embryology.

Later experiments also showed that two complete embryos resulted from isolation of the first two blastomeres only when the first cleavage occurred in a plane that bisected. the gray crescent area. In those instances where the first cleavage plane occurrcd at some angle to the plane of bilateral symmetry instead of parallel to it, only the blastomere containing the gray crescent material developed into a complete embryo as diagrammed in Figure. The blastomere that lacked the gray crescent developed only into an undifferentiated mass of epidermal cells. These results, along with other studies, served to focus attention on the gray crescent area in later experimental work.

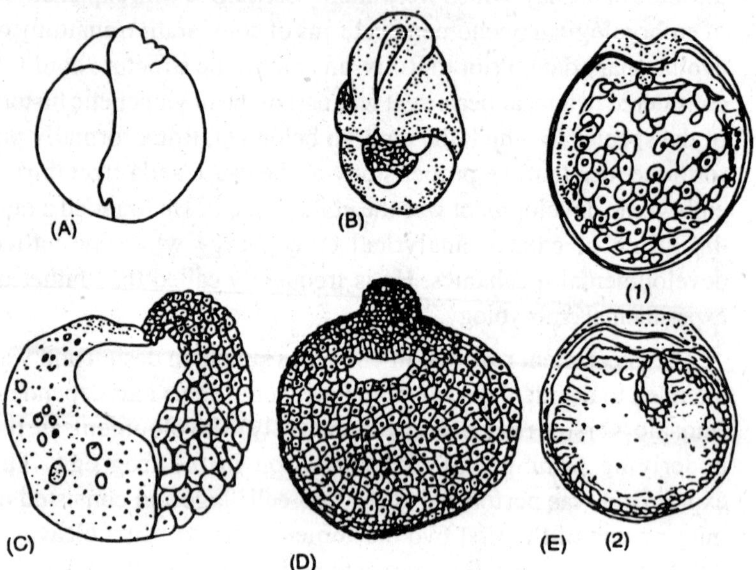

Figure 6.1 : (A) Half embryo of frog, resulting from injury to one of the first two blastomeres; (B) anterior embryo, so-called, after injury to one of the first two blastomeres of an egg in which the first cleavage had been at right angles to median plane. This embryo may also be interpreted as a whole embryo in which the lateral lips of the blastopore have been prevented from coming together by the material of the injured half; (C) section of blastula stage of ½ blastomere; (D) section of ½ embryo like that shown in A. (E) Cross sections through dorsal embryos arising from isolated Triturus blastomeres. (1) Half embryo; (2) quarter embryo, some magnification, (dorsal meaning the gray crescent material was included).

Fusion of Two Embryos; Additional Evidence of Regulative Ability

Two whole amphibian eggs can be merged to form a single embryo of double size. Two 2-cell stages are cross united in the *manner.* The result is regulation to form a single embryo, not a double "monster." Again, this result confirms the theory of interdependence of developing parts rather than theory of independent, self-differentiation of parts.

Experiments on the Gastrula; Interchangeability of Presumptive Neural Plate and Epidermis

The early gastrula, as shown by the fate map, has a roof over the blastocoel composed of cells destined to give rise to neural plate and epidermis. Prior to extensive involution of the presumptive chordamesoderm at the dorsal lip of the blastopore, the roof of the blastocoel can be rotated 180° such that presumptive neural plate and epidermis have exchanged locations. The result of this operation is a completely normal embryo indicating that, at this time, the two tissues are interchangeable (regulative).

Inductive interaction between cells is shown by transplants of the dorsal lip

The developmental fate of the cells turning in at the dorsal lip of the blastopore is largely chordamesoderm. If the chordamesoderm is transplanted to the ventral epidermis of an early gastrula host embryo, the transplant tissue will turn under and come to lie beneath the ventral epidermis of the host embryo. At this point an entire secondary neural axis will arise on the ventral side of the host. This experiment was first performed by Spemann and Mangold, who went on to demonstrate that the neural tube of the secondary embryo is of host origin and the mesoderm is of graft origin. The Spemann — Mangold experiment involved the use of two salamander species of differing pigmentation as donor and host tissues. Sipenánn gave the dorsal lip of the blastopore the functional designation of inmary organizer," reflecting its role in the organization of the neural axis. The presumptive chordamesoderm, upon transplantation or explanation to culture medium, is capable of self-differentiation into those structures assigned to the dorsal lip by fate map studies.

The action of the dorsal lip is apparently, from the experiment above, to organize the overlying presumptive ncural plate into the neural axis. This is borne out by the following observations:

1. The neural axis fails to develop in those embryos whose primary organizer regions have been removed.

2. Accessory neural axes are induced in overlying presumptive epidermis in the presence of implanted dorsal blastoporal lip material.

3. The presumptive epidermal and neural areas are interchangeable in the early gastrula, as shown by experiments involving rotation of the roof of the blastocoel through 180°.

4. In embryos induced to form exogastrulae, in which the chordamesoderm self-differentiates but does not come to lie beneath the presumptive neural plate cells, fail to differentiate as neural cells.

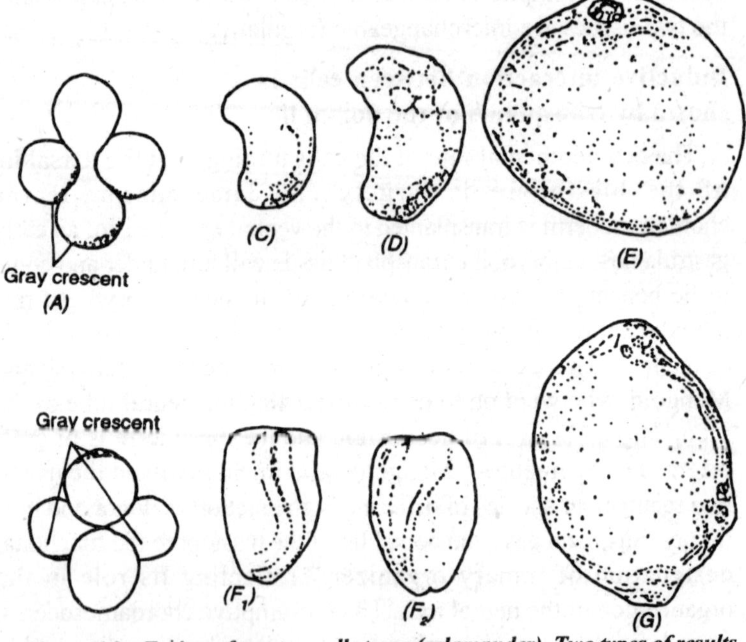

Figure 6.2 : Fusion of two two-cell stages (salamander). Two types of results are found, depending on the first cleavage of the two fused eggs.

The Chordamesoderm is Regionally Specific

Transplant studies show that posterior regions of the chordamesoderm induce posterior neural structures; anterior portions to form. This can be shown by defect experiments, in which defects are made in the chordamesoderm at different times during gastrulation. Defects are thus caused at different levels in the chordamesoderm and produce corresponding defects in the overlying neural tube. The action of the dorsal lip material (primary organizer) is an example of embryonic induction, in which an inductor tissue evokes a response (differentiation) in tissue competent to respond to the stimulus. This competence extends to presumptive neura platc areas and to presumptive epidermis. Competence to respond to the primary organizer is lost in later (neurula) stages.

In summary, the. primary organizer induces **the neural** axis of the embryo. The organizer activity is confined to the region of the dorsal lip of the blastopore. The organizer is selfdifferentiating and regionally specific in its action. The location of the dorsal lip and, therefore, the organizer corresponds to the location of the gray crescent material of the uncleaved, fertilized egg.

Cortical Transplants Provide Evidence for Regionalization of Egg Cytoplasms

As described earlier, the gray crescent is a cortical area characterized by a retreat of pigment from the equator at fertilization. It lies at the boundary between the black and white hemispheres of the frog egg and marks the future dorsoposterior side of the embryo. It will be re-called that the gray crescent region of the fertilized frog egg corresponds to the region of the primary organizer and the chordamesoderm. Development of isolated blastomeres is complete is both isolated cells only if both contain gray crescent material in 'nearly equal amounts. These observations focus attention on the gray crescent cortex of the egg as the initial organizer center.

Recently it has appeared possible to transplant or remove the cortical gray crescent material. The results of these operations are summarized. The gray crescent material behaves in much the same way as the dorsal lip material with regard to neural induction. Removal of the gray crescent (up to the eight-cell stage) terminates neural development. Prior to the eight-cell stage, implanting an extra

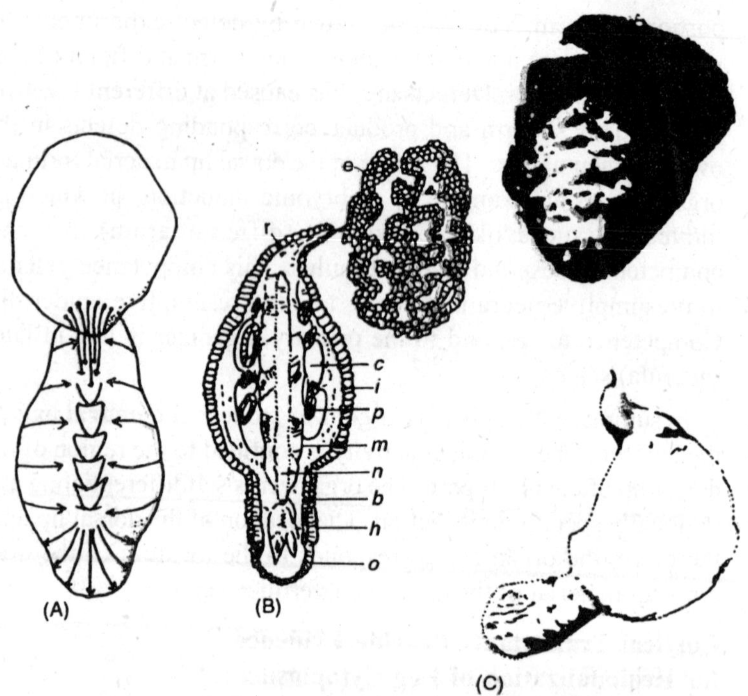

Figure 6.3 : Complete exogastrulation of a salamander germ.

gray crescent produces an extra neural axis. The gray crescent cortex has apparently discharged its function by the eight-cell stage, after which removal or mplantation of extra material does not affect development. The cells of the dorsal lip will possess organizer activity even hough the gray crescent (at eight cells) has been largely or entirely removed. In many respects, the gray crescent material is analogous to the micromere cortex of the sea urchin egg, in that it seems to be the center of egg polarity at early stages and possesses inductive potential.

Changes in Composition of the Gray Crescent Cortex

The cortex of fertilized eggs in the one-cell and eight-cell stages has been tested for organizer activity in other independent studies. These more recent studies involved implantation of the cortical material in the host blastocoel. The implant comes to lie beneath the ventral epidermis. The gray crescent cortex from one-to eight-

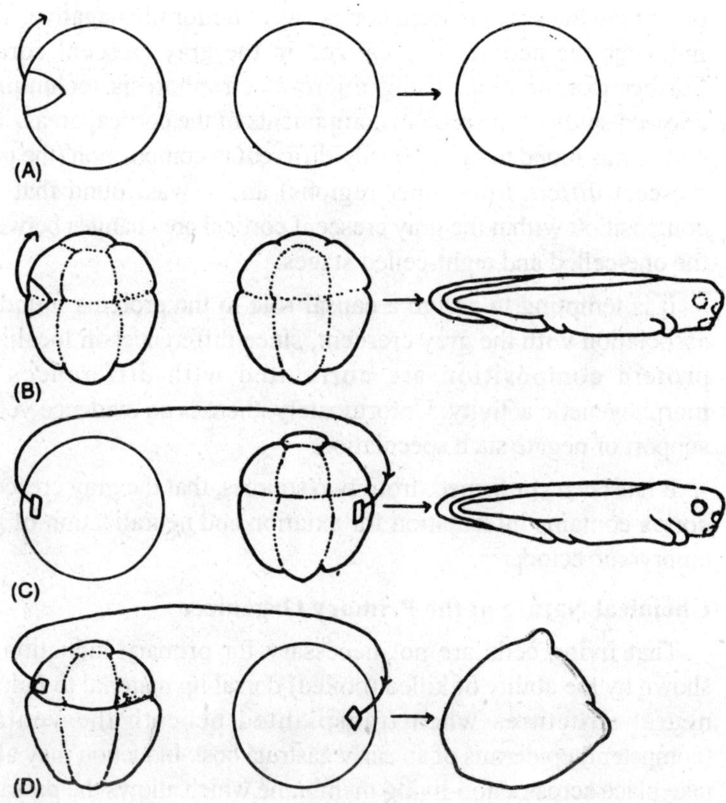

Figure 6.4 : Cortical transplant in* Xenopus. (A) *Excision of the cortical gray crescent area the one-cell stage; no gastrulation; (B) same experiment at the eight-cell stage; normal embryo; (C) graft of the gray crescent cortex of the one-cell stage to the ventral part of the eight-cell stage does not result in the induction of a secondary embryonic axis; (D) graft of the gray crescent cortex from the eight-cell stage to the ventral margin of one cell stage a secondary embryonic axis.

cell stages was able to induce neural structures under these conditions. The inductive potency of the cortex increases from one-cell to eight-cell stages. In these studies, the blastula stage was obviously able to respond to the cortical stimulus, perhaps because of the position of the implant in the blastocoel (other studies above found embryos beyond eightcells refactory to the action of implants in the cortex of cortical material). The controls in these experiments, involving implants of cortical material derived from regions other than the gray crescent cortex, were uniformly negative. This indicates the activity is localized in the gray crescent cortex. Further examination, using micro-electrophoresis techniques, allowed study of the protein components of the cortical areas. The cortex was found to be regionally different in composition (the gray crescent differs from other regions) and it was found that the composition within the gray crescent cortical are changes between the one-celled and eight-celled stages.

It is tempting to assign a causal role to the proteins found in association with the gray crescent, since differences in localized protein composition are correlated with differences in morphogenetic activity. Unfortunately, there is no evidence yet to support or negate such speculation.

It has been confirmed, from two sources, that the gray crescent cortex contains information for axiation and neuralization of the embryonic ectoderm.

Chemical Nature of the Primary Organizer

That living cells are not necessary for primary induction is shown by the ability of killed (boiled) dorsal lip material to induce neural structures when transplanted beneath the ventral (competent) epidermis of an early gastrula host. Induction may also take place across a non-living membrane which allows the passage of macromolecules but not cells. However, it has been difficult to establish that induction across membranes of known porosity does not involve the intercellular contact of fine cell processes which are able to insert themselves through the membrane pores. Induction will not take place across cellophane, which allows neither macromolecules nor cell extensions to penetrate. It is therefore uncertain whether or not normal induction involves the release and uptake of materials from inducer tissue to competent tissue, and whether or not cell contacts are required for induction under normal circumstances.

With the above restrictions in mind, the task of identifying the chemical naturally responsible for neural induction is a Viable one. Many extracts and substances have been tested and many were active. The problem is still to find a means of examining the natural inductor (the dorsal lip) for the molecules it **may release** during induction. Because of the small quantities of material available, conventional approaches are difficult, especially when it is realized that the active material may be present in low concentration and hidden by the diverse organic molecules normally encountered in cells.

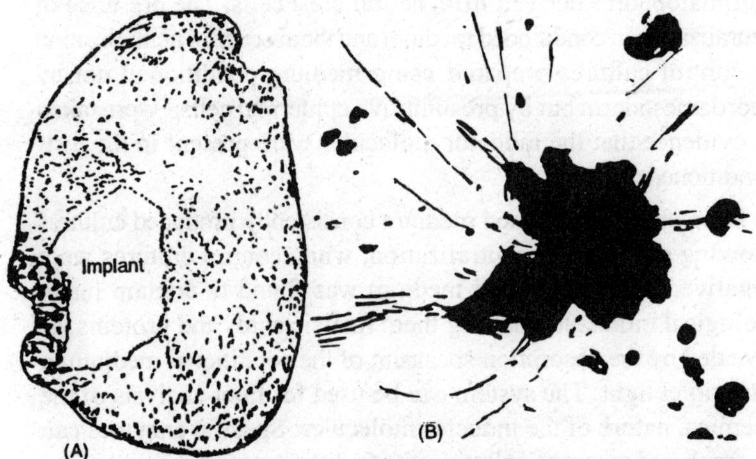

Figure 6.5 : (A) Induction of secondary neural plate in an axolotl embryo by means of an implanted piece of agar containing substances extracted from muscle by boiling the muscle in water. (B) Neural tissue with radiating nerve fibers and melanophores developed from a piece of young Triturus ricularis ectoderm cultivated in conditional medium.

A technique has been devised whereby isolated dorsal lip tissue can be cultured in defined medium, in drop cultures. Under these conditions, the explant will selfdifferentiate into a number of mesodermal structures. Since self-differentiate of the tissue occurs, it is reasonable to assume that other events associated with chordamesoderm development will also occur, including the release of molecules concerned with inductive changes in presumption neural plate. These "inductor molecules" would presumably be located in the culture medium, since the dorsal lip cells were cultured without responsive cells. Using this system and attendant assumptions about the release of active molecules, the following biological assay was developed. Medium in which presumptive chordamesoderm had been growth for a number of days was recovered, free of cells.

This medium contained the original inorganic components, plus any molecules, contributed by the differentiating chordamesoderm cells. In new cultures the chordamesoderm medium (termed conditioned medium) was used to culture pieces of presumptive epidermis. After some days of culture, the tissue was examined for evidence of neural development (presence of cells with nerve fiber outgrowths; chromatophores derived from neural crest cells. The presence of neuralization in conditioned medium and the absence of neutralization in control cultures prepared using medium conditioned not by chordamesoderm but by presumptive epidermal cells," were taken as evidence that the inductor molecules were present in the test-conditioned medium.

In practice, conditioned medium consistently produced cultures showing evidence of neutralization, while control cultures were negative. The conditioned medium was found to contain many biological molecules, among them nucleic acids and proteins, as revealed by the absorption spectrum of the conditional medium in ultraviolet light. The system can be used for finer analysis of the chemical nature of the inductor molecules: Specific enzymes can be employed to specifically inactivate different kinds of biological molecules. Proteolytic enzymes (trypsin) would be expected to remove inductor activity associated with proteins. Nucleases (RNase and DNase) would be expected to remove activity associated with nucleic acids. Actual experiment shows that only trypsin completely abolishes the inductor activity of conditioned medium, though RNase diminishes the activity without abolishing it completely. These experiments suggest that the material involved in the induction of the neural axis by the underlying chordamesoderm is protein in nature, possibly a ribonucleoprotein.

Inductions Using Foreign Materials

Obviously, the amount of tissue available for analysis in the dorsal lip of the blastopore is extremely limited. In the course of experiments on killed inductors (cell extracts, or heated preparations), it was found that mammalian tissues yielded preparations having inductive activity when tested on amphibian embryos. Thus, boiled guinea pig bone marrow caused the competent, early gastrula, presumptive epidermis to develop into spinocaudal structures (tail musculature and other mesodermal derivatives). Other tissues, such as guinea pig liver, yielded material causing the induction of anterior neural structures. The active materials all seem to be protein in nature. Later, it was discovered that active material could also be extracted from whole amphibian gastrulae.

These abnormal inductors have been highly purified and preliminary word has been done on the mode of action of the proteins. The spinocaudal factor (mesodermal or vegetalizing factor was inhibited by nucleic acids. The inhibition was due, at least in part to the binding of the factor to the nucleic acid (DNA or RNA). The source of the nucleic acid was not of consequence, chick DNA or RNA serving as well as amphibian DNA or RNA. This has been interpreted to mean that the inductors might be acting by processing RNA some way, facilitating its transport to cytoplasmic regions. These speculations have little to espouse them. There is little evidence for the activity of these factors in the normal inductive process. The situation is reminiscent of the situation encountered in artificial parthenogenesis. Many different agents can act to activate the egg. None is necessarily involved in normal fertilization processes. The ability of an "inductor" to alter the fate of a cell is of interest as a system of cell differentiation, but does little to elucidate what actually happens during the normal determination of the presumptive neural plate of the amphibian gastrulae.

Interestingly, these kinds of results have led some to theorize that induction involves changes in intracellular concentration of various ions or changes in *intracellular* pH. Lithium, sodium, or calcium can all induce differentiation of neurons from presumptive epidermis. Later treatment with the same ions also induces differentiation of these same neurons into pigment cells. The observations are supported by the occurrence of great changes in concentrations and proportions of cations *in vivo* during the induction of the nervous system.

The effects of the conditioned medium and other preparations are apparently not medicated through damage to the competent ectoderm cells, but through the interaction of the molecules with the cells. There is reason to believe that inductor molecules act indirectlyy on competent tissue to cause a response. The extent to which the abnormal inductors are identical to the natural substances from the dorsal lip is not known.

Inductive Action is Indirect and Mediated Through the Responsive Genome

These analyses involve the use of two species; one, the source of the inductor; and the other, the competent responding tissue. The response to the inductor is always in accord with the genetic information contained in the responding tissue. For example, salamander larvae possess a structure on either side of the head just behind the jaw angle and beneath the eye. This structure is called a balancer. Anuran embryos possess homologous structures beneath the mouth variously called mucous glands, adhesive organs, or oral suckers. These structures (balancers and mucous glands) 'are induced in overlying epidermis by inductive action of the anterior roof of the archenteron. Speaking first of balancers, there exist some species of salamander that lack these organs. If epidermis from any part of the body of a species normally possessing a balancer is transplanted to replace the balancer epidermis of a species not possessing a balancer, a balancer will develop. In the reverse experiment, epidermis from a species not possessing balancer fails to develop a balancer when placed over the balancer inductor in the species normally possessing balancers. The balancer inductor is obviously operative in both species. The ectoderm of the species lacking balancers is genetically not competent to respond to either inductor, whereas the epidermis from the species having balancer is competent in either location. The main point is that the genetic lack of competence is not overridden by the inductive stimulus which is present in both species. Inductors cannot alter the genetic nature of the responding tissues.

Similar experiments involve the exchange of epidermis from the flank of frog and salamander embryos to the balancer or mucous gland region. One then has a salamander embryo (neurula) with

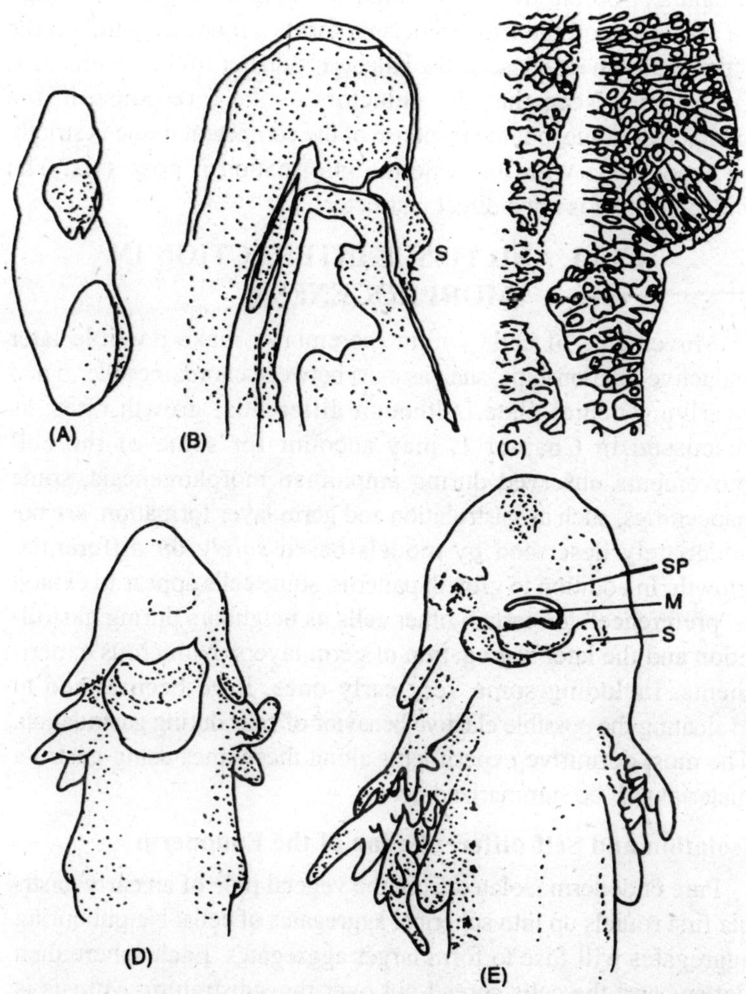

Figure 6.6 : Xenoplastic transplants; ventral skin of Rana esculenta implanted into Triturus gastrula. A, tail bud stage; B, later stage, longitudinal section; C, adhesive disc regions-of the embryo of B greatly magnified; D, E urodele larva with an implant of anuran epidermis in the mouth region; F, showing sucker discs, tadpole mouth with horny jaws (M) and horny spines (SP) on the lips. S, sucker discs.

frog belly epidermis overlying the balancer inductor and a frog embryo with salamander belly epidermis overlying the mucous gland inductor. The result is that the salamander epidermis forms a balancer on the frog in response to the mucous gland inductor of the frog, and the frog epidermis forms a mucous gland on the salamander in response to the balancer inductor of the salamander. Again, it is seen that the inductors evoke a response in the competent tissue, but the response of the competent tissue is strictly in accordance with the genomic information it possesses. The inductor itself is not a direct instructor.

CELL AND TISSUE INTERACTION IN MORPHOGENESIS

Movements of cells within the embryo make possible later inductive relationships, such as exist between chordamesoderm and overlying neural plate. Although differential growth rates, as discussed in Chapter 1, may account for some of the cell movements observed during amphibian morphogenesis, some happenings, such as gastrulation and germ layer formation, are not adequately described by models based *solely on* differential growth. In addition to growth patterns, some cells appear to exhibit a "preference" for certain other cells **as** neighbors during gastrulation and the later segregation of germ layers. Numerous experiments, including some very early ones, have been aimed at evaluating the possible elective behavior of cells during gastrulation. The most definitive experiments along these lines using gastrula material will be summarized here.

Isolation and Self-differentiation of the Endoderm

Purc cndoderm isolated from the vegetal pole of an early gastrula first rounds up into spherical aggregates of cells. Neighbouring aggregates will fuse to form larger aggregates. Each sphere then flattens and the cells spread out over the substratum. Mitosis is infrequent, and the cells glide over the glass surface by producing pseudopodia. A few individual cells may separate from the mass and migrate independently. The tendency to spread on the glass subtratum corresponds to the time (in a normal embryo) when the edges of the floor of the-trunk endoderm move dorsally, eventually fusing on the midventral line to form the intestinal tube. Though the migration in culture is only in the horizontal plane, the topography of tissues within the whole embryo may guide the endoderm cells into the proper three-dimensional movements during normal development. It was. found, for example, that the migrating endodermal cells will spread over the outside of a tissue substratum and form an inverted intestinal epithelium. If no substratum is present and the aggregates of endoderm cells are made to float freely in the medium, no epithelial sheet is formed and the aggregated cells give rise to a cytologically differentiated epithelium containing spaces filled with secretions. The ability of the endoderm to so differentiate in culture indicates that the medium used as without adverse effect on the cells and that the endoderm his self-differentiating capacity.

Changing affinition of ectoderm and Endoderm During Gastrulation

Ectoderm and underlying endoderm can be excised together from an early gastrula from the mediocaudal region opposite the blastopore. Accident inclusion of ventral mesoderm is to be avoided. The two cell types are loosely connected at first. The white endoderm cells form a pile within the pigmented ectoderm cells, which tend to curl closely around the endoderm. After one to two days the two cell types separate from one another, forming discrete spheres of ectoderm and endoderm. If a suitable substratum is present, the endoderm cells will then migrate over it is with pure endoderm isolates, and differentiate as intestinal epithelium. The ectoderm remains as a ball of epidermal cells. The separation of the two types of cells was achieved by directed autonomous cell activities and not by differential growth or budding. These kinds of separations occur between various cell types during normal development and car be thought of as arising from a negative affinity between ectoderm and endoderm. This affinity changes with time, as evidenced by the initial covering of endoderm by ectoderm, followed by the separation of the two. Isolated ectoderm three to four days old will not adhere to endoderm even when the endoderm is freshly isolated from the early gastrula.

Role of Negative Affinity in Gastrulation

The temporary incompatibility of ectoderm and endoderm seems to play an important role in steering the involution process during gastrulation. The problem of why involution rather than exogastrulation normally takes place has not as yet been clarified. In any event normal gastrulation seems to operate initially by way of an active moving apart of heterologous tissues.

Reassortment of Tissues in Explants Involving all Three Germs Layers

Endoderm and mesoderm combinations are obtained by isolating a laterocaudal piece of an early gastrula containing elements of the lateral plate mesoderm, which normally gives rise to connective tissue. Ectoderm is also included in the isolate. The isolated mass first rounds up into a sphere. The endoderm remains incompletely covered by the ectoderm. Again, after one to two days, the endoderm protrudes from the sphere and a constriction develops at the junction of the ectoderm and endoderm. Instead of progressing to complete isolation, the constriction will later relax. A vesicle is then formed with an interior of mesenchyme cells which form a loose network in a secreted fluid. The aggregates of ectoderm and endoderm cells do not remain solid, but form the walls of the vesicle. The point of juncture of the ectoderm and endoderm is marked with a slight fissure and the two are held by the internal mesenchyme. If a larger piece of ectoderm is provided, the structure resembles that diagrammed. The vesicle is completely covered by ectoderm, in two layers. The mesoderm lies between the inner ectoderm and the endoderm, which have separated a provide a cleft into which the mesenchyme can move. The inner endoderm forms a lumen lined with intestinal cells and containing a secreted fluid. The arrangement of tissues and the inward orientation of the endodermal cells in producing the intestinal epithelium are typical of the spatial arrangements found in normal embryos.

Combinations of Ectoderm and Mesoderm and Induction

When small amounts of ectoderm are isolated with dorsal lip material normally forming somites and notochord, a variety of forms results. Endoderm is excluded from these cultures. These mesodermal-ectodermal isolates first round up into spheres; then the mesoderm elongates, separates from the ectoderm, and self-differentiates in contact with the substratum into somites and notochord. The epidermis then reassociates with the mesoderm over a widening area and, subsequently, segregates into epidermis and neural tissue (through induction by the mesoderm). Thus, the affirnity of ectoderm for mesoderm progresses from a negative to a positive affinity.

The degree of specificity of cell affinities (or cell adhesion) is of the order encountered in the interaction of antigen and antibody molecules. The phenomenon is encountered in many development systems, in both plants and animals. In simple terms, it means that cells are able to "recognize" neighboring cells or neighbouring cell-bound molecules and "elect" to adhere to these or not. The phenomenon is, undoubtedly, a surface phenomenon, dependent on surface molecules present in or protruding through the surface membrane.

SELF-DIFFERENTIATION OF FIELDS AND STEPWISE DETERMINATION

An explant of presumptive mesoderm of the early gastrula is capable of self-differentiation into a variety of mesodermal tissues. The endoderm is capable, at this same time, of cytodifferentiation into intestinal epithelium. Ectoderm, destined to form either epidermis or neural tissue, is dependent upon induction by the chordamesoderm for differentiation into neural tissue. The presumptive mesodermal areas of the early gastrula are capable of-self-differentiation and are referred to as fields, such as the chordamesoderm field and the heart field. If an amphibian embryo is induced to exogastrulate (using Li), the chordamesoderm will fail to underlie the presumptive neural plate area, which then develops as epidermal tissue while the chordamesoderm self-differentiates into notochord, somites, nephric structures, and so forth. The failure of the presumptive neural plate to differentiate is due to the failure of the chordamesoderm to provide the necessary inductive stimulus, as described above. If a piece of presumptive neural plate is isolated prior to gastrulation, the result is the same. If the isolation is made after gastrulation, the explant will develop into nervous tissue. It is said to have become determined. This determination does not take place in isolated, early ectoderm.

In the embryo the entire neural axis (neural field) is determined by inductive actions along the length of the underlying chordamesoderm. In a corresponding manner, the ectoderm developing as epidermis loses its ability or competence to respond to neural inductors. As time progresses the neural axis becomes divided into subfields (forebrain, midbrain, and hindbrain; spinal cord). The regions of the neural field then act as in ductors, causing the lens to develop opposite the optic vesicle and the otocyst to form toward the posterior end of the hindbrain. The lens then becomes determined, for example, and will form lens tissue in isolation. In the intact embryo, the eye lens exerts an influence (induction) on the overlying ectoderm, causing the development of the cornea. The process of differentiation when seen in this context becomes a series of stepwise determinations and inductions, beginning with the initial action of the chordamesodermal field (determined during oogenesis) on the overlying ectoderm.

LIMB DEVELOPMENT: AN EXAMPLE OF A FIELD

The beginnings of forelimb development are to be seen in the somatic mesoderm ventrolateral to the pronephros and behind the gill region. The mesoderm becomes thickened, as does the overlying epidermis. A similar development takes place just anterior to the anus. These thickenings are the forelimb and hindlimb buds, respectively. The mesoderm element in the anterior limb bud is determined at an early stage, shortly after the closure of the neural folds. Pieces of somatic mesoderm removed from the forelimb region can be transplanted to other areas of the body beneath the epidermis, where they will cause the development of heterotopic limbs (limbs forming in areas not normally giving rise to limbs). That any portion of the epidermis can, at this time, participate in limb formation is shown by experiments placing epidermis from various parts of the neurula over the limb mesoderm. All such pieces, regardless of source, are able to cooperate with the mesodermal element to produce a normal limb. This does not mean that the ectoderm of the amphibian limb bud is passive in limb development. A limb structure will not develop from isolated mesoderm; a covering of ectoderm is required even though ectoderm from a variety of sources will suffice for this purpose. The role of the ectoderm is more pronounced in amniote embryos.

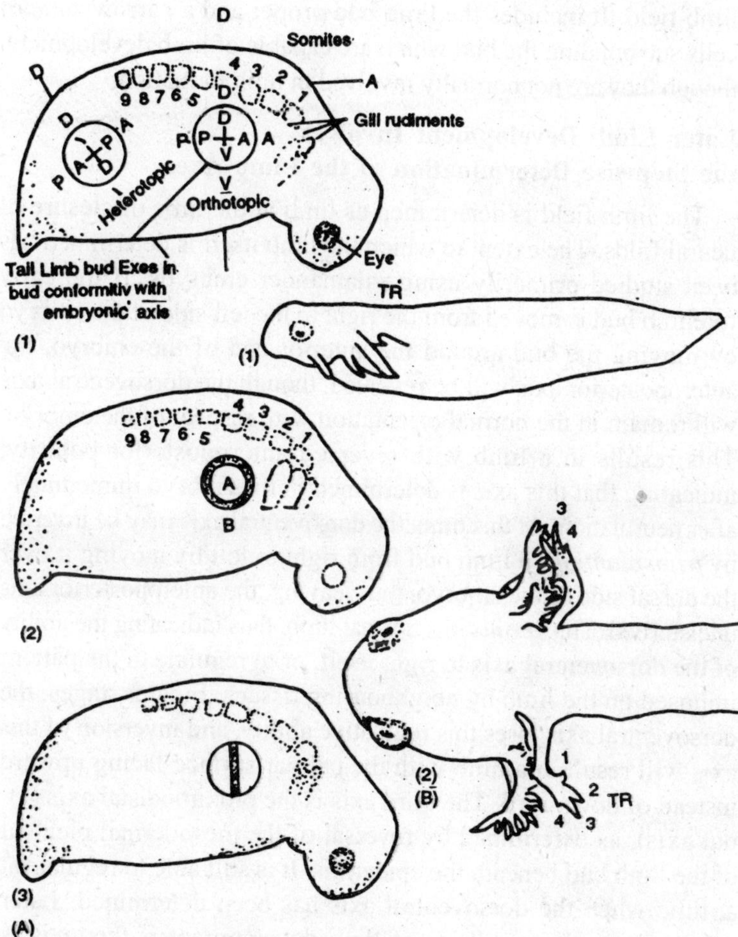

Figure 6.7 : (A) Experiments on the limb-bud differentiated in salamander (Ambystoma) during early tail-bud stage.

The Early Limb Bud is a Regulative System

The early limb bud can be divided into two areas, or two limb buds can be placed side by side, slightly overlapping in normal orientation, or one-half of the limb bud can be removed. In all cases, a complete single limb will develop. The system is a regulative one. If the area of the limb bud is removed entirely, a peripheral area not normally involved in limb development, will replace the lost limb bud. This larger area of limb potential is the limb field. It includes the limb bud proper and a narrow zone of cells surrounding the bud which are capable of limb development, though they are not normally involved in limb formation.

Later Limb Development Involves the Stepwise Determination of the Limb Axes

The limb field is determined as limb at the time of closure of neural folds. The extent to which the limb itself is determined has been studied primarily using salamander embryos. If the early forelimb bud is moved from the right to the left side of the embryo by moving the bud around the anterior end of the embryo, the anteroposterior axis will be reversed, though the dorsoventral axis will remain in the normal orientation with respect of the embryo. This results in a limb with reversed anteroposterior polarity, indicating that this axis is determined in the embryo immediately after neurulation. At this time, the dorsoventral axis may be inverted by *transplanting'* a limb bud from right to left by moving it over the dorsal side of the embryo, thus leaving the anteroposterior axis undisturbed. This results in a normal limb, thus indicating the ability of the dorsoventral axis to right itself, or to regulate to the pattern imposed on the limb by neighbouring tissues. In later stages, the dorsoventral axis loses this regulative ability, and inversion of this axis will result in a limb with the palmar surface facing upward instead of downward. The third axis is the proximodistal axis (in-out axis), as determined by reversal of the mesodermal element of the limb bud beneath the epidermis. It is still able to regulate at a, time when the dorsoventral axis has been determined. Later stages show abnormalities of limb development if this axis is inverted, indicating a determination of this axis. These experiments are difficult to interpret precisely, since a limb cannot actually reverse itself and grow into the body; to do so would mean a loss of contact with the ectoderm essential for normal limb development, in addition to encountering structural barriers to limb growth from other Body tissues.

The three major axes of the limbs are seen to be determined at separate times, and the limb bud as a whole is determined in a stepwise fashion. The later axial sequence of limb determination is in a proximodistal direction. The girdle is determined first, the phalanges last.

OTHER FIELDS

Stepwise Determination is Evident in the Development of the Central Nervous System

The normal forelimb movements of urodele larvae depend on innervation by three pairs of spinal nerves (3, 4 and 5) comprising the branchial plexus. If this area of the neural plate is exercised and replaced with a more posterior segment, the graft will morphologically and functionally fill the role of controlling the limb movements. A similar transplant at the tail-bud stage results in limb innervation, but leads to abnormal limb movements. The posterior segment can no longer participate in the development of the branchial plexus.

At the tail bud stage, the section of neural tube which is to form the mudulla may be excised and rotated 180°. The replaced graft develops into a morphologically normal medulla, and all nervous responses of the operated larvae may be perfectly normal. Experiments on later tail bid larvae lead to abnormalities of medulla morphology and function.

Consideration of symmetry determination in other fields (e.g., heart field) would yield similar conclusions; the field is initially regulative after being specified as a field and later becomes a determined mosaic of smaller parts, which again regulate within the subfields until they also become specified, presumably by induction from neighbouring cells. The beginning of this sequence of dependent differentiation is, again, the initial induction of the nervous system by the chordamesoderm and the continued self-differentiation of the endomesoderm.

SPECIFICATION OF SYNAPSES AND THE DEVELOPMENT OF INTEGRATED BEHAVIOUR

Background Considerations

In some invertebrates, where the total number of neurons in the animal is relatively small, the neural connections (between nerve fiber and muscle, sense organs, or other interconnecting fiber) can be mapped to some degree. Neural connections are reproduced among these animals with great fidelity, presumably on instructions from the genome. In vertebrates, there are far too many neurons for one to know with certainty the degree of order among neural connections specified by the genome.

Two extremes exist. On the one hand, neural connections might be made in random fashion. The useful connections could then be sorted out by some learning procedure. On the other hand, the entire circuitry might be specified in the genome and manifest in specific surface molecules which make each nerve cell and its connections unique. The truth most probably lies somewhere between the two extremes. Those against genetic specification sometimes argue that there are 'more neurons and synapses in a vertebrate brain than there are genes in the genome. However, in a number of cell recognition systems, the recognition molecules are protein-polysaccharide complexes. Specificity has been associated with the branching arrangement of the polysaccharide moiety, a property that could manifest many configurations within the instructional frame-work of a single gene. The possibility exists for complete genetic specification, though this is perhaps not the most likely situation. Alternatively, there is considerable evidence against the hypothesis of random connections later sorted out by learning activities.

The development of behaviour is obviously dependent on the development of the nervous system of receptors and effectors and interconnecting pathways (neurogenesis). Motility and bioelectric activity are essential to behavioural patterns. There is a close correlation between structural and functional maturation. Young neurons are capable of impulse transmission, and primitive synaptic connections serve to mediate early motility. Each behavioural advance follows closely on the completion of new synaptic connections. As will be seen below, sensory input and practice, or trial and error, have little to do with the development of integrated behaviour in vertebrates. In salamanders, behaviour is integrated as meaningful swimming movements from the time of hatching. In higher vertebrates such as birds and mammals, initial movements are unorganized. In the bird, these random movements are superceded by quite different, intricate, and coordinated movements that precede hatching. The latter movements do not grow out of the former, since the uncoordinated movements continue to take place even after hatching. They appear to be the result of indiscriminate and massive electrical discharges that excite many motor neurons and cause movement, which may be important for the normal differentiation of joints. The intricate hatching movements appear to be integrated from their beginning without benefit of practice movements in earlier stages. These observations tend to deny any role of sensory input in development of early integrated behaviour. It is now widely held that the neural machinery for integrated behaviour differentiated autonomously, as a "printed circuit."

Classic Experiments with Specification of Sensory Connections

These experiments deal with the regeneration of the optic nerve fibers of larval and adult salamanders and frogs. The eyes originate as a pair of lateral out-pocketings from the walls of the diencephalon. The optic vesicles reflect back on themselves, forming the two-layered optic cups. The inner layer of the cup is the retinal layer and contains the sensory elements (rods and cones), the interconnecting neurons, and the optic nerve cell bodies which send their axons to the optic lobes (optic tectum) in the midbrain region. Experiments with the optic tectum in the midbrain have established that the retinal field is projected, point by point, onto the optic lobes. Specific stimulation of the retinal cells (one or two cells at a time) gives signals to specific cells of the lobe corresponding to the portion of the retinal field being stimulated. The optic fibers are predetermined as to their point of termination in the optic lobe even before they have grown back to the midbrain. This can be shown by rotation of the optic cup prior to optic nerve growth. This operation results in inverted vision, leading to the conclusion that the optic nerve fibers deviated from their normal path to journey from their position in the inverted retinal layer to their normal terminals in the tectum.

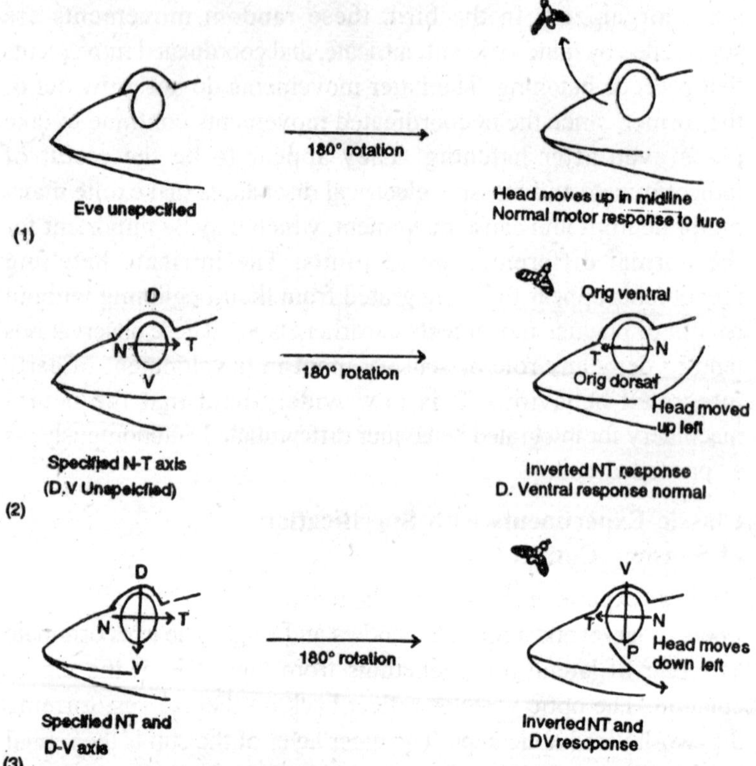

Figure 6.8 : Diagram of development of retinal polarity in eyes of amphibians rotated at various embryonic stages. Embryonic state of determination at rotation in left column; resulting adult behaviour in right column. DV, dorsoventral; NT, nasotemporal. The fly acts as a lure.

Crushing of the optic nerve in salamander larvae or adult frogs can result in optic nerve regeneration and restoration of normal vision and normal responses to visual cues in the environment. Rotation of the eye in the orbit after crushing the optic nerve also results in the restoration of vision in a significant number of operated animals. The vision of the inverted eye is, however, inverted, as are the responses to visual cues in the environment. The implication of these studies is that the optic nerve fibers returned to their original connections in the optic lobes through a thick mat of apparently randomly regenerating nerve fibers. Now the environmental stimulations impinge on inappropriate portions of the retina (a dorsal stimulation now focuses on the ventral retinal field, for example). Responses to the stimuli are correspondingly inverted. The inappropriate responses continue throughout the life of the adult frog. Most animals continue to snap at lures or food (flies) in a reverse manner; a fly dangled dorsal to the nose will be lunged for between the front legs. These responses in some animals were replaced by indifferent reaction, as though the frog had simply given up on the impossible chase. Thus, there may be a tendency in some to ignore the lure or to inhibit the responses. However, in no animal was a positive attempt at correction of the defect noted.

Evidence from Lesions in the Optic Tectum of the Optic Lobes

Specific lesions (scotomas, or blind spots) produced in the tectum result in production of expected visual deficiencies in animals with regenerated optic nerves. An anterior lesion in the tectum abolished responses in the anterior region of the visual field, and so with lateral and posterior lesions. In those animals with inverted eyes, the lesion in the posterior region produced deficient responses in the anterior visual field. In summary, it can be concluded that the ingrowing optic fibers reestablish functional connections in the same topological areas of the optic lobe where they originally terminated during normal neurogenesis.

Implications of These Studies

The foregoing data support the contention that each retinal locus possesses functional connections with brain centers differing from all other loci. The data also support the contention that the orderly restoration of central reflex connections, which occur regardless of the orientation of the retina, must be independent of functional adaption or learning. It is also implied that the retinal fibers must possess specific properties by which they are recognized in the optic lobe according to their respective retinal origins. In studies on regeneration of the optic nerve in fish, these conclusions have been borne out by direct anatomical observation, not only with respect to the terminal connections established in the tectum, but also with respect to the pathways taken by the optic fibers to reach their central, terminal points.

Experimental Evidence; Motor Activity

The concept of the "printed circuit" of neural activity as a part of the genetic endowment of a species was supported by early narcotization experiments on salamander embryos. In this study a clutch of salamander eggs was divided into two groups. One group was kept as a control. A second group was anesthetized with chloretone from the preswimming stages to beyond the swimming stage. When the anesthetized tadpoles were removed from the anesthetic, they were found to swim in a fashion equalling the coordination of the control group.

Additional Information from Inverted Limbs

The patterning of the central neural pathways would thus seem to depend on specific neuronal connections. This type of selective connection (or affinity) is presumably based on molecular recognition of one nerve cell by another, or of recognition of particular muscles by nerves. Evidence for a chemoaffinity (as opposed to trial and error) mechanism operating between nerve fibers and between nerve and muscle is found in studies of inverted salamander limb buds. These limb buds were inverted at a time when their anteroposterior axis had been determined, and thus grew out in a reverse position. It was found that from the beginning of motility the limbs also moved in reverse. This implies that the spinal center for locomotion develops independently of the inverted limb and produces a "malfunction" that is never corrected. In another experiment, the legs were deprived of sensory nerves before leg movement had started. Coordinated locomotor function was not impaired in the treated limbs. It has also been found that the nerves of the lumbosacral plexus (8, 9, 10) will grow around a mica barrier, taking an abnormal path to the developing hindlimb.

The normal innervation of the hindlimb is possible if the barrier is not too extensive. This points to a selective affinity of these nerves for muscle fibers of the hindlimb.

It has been found that a forelimb transplanted to the head region will be innervated by cranial nerve fibers, sensory and motor. The limb will not function in coordinated fashion with other limbs, but rather tends to move in concert with anterior structures (e.g., movements of the gill chamber) also innervated by the nerves supplying the abnormally placed limb. The abnormally placed limb is innervated non-specifically in an abnormal situation. Under these conditions it functions as though it were a part of the motor apparatus in the abnormal position and not in co-ordination with other normally placed limbs. The basis of the apparently non-specific attraction of cranial nerves to the abnormally placed muscle is puzzling and represents a question to be resolved.

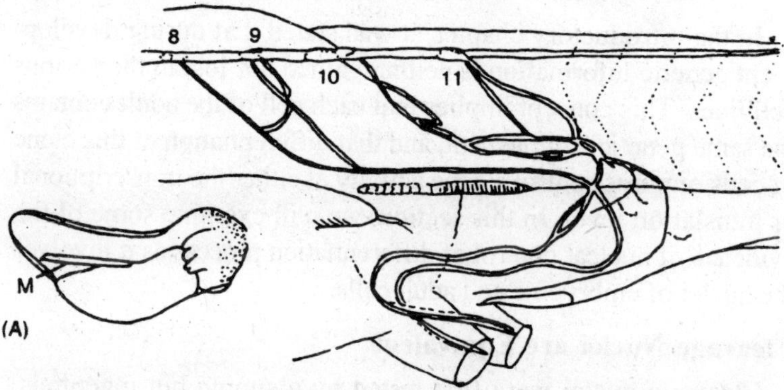

Figure 6.9 : Response of outgrowing nerve fibers to physical barrier in normal pathway. (A) A mica plate (M) inserted in the path of outgrowth of the spinal nerves to the hindlimbs in a frog embryo: (B) the nerves have grown around the obstacle and have reached the hindlimbs.

Gradual Specification of the Nervous System

Beginning with the induction of the central nervous system by the dorsal lib of the blastopore, the development of the functional nervous system proceeds through a period of plasticity to an extremely high degree of specification. Nerves maintain the same specific connections made during development after regeneration, so that motor nerves innervate the appropriate muscle, and sensory nerves innervate the proper end organ in establishing reconnections. Clinical attempts in humans to supply facial muscles with cervical nerves (as when the facial nerve , is paralyzed) may result in innervation of facial muscles by the cervical nerve. However, the facial muscles. function in concert with cervical voluntary muscle rather than with other facial muscles. This situation is not corrected centrally and persists throughout life. In the section on human development additional information is available on plasticity during development and on the essentially inflexible situation found in the adult. The basic mechanism governing nerve cell outgrowth and synaptic connections is essentially unknown and represents one of the most fascinating and challenging areas of experimental biology.

GENOMIC CONTROL OF DEVELOPMENT

In the introductory chapter, it was stated that during development genetic information is neither gained nor lost in the various cell lines. This concept implies that each cell of the adult contains the same genetic complement, and that differentiation of this clone of cells requires control a gene activity at either the transcriptional or translation level. In this section, we will examine some of the evidence of nuclear control of differentiation process as it involves the nuclei of embryonic and adult cells.

Cleavage Nuclei are Equivalent

Cleavage nuclei were first tested by a simple but ingenious. experiment. The fertilized salamander egg was constricted by a hair loop into a dumbbell shape. The fusion nucleus was located in one portion that proceeded to cleave, while the portion without the nucleus remained unsegmented. The constriction is made parallel to the anterior-posterior axis of the embryo and bisects the gray crescent. After cleavage to perhaps 32-64 nuclei, the constriction allows one of the cleavage nuclei to pass to the enucleated egg. The selection of the nucleus which passes to the undivided side is completely random. The newly nucleated portion of the egg then begins to segment, and the loop is pulled tight to completely separate the two halves. The result is the formation of two identical twins, one of which will be somewhat younger as regards the **stage** of development. Since the selection among the cleavage nuclei was completely at random, it follows that all cleavage nuclei are equivalent and totipotent at the stage at which the nucleation of the uncleaved portion of the egg took place.

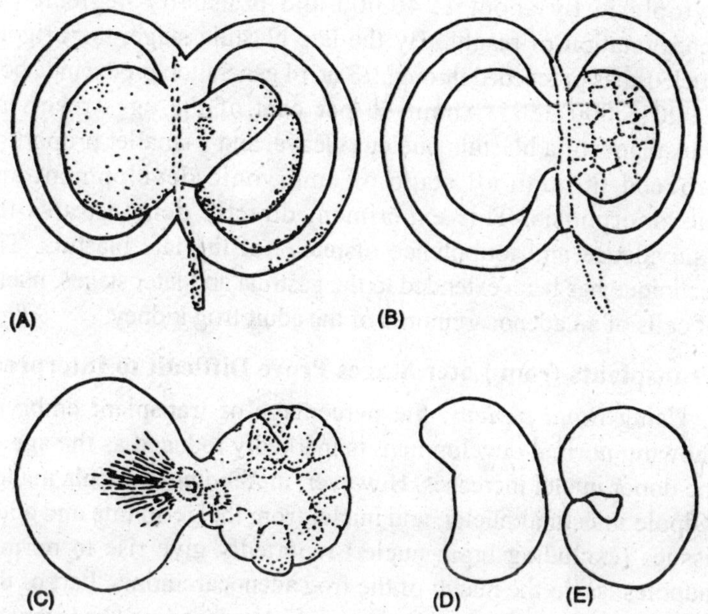

Figure 6.10 : Nuclear equivalence during cleavage. A restrictive noose is placed around the egg at the first cleavage (A, B). The nucleate half cleaves. Later (C) a cleavage nucleus passes into a nucleate half. resulting in older and younger twins.

Equivalence is Extended to the Blastula Through Nuclear Transplantation

In the 1950s the technique of nuclear transplantation was developed using the frog egg. This procedure allows for the direct testing of embryonic nuclei for equivalence and totipotence. In essence, the technique involves the enucleation by microsurgery of an artificially activated egg by removal of the second polar spindle and associated chromosomes. This is followed by the introduction of a test nucleus into the egg via a micropipet. The test nucleus is taken from any source by pulling a cell into a small-bore pipet with gentle suction. This procedure usually breaks the cell membrane. Transplantation of isolated nuclei without transfer of cytoplasm has not been accomplished, since nuclei isolated in artificial media are inactivated as far as future nuclear division are concerned. The transplanted cytoplasm is diluted by the egg cytoplasm by about 1: 40,000 and is usually neglected in interpretation of results. By the late blastula stage, the original nucleus has proceeded through 13 or 14 generation producing about 5,00016,000 cells. About 80 per cent of the eggs receiving transplants of a blastula nucleus cleave, and a smaller proportion proceed through all stage of embryonic development and metamorphosis. This experiment directly demonstrates the equivalence and totipotence of nuclei of the late blastula. The technique has been extended to the gastrula and later stages, nuclei of cells of an adenocarcinoma of the adult frog kidney.

Transplants from Later Stages Prove Difficult to Interpret

Using *Rana pipiens,* the percentage of transplant embryos showing normal development is markedly reduced as the age of the donor nuclei increases. However, in *Xenopus,* gastrula nuclei, tadpole intestinal nuclei, and nuclei from the germ line and adult tissues (excluding brain nuclei) reportedly give rise to normal tadpoles, as do the nuclei of the frog adenocarcinoma. Part of the difficulty with nuclei from embryos of later stages may be technical and involve difficulties in handling the small cells without injury to the nuclei and chromosomes. There is also a biological difficulty resulting from the faster generation times during cleavage as compared to later stages (about once every hour or two versus once every two or more days). The replication of chromosomes may fail to keep up in transplanted nuclei from older embryos or adults, leading to partial replication of chromosomes may fail to keep up in transplanted nuclei from older embryos or adults, leading to partial replication of chromosomes and loss of chromosome material. Fragmentation of chromosomes is observed in *Rana* nuclei transplanted from later stages.

Success obtained with older material might be due to parthenogenesis, resulting from failure of the experimenter to remove the egg nucleus. Such operational errors have been recognized and eliminated by using markers in the transplanted nuclei. Both triploidy and number of nucleoli have been used as cytological markers for transplanted nuclei. Genetic markers could be used as well. The marker appears in all the cells of the embryo resulting from nuclear transplantation if the transplant nucleus has indeed participated in cleavage in the absence of the egg nucleus. The successful nuclear transplants in the *Xenopus* system, as well as those using adenocarcinoma nuclei of frog kidney, utilized marked nuclei. There is no mistake about these positive results. It has been argued, however, that the percentage is so low as to raise the question of the involvement of exceptional, undifferentiated cells in the successful experiments.

The Basic Question Involves two Concepts

The first is the question of the totipotence or pluripotence of the somatic cell nucleus. The second is the question of the reversibility of nuclear changes (differentiation) which occur during development. Somatic nuclei may be possessed of all their nuclear genome and may thus potentially function as zygote nuclei. However, the process of differentiation, involving selective inactivation of most of the genome, may require special circumstances for reversal which are not met by the activated egg cytoplasm. Indeed, the nuclear changes may not be reversible at all. This is certainly the case in somatic tissues of some insects which develop giant polytene chromosomes. In these cells the entire genome is represented, but each chromosome has been replicated throughout its length perhaps 1000-fold, leading to structural specializations which preclude its function as zygote nucleus, perhaps on purely mechanical grounds. Systems other than nuclear transplantation (such as the development of tumors of primordial germ cells) also indicate totipotence of nuclei from differentiated tissues. It is necessary to consider all the evidence at hand and not just nuclear transplantation data alone, in arriving at the conclusion that the genome is conserved during development.

The Cytoplasm Controls Nuclear Activity

At the molecular level, the transplanted nuclei undergo changes similar to those noted in the male pronucleus after normal fertilization. The sperm nucleus first swells and then begins synthesis of DNA. A transplanted nucleus from the midblastula stage, normally synthesizing DNA, will increase in volume and continue DNA synthesis at the times specified by the egg cytoplasm. Neurula nuclei, normally synthesizing ribosomal RNA but infrequently DNA, will, upon transplant to an activated enucleated egg, cease ribosomal RNA synthesis and begin DNA synthesis after the nuclear-volume increase. During cleavage, these nuclei synthesize some messenger RNA. The transplanted neurula nuclei will again synthesize ribosomal RNA upon reaching the gastrula and neurual stages, following the transplant. Nuclear transplants may also be made to primary oocytes (actively synthesizing RNA, not DNA) and to unfertilized, unactivated eggs (making neither DNA no RNA). In growing primary oocytes, transplanted nuclei from blastulae are induced to cease DNA synthesis and commence RNA synthesis. In unactivated eggs, nuclei are quiescent with respect to RNA synthesis. The transplant chromosomes condense to resemble the egg meiotic chromosomes. Foreign nuclei (mouse liver) transplanted to enucleate, activated frog eggs are induced to synthesize DNA and to stop RNA synthesis. Clearly, changes in nuclear activity are dictated by the cytoplasm, and in a universal language as well. The several responses of nuclei to different cytoplasms argues for pluripotence of these nuclei.

Preprogramming of the Oocyte and RNA Synthesis During Development

Transcription of the genome occurs during oogenesis, as well as during embryogenesis. The question arises as to the qualitative nature of the mRNA formed at various times between oogenesis and the completion of differentiation. Some mRNA is transcribed during oogenesis for later use by early embryos (through blastula). To this extent, the egg may be said to be preprogrammed with differentiation controlled at the translational level. The paragraphs below examine gene activity during oogenesis through late tadpole stages, with respect to synthesis of the various classes of RNA (ribosomal, transfer and messenger).

During oogenesis lampbrush chromosomes are present, as are numerous nucleoli. The nucleoli have been found to represent amplified DNA sequences engaged in the production of ribosomal subunits. This gene amplification represents a specialization for the accumulation of the large amount of ribosomal RNA required during early development through to the hatching tadpole stage. The rate of ribosomal RNA synthesis is maximal at the lampbrush stage and predominates to the point of obscuring synthesis of messenger RNA. In mature oocytes, 95 per cent of the total RNA is ribosomal. Though measurement of the template mRNA is difficult in the presence of large amounts of ribosomal RNA, it has been estimated that about 2.5 per cent of the total RNA of *Xenopus* oocytes is template active. This template or messenger RNA seems to have been synthesized during the diplotene lampbrush stages, particularly stage 4, and constitutes the bulk of the messenger RNA inherited by the embryo as maternal template. In terns of unique-sequence DNA transcripts oocyte RNA contains about 9 per cent of the information content of uniquesequence DNA. This is remarkable close to the value for *ilrechis* where a similar complexity is found. At ovulation, a burst of messenger RNA synthesis occurs under the influence of pituitary hormones. It is of some interest that the egg cytoplasm does not acquire the ability to induce DNA synthesis in transplanted nuclei until after break-down of germinal vesicle and ovulation occur. Preovulation oocytes do not support DNA synthesis in transplanted nuclei. This property appears after injection of pituitary hormones and may be dependent upon the burst of messenger RNA synthesis at ovulation. Maturation itself is not dependent on the hormone-induced RNA synthesis.

In the sea urchin, it was seen that early development was dependent upon template RNA **synthesized** during oogenesis. Later development required new message transcription, beginning at the late blastula stage. A summary of RNA synthesis in amphibian embryos *(Xenopus)* shows similar patterns. An early

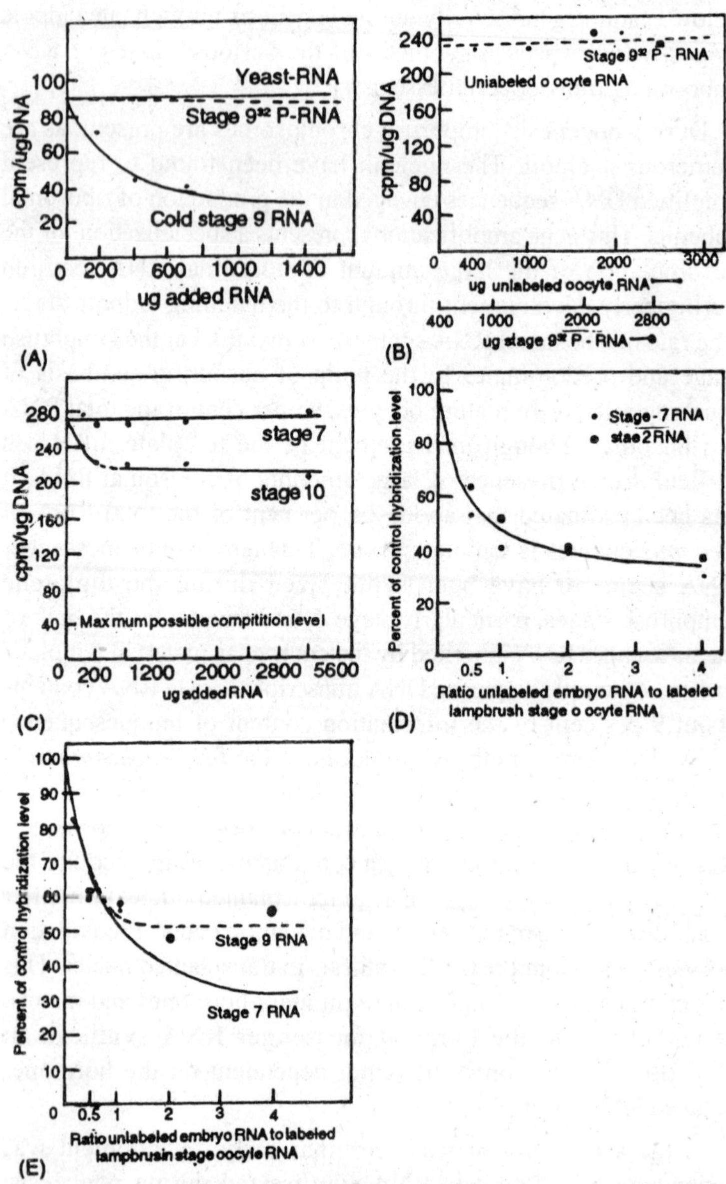

Figure 6.11 : (A) Competitive NA: RNA binding experiments indicating degree of homology between RNAs of various embryonic stages and RNA of lampbrush oocytes of Xenopus.

synthesis of messenger (template) RNA exists; which increases in intensity during cleavage to midblastula. During late portions of the blastula stage an abrupt increase in gene transcription occurs over the whole embryo. The newly synthesized messenger RNA contains a new program of genetic information. Transfer RNA synthesis is activated during this same period. During cleavage, the synthesis of ribosomal RNA is at a low level, if present at all. New ribosomal RNA is synthesized at gastrulation and becomes essential at the hatching tadpole stage. Ribosomal RNA in *Xenopus* has been studied using anucleolate mutants. These mutants are actually deficient in ribosomal DNA though a deletion of area of the genome responsible for organizing the nucleous. The heterozygous mothers of homozygous anucleolate embryos synthesize a normal complement of ribosomes. The embryos homozygous for the deficiency, however, do not make new ribosomal RNA and die as early tadpoles even though messenger RNA is synthesized in normal amounts.

The effects of transcription inhibition by actinomycin D has also been studied in amphibian embryos, including *Xenopus*. Actinomycin does not affect cleavage, though gastrulation and neurulation—are completely blocked. Inhibition of translation using puromycin blocks cleavage in *Xenopus,* as it does in the sea urchine embryo.

Organization of the Xenopus Genome

Studies involving reannealing of sheared *Xenopus* DNA fragments indicate interspersion of longer section of single copy DNA with shorter, repetitive segments. The sheared fragments of various lengths were incubated to a Cot value to include only repetitive segments, using 450 nucleotide long DNA fragments in excess to drive the reaction. As the length of the fragments increased, these longer fragments contained more and more unique-sequence DNA, a result expected if the single copy sequences were interspersed with repetitive sequences.

The use of Xenopus Oocytes in mRNA Assay; the Question of Translational Control

Oocytes contain mRNA which is transcribed during oogenesis

and "masked" for controlled use during early development. The nature of the mask is not known. However, mRNAs ("unmasked") from various diverse sources can be microinjected into oocytes and will be translated along with the messages normally available for protein synthesis in these cells. The oocytes are readily permeable to amino acids, and the newly synthesized proteins can be labeled and separated from one another by various chromatographic or immunological procedures. A number of species of eucaryotic mRNA have been used, in purified form, to test the oocyte system. Included are mRNAs for calf lens protein, duck, rabbit and mouse globin chains, trout protamine and rabbit hemoglobin. To reemphasize, the protein products of translation of mRNAs are stable and have been characterized as belonging to the species providing the mRNAs and not to the frog. Since oocyte is not engaged in synthesis of any of the proteins coded by the exogenous mRNAs, recognition of the translation product is possible. The fidelity of translation has been examined and found to be of the same order as when the mRNA is translated in the donor cells. This reflects a marked lack of species specificity in the process of translation mRNA.

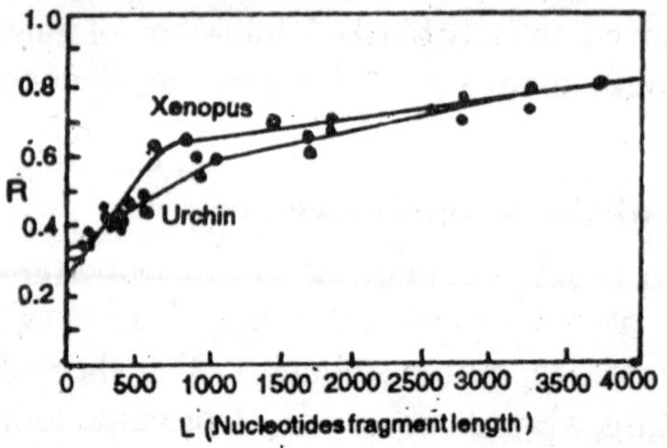

Figure 6.12 : Interspersion of single-copy and repetitive DNA in Xenopus. Relation between fragment length and hydroxyapatite binding in the DNA of the sea urchin (Strongylocentrotus purpuratus), compared to similar curve for Xenopus DNA.

The oocyte system is very efficient, and messages are translated with the same rapidity encountered in normal donor cells. Small amounts of mRNA in a crude RNA preparation can be detected in this way, and the system has proved to be most useful in this regard.

Quantitatively, using single injected messages, a linear relationship between mRNA injected and protein synthesized exists up to a saturation level. Even at saturation the amount of endogenous oocyte protein synthesized is not altered. This would indicate that the oocyte has a definite reserve translation capacity beyond normal endogenous levels, which may not be the same for all mRNAs injected. Some have argued that the presence of this spare translation capacity rules against controls at the translational level. To put it another way, it appears that any mRNA present in the cytoplasm will be translated, regardless of origin. The translation activity of exogenous message continues for days in injected oocytes. Normal translation activity is controlled by "masking" endogenous mRNA. The proper masking control for exogenous message seems not to exist. Translation can proceed in embryos in the absence of transcription (actinomycin studies) in controlled fashion, and one must conclude that the "foreign" message is somehow treated differently from that produced by the oocyte nucleus. A number of controls ("masks") have been proposed. It is possible that oocyte messages are transcribed, but are retained in the nucleus until time for translation. It is also conceivable that messages are produced by the oocyte nucleus and immediately combined with a cytoplasmic repressor that is removed at the proper time, such as after fertilization. These controlling events may be inoperative in the injection of foreign messages into the oocyte cytoplasm.

Both transcriptional and post-transcriptional controls are utilized by cells. A major problem for developmental biologists is evaluation of the relative importance of these levels of control in bringing ' about and maintaining a differentiated state. Repressing a gene at the level of transcription of DNA might seem more economical than synthesis of message to be followed by the masking or inactivation of that message. Transcriptional control is seen in terminal stages of development, in which all genes save one sequence may be inactive. In early development some control seems to be at the level of controlling translation of preexisting maternal message, as occurs in sea urchins and amphibians.

Between the two extremes, the cell probably utilizes both methods. Under certain conditions, transcription may be speeded and translation of mRNA accelerated, either by increased translational rate, or by decreased degradation of the message. Controls are therefore complex and involve levels of controls not only at the DNA and at the ribosome, but also in the length of functional life of the mRNA molecules. Most differentiated tissues do develop very stable mRNA molecules for production of tissue-specific proteins. 'The cells of the eye lens, as epithelial cells, synthesize the crystalline protein of the lens fibers. Actinomycin inhibits this synthesis in the lens epithelial cells, but not in the fiber cells into which the epithelial cell develop. The fiber cells possess an extremely long-lived mRN that operates in the absence of any transcription for long periods of time, obviating the need for nuclear activity. A similar situation exists in cells synthesizing hemoglobin. In this respect, translation control and long-lived messages seem to be characteristic of the beginning and the end of development.

Transcriptional control seems to operate during differentiation, though information in support of such generalizations awaits a thorough analysis of at least one example of cell differentiation.

Sources of Information and Raw Materials for Early Protein Synthesis

Most of the evidence concerning the function and fate of early messenger RNA tends to support the suggestion that these molecules are largely stored for later use in protein synthesis.. The observation that both enucleate and actinomycintreated embryos synthesize as much protein as control embryos during cleavage suggests that the amount of protein synthesis dependent upon newly synthesized messenger RNA is, at least quantitatively, insignificant. Protein synthesis, as measured by incorporation of labeled amino acids, takes place in the unfertilized egg. No increase in protein synthesis occurs after fertilization. What is actually being measured by following incorporation of radioactive amino acids into protein is the synthesis of new protein molecules from a pool of amino acid precursors derived from the breakdown of yolk platelets. The yolk protein is thus broken down and resynthesized into different protein molecules according to the needs of the embryo. Some protein molecules may be qualitatively the same as those made in the oocyte. New types of protein appear at gastrulation, as evidenced by serological experiments. These experiments demonstrate that antigens are present in the gastrula and neurula which are absent from the earlier stages. These proteins may be translated from the messages synthesized during the burst of messenger RNA synthesis that occurs just prior to gastrulation. They may also be the resultd of the unmasking and translation of oocyte mRNA already present. In any event, the rate of protein synthesis does increases during gastrulation.

7

Transformation

A remarkable series of changes takes place when an aquatic, fishlike tadpole is transformed into a land-dwelling frog. Throughout embryonic and larval life the development of the frog has been almost entirely a gradual, unfolding process of growth and differentiation, but during the metamorphic period growth and differentiation, but during the metamorphic period occur simultaneously with dramatic suddenness. The term "metamorphosis" has broad zoological usage. It is used to designate any group of developmental changes that are completed within a period of time which is brief in comparison with the full developmental period of the individual concerned. A variety of animals undergo metamorphoses of diverse sorts. Each of the events of amphibian metamorphosis contributes toward the preparation of the developing individual for life on land, but one cannot say that preparation is confined exclusively to the metamorphoic period, since, after all, the limbs and the lungs have been differentiating during most of the larval period.

Staging of Anuran Development

Development is, of course, a continuous process, but in **order** to make critical comparisons between different species or between different individuals of the same species it is desirable that the developmental period be divided into discrete steps or stages and that they be described in a staging table. A number of such tables have been prepared for different amphibians. The ones for anurans with aquatic larvae are quite similar to one another. Gosner (1960) has combined two of the best of them those of Limbaugh and Volpe (1957) and Taylor and Kollros (1946) - into a simplified and generalized series that should be readily adapted for use with any frog or toad having free-swimming larvae. The larval and metamorphic stages of Gosner's series are presented here because they illustrate the sequence of external changes that are most easily observed during typical anuran metamorphosis.

That stages 23, 24 and 25 are marked by the formation of the operculum and the consequent covering over of the external gills by its anterior component which grows backward from the hyoid arch. By stage 25 the anterior and posterior components of the operculum fuse except for a small funnel-shaped opening to the outside, the spiracle.

At about stage 23 the oral disc and rows of keratinized labial teeth and horny beaks (Fig. 9.3begin to form. In stages 23 to 25 the initial formation of pigmentary patterns takes place, chromatophores of several types appearing at about stages 23 and 24.

In distinguishing between families the diagnostic feature is the form of the oral disc. Its essential peculiarities are present by about stage 26, although changes occur subsequently in the number and form of oral papillae. The tooth rows develop gradually. Although the "mature" tooth row formula of a species is usually established in the early larval stages, the relative proportions and numbers of the rows sometimes change during ontogeny.

Independent feeding commences sometime between stages 25 and 26. Primarily on this basis stage 26 is arbitrarily designated as the first larval stage.

Identification of stages 26 to 40 is made by examination of the hind limbs. Stages 26 to 30 are distinguished by changes in the ratio of length to diameter in the hind limb primordium. At stage 31 the "foot" is paddled-shaped, and in subsequent stages the configuration of the paddle is altered as individual toes are differentiated. The distinguishing criteria of stages 23 to 40 are proportional changes in the length of individual toes and in the appearance of metatarsal and subarticular tubercles.

Etkin (1932,1955 and 1964) regards anuran metamorphosis as consisting of two phases, prometamorphosis and metamorphic climax. Prometamorphosis begins at stage 36 and is marked by the rapid elongation of the hind limbs. During stage 40 the cloacal tail piece is resorbed, shifting the position of the anus. The completion of this shift marks the beginning of stage 41. The operculum thins and becomes translucent over the developing forelimbs, forming a "skin window" through which the forelimbs erupt.

The appearance of the forelimbs marks the beginning of stage 42, the first stage of metamorphic climax. Stages 42 to 46 are characterized by the remodeling of the head and are distinguished primarily by changes in the mouth. Larval mouthparts are lost. The tympanum is formed. At stage 46 metamorphosis is essentially complete. Newly transformed young may or may not resemble the adults sufficiently to permit positive identification.

The extensive alterations in external features noted are accompanied *by* equally profound changes in internal anatomy such as the adaptation of the aortic arches and the hyoid cartilages and muscles for pulmonary respiration, the loss of the lateral line system, the development of a muscular tongue, and the shortening of the gut. In this chapter, however, we shall give primary attention to external morphology.

Typical Development Among Urodeles

In the urodele the events of metamorphosis appear to *be* much *less* striking than in the anuran since the superficial resemblance of the salamander larva to the adult is much greater than that of the tadpole to the frog.

Rather abbreviated sequences of metamorphic stages have been described for *Eurycea bislineata* by Wilder (1925), for *Ambystoma maculatum, Notophthalmus' virides cens, A. jeffersonianum* by Grant (1930a and 1930b), and for *Gyrinphilus palleucus* by Dent and Kirby-Smith (1963) but external morphological changes are not sufficiently marked to substantiate a long series of stages such as that described for anurans. The only truly obvious change that is a consistent feature of metamorphosis among all urodeles is the resorption of the gills. Other consistent but less obvious external features are the resorption of the tail fin and the larval folds of the lower jaw, fusion of the gill slits, and the differentiation of eyelids. Also, colours and colour patterns typical of certain species change from larval to adult shades and configurations. In addition to the events common to all urodeles, there are numcrous changes in features peculiar to certain groups. For example, the Plethodontidae usually develop nasolabial folds during the latter states of metamorphosis.

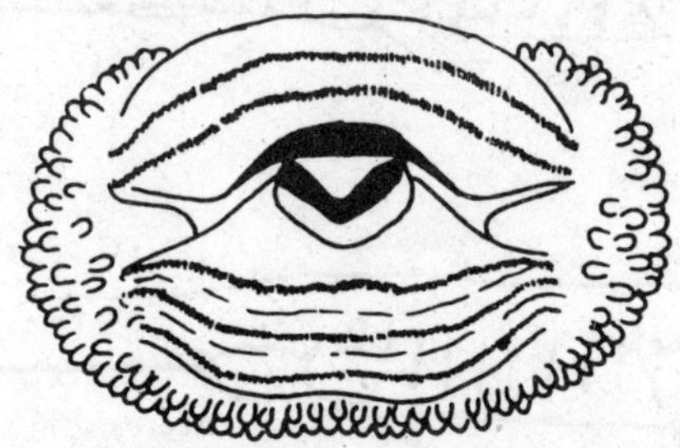

Figure 7.1 : Detailed diagram of oral disc from tadpole of Leptodactylus melanotus, a typical aquatic anuran larva. On the lateral and ventral borders are oral papillae.

The internal changes of urodele metamorphosis are most extensive in the head region. Valves develop around the nares to prevent the entrance of water if the adult becomes submerged.

Although *Notophthalmus* is the generic name currently accepted' by systematists for the eastern spotted newt, this animal has at different times also been called *Diemictylus* and *Triturus*. It became well established as subject for experimental studies during the time it was known as *Triturus*, and many continue to refer to it by that name in the literature of experimental zoology.

Alterations take place in the skull and in the hyobranchial apparatus. The skeletal changes are accompanied by alterations in associated musculature. In the integument there is a loss of large glandlike cells, the Leydig cells, and the formation of a keratinized stratum corneum.

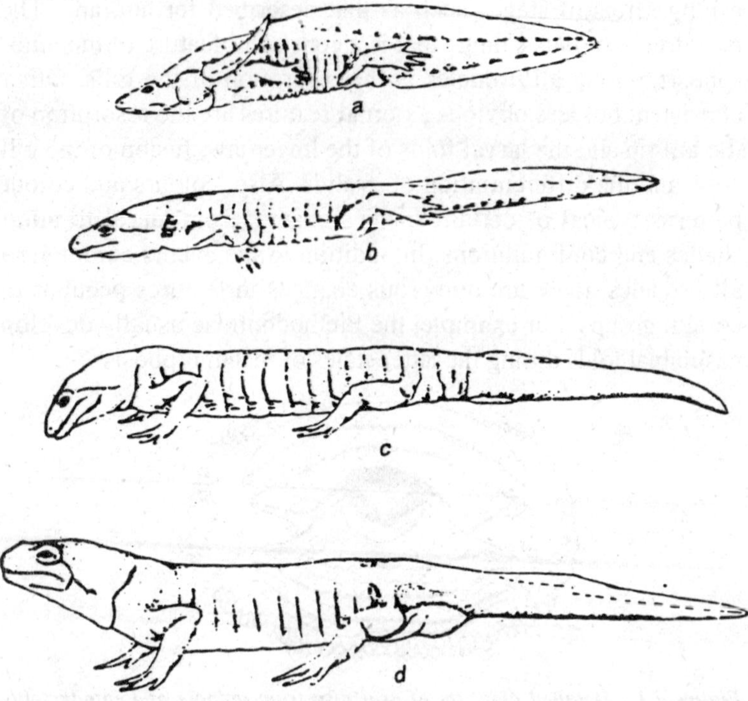

Figure 7.2 : Ambystoma rosaceum at a: larval; b: metamorphic; c: venile; and d: adult,stages.

Variation in Amphibian Life Histories

Although there are many typical anurans and urodeles whose life histories follow the patterns that have just been described, one does not venture far into amphibian systematics and biology without discovering that there are wide variations upon the basic theme. In the evolution of the vertebrates the amphibians provided the link between the fishes and the reptiles.

One tends to think of the amphibians being in the process of withdrawing from the water for life on land. A survey of the various taxonomic groups discloses that there is a fairly complete gradation in a broad range between amphibians that live completely in the water and those that live exclusively on land. The various levels of this gradation, however, neither represent a single orderly

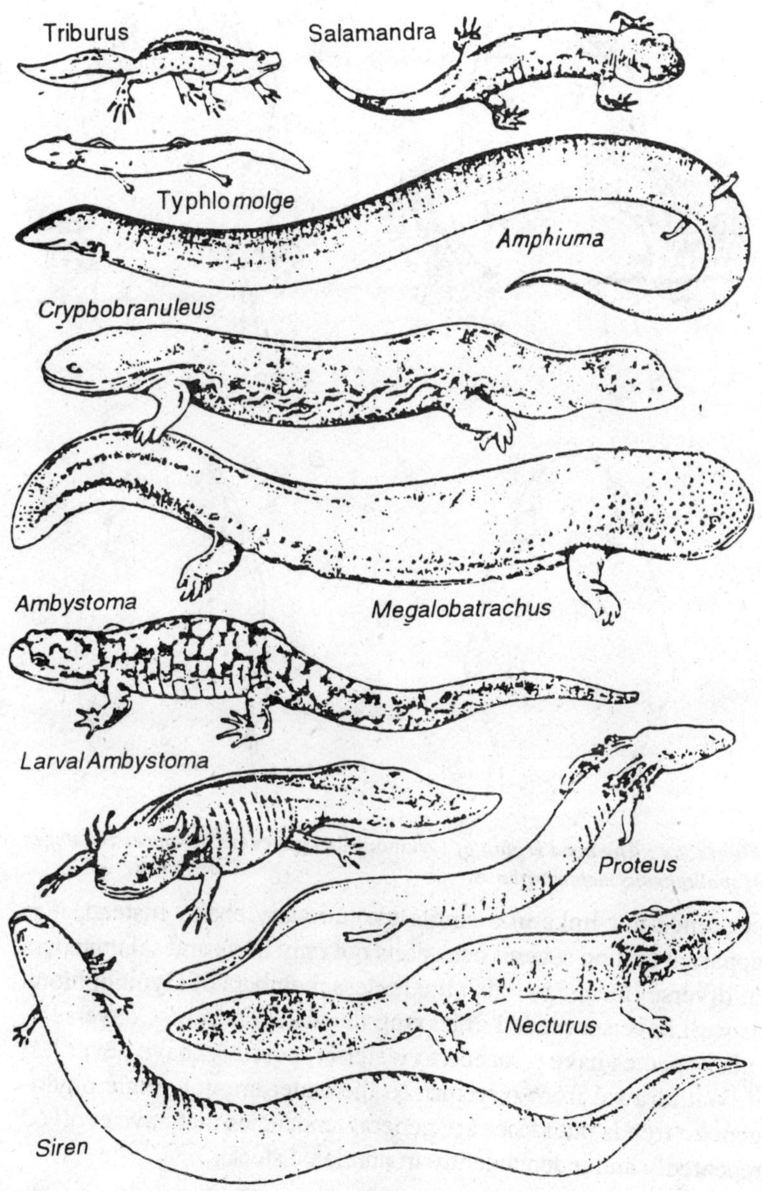

Figure 7.3 : Some of the various urodele amphibians.

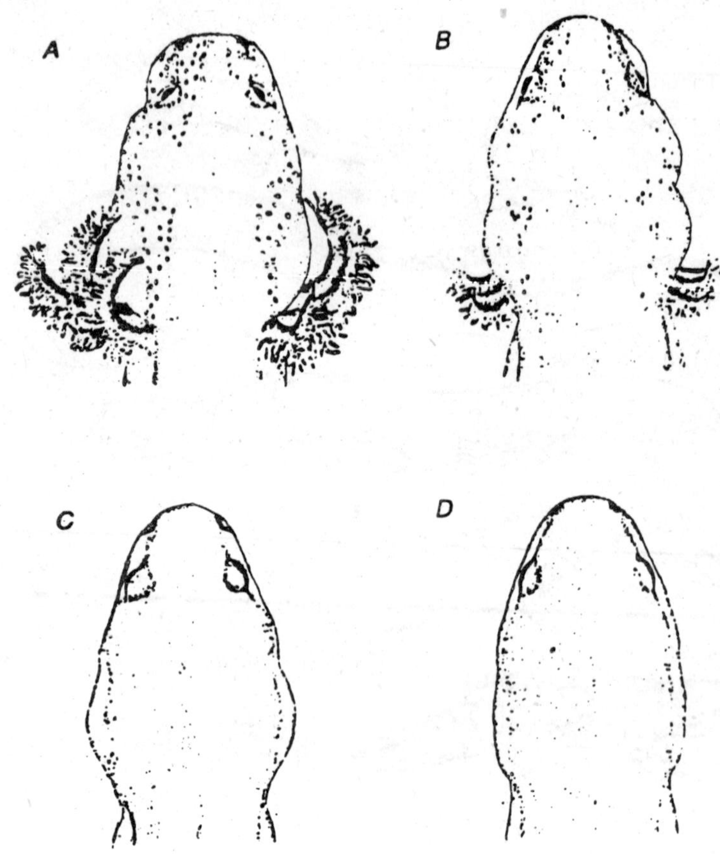

Figure 7.4 : The head region of **Gyrinophilus palleucus** *at successive stages of spontaneous metamorphosis.*

sequence nor links in a single evolutionary chain. Instead, it is apparent that on several occasions not only frogs and salamanders of diverse lineage but also the legless members of Gymnophiona as well have succeeded in leaving the water entirely. Conversely, other species have returned to water or, possibly, have never left it. Withdrawal from or return to the water are not single phylogenetic trends but rather are general tendencies that have evolved repeatedly and independently in unrelated stocks.

Among the 19 general of the order Gymnophiona one finds **sole** with aquatic larvae, others with direct development, and still others that are ovoviviparous. Yet they are, in effect, small and degenerate groups, and it has been decided not to give them further attention in this chapter.

Completely Aquatic Amphibians

The completely aquatic amphibians may be divided into two categories: (1) those with aquatic larvae that complete metamorphosis in the water and then remain in it as adults, and (2) those that are neotenic.

None of the urodeles quite fit into the first category. The spotted newt, *notophthalmus viridescens, is* completely aquatic as a larva and as an adult but following metamorphosis typically spends one to three years on land as a red eft. The eft has a tongue and a terrestrial integument lacking lateral line organs, but passes through a second metamorphosis before returning to the water during which the tongue is lost and lateral line organs are reacquired. *Leurognathus maramorata* of the lungless Plethodontidae is rarely found outside the water but has no special aquatic adaptations as an adult.

Among the Anura the Pipidae, such as the South African clawed toad *Xenopus laevis,* never leave the water. Both larvae and adults are tongueless and have lateral line organs. Occasional aquatic genera are also found among other families such as *Batrachophrynus* and *Pseudobufo* of the Bufonidae and *Telmatobius* of the Leptodactylidae.

Neoteny

There is some confusion in the use of the terms "neoteny" and "paedogenesis." Neoteny is a condition in which larval characters are retained for prolonged periods of time. Paedogenesis is the process by which larval individuals reproduce. A paedogenetic individual is of necessity neotenic. If a race is to be permanently neotenic it must obviously be also paedogenic.

Paedogenesis is not found among the Anura, although naturally occuring, non-metamorphosing anuran larvae have been reported. In some instances the larval periods of certain species or individuals have been prolonged sufficiently for them to be classed as neotenic.

TABLE 7.1 : DEGREES OF NEOTENY AMONG THE URODELA

		Family	Genus	Species	Region\
				Lacertina	Southeastern U.S.
		Sirenidae	*Siren*	*intermedia*	Southeast and Central U.S.
			Pseudobranichus	*straitus*	Southeast U.S.
				maculosus	Eastern U.S.
			Necturus	*punctatus*	Southeastern U.S.
		Proteidae	*Proteus*	*anguinus*	Central Europe
1.	Permanent larvae		*Cryptobranchus*	*alleganiensis*	Eastern U.S.
		Cryptobranchidae		*jáponicus*	Japan
			Megalobatrachus	*davidianus*	China
				means	Southeastern U.S.
		Amphlumldae	*Amphiuna*	*tridactylion*	Southeastern U.S.
			Typhlomolge	*rathbuni*	Texas
			Haideotriton	*wallacei*	Georgia and Florida
2.	Consistently netenous in natural habitat,			*Tynerensis*	Oklahoma
		Plethodontidae		*neotenes*	Texas
			Eurycea	*nana*	Texas

Table 7.1 Contd.

Table 7.1 Contd.

but metamorphosis can be induced			*troglodytes*	Texas
		Gyrinophilus	*palleucus*	Tennessee
	Ambstomatidae	*Siredon*	*pisciformis*	Mexico
		Dicampton	ensatus	West Coast of U.S.
			Tigrinuon	United States
	Ambystomatidae	*Ambystoma*	*Talpoideum*	Southeastern U.S.
			gracile	West Coast of U.S.
		Rhyacosiredon	*4* species	Mexico
		Notophthalmus	perstriantus	Eastern U.S.
Occasionally neotenous in Nature			*viridescens*	Eastern U.S.
			alpestris	Central Europe
	Salamandridae		*cristatus*	Western Europe
		Triturus	helveticus	Western Europe
			Taenialus	Central Europe
	Plethodontidae	*Euirycea*	*multiplicata*	Oklahoma, Arkanasas, and Missouri
	Hynobidae	*Hynobius*	*lichenatus*	Japan

Table 7.1 presents a listing of caudate species reported to be neotenous. All are probably paedogenic as well.

Of the genera listed as permanent larvae, Noble (1931) - upon consideration of such metamorphic features as the development of limbs, maxillary bones, loss of gills, and reduction of branchial arches-proposed that *Siren* and *Pseudobranchus* be considered as forms that cease to differentiate at a very early stage of larval life; *Proteus* and *Necturus* as forms that reach a later stage of urodele ontogeny; *Cryptobranchus* as a form that had begun its metamorphosis; and *Megalobatrachus* and *Amphiuma* as forms that have nearly completed their metamorphosis.

The outflow of water from the mouths of urodele larvae through the internal nares (choanae) is usually prevented by the action of a simple flap of connective tissue that serves as a valve.. As metamorphosis a more elaborate valve activated by smooth muscle is developed. *Necturus* and *Proteus* have choanal valves and skin of the larval type (with Leydig cell and without stratum corneum), two pairs of gill slits, and three pairs of external gills (no urodele has internal gills). Moving in the adult direction, *Cryptobranchus* and *Amphiuma* each have one pair of gills slits. *Megalobatrachus* has none. These animals have not developed eyelids. The larval character of *Siredon* and *Pseudobranchus is* indicated by the absence of hind limbs and the presence of choanal valves, external gills (three pairs in *Siren* but only one in *Pseudobranchus),* and open gill slits. The skin of *Siren* has adult structure, but that of *Pseudobranchus* is larval.

The Thyoid Gland and Neoteny

With the coming of knowledge regarding the relation of the thyroid gland to metamorphosis, questions were raised regarding neotenic forms. Do they fail to metamorphose because of deficient thyroid function or haye the tissues hat ordinarily respond to the thyroid lost their sensitivity to it? In general, the second hormone explanation seems to be most nearly correct, *Necturus* failed more to respond to treatment with thyroxin alone, although it was in combination with adrenalin. The treatment was lethal, and no other metamorphic changes were noted. Etkin (1955) ascribes these results to generalized effects of unfavourable conditions. Gill reduction without other changes was produced in *Siren* and *Pseudobmnchus* by treatment with iodothyrine. This, also, may have been a generalized rather than a specific response. Immersion in solutions of desiccated thyroid gland hastened the shedding of skin but had no further effect on *Cryptobranchus*. Equivalent results were obtained in *Amphiuma* and thyroxin. Although *Proteus* gives ho metamorphic response to treatment with thyroxin, its skin undergoes changes in the adult direction upon transplantation to metamorphosing salamanders *(Triton, Salamandra,* or *Ambystoma).*

The placement of the caverniculous salamanders *Typhlomolge* and *Haideotriton* in category 2 is perhaps questionable. In 1957 Dundee immersed a single small (33 mm snout-vent length) specimen of *Typhlomolge* in a 1:1,000,000 aqueous solution of racemic thyroxin. When no results were noted the concentration was increased first to 1:500,000 and then to 1:100,000. Immediately the labial folds, gills, and fins began to undergo gradual atrophy. Maxillae were developed and the beginnings of maxillary dentition were seen. Before the animal died at the end of 19 days, the fins and labial folds were resorbed, and the gills were reduced to mere stubs. The skin was unchanged, and no further metamorphic events were noted. It is possible that if the experiment were repeated using larger animals metamorphosis might be brought to completion. It is well-known that distortion of the metamorphic pattern results when very young larvae are treated with thyroxin.

The evidence favouring the inclusion of *Haideotritition* in category 2 is much stronger. Dundee (1961) immersed five specimens of *Haideotriton* in concentrations of thyroxin ranging between 1:100,000 and 1:2,000,000. All concentrations produced metamorphic changes with about equal effectiveness. In all instances, there was a loss of fins, labial folds, lateral line organs, gills, and the coronoid bone. There were no further changes in the skull, no changes in the skin, and the eyelids were not developed. All five animals died within 25 days of the beginning of the treatment. Like the spccimen of *Typhlomlge,* they were relatively small individuals, the larges being 27 mm in length. A mature

TABLE 7.2 : EXAMPLES ILLUSTRATING THE TREND TOWARD DIRECT DEVELOPMENT WITHIN THE ANURA

Frog	*Eggs Deposited in*	*larval Period*	*Metamorphic Modifications*
Rana pipens	Ponds	Typical aquatic	None
Hyla septentrionalis	Water containing cavities of bromeliads	Typical aquatic (rapid development)	None M
Hyla Faber	Water-filled nests walled off from larger ponds or poles	Typical aquatic	None
Hyperolius tuberillinquis	Vegetation overhanging water aquatic larval period	Upon hatching larvae fall into water for typical	None
Leptodactylus alWabris	Froth-filled nest near pond or pool	Fluctuation of water level washes larvae into pond	None
Hemisus marmoratum	Underground nests near ponds or pools	Female digs tunnel to pond through which larvae wriggle	tacks external gills but has horny mouth parts
Thoropa petropol itana	Spray-derenched rocks rocks	Tadpoles remain on wet	Mouth adapted for clinging to rocks, tail fins reduced

Table 7.2 Contd.

Table 7.2 Contd.

Leioplema hockstetteri	Damp situations usually (but nort always) floodedd before metamorphosis	Aquatic if flooded to have respiratory function.	Lacksgills; tail considered
Leptodactylus nanus	Froth within earth-covered nest distant from water	Tadpoles remain within cavity	None
Arthroleptella light footi	Damp moss forelimbs emerge	Larvae wriggle on moss for short time before covered by operculum.	No gills, gill slits, or larval mouth parts; forelimbs
Cornufer hazelae	Axils for fern fronds	None	No gills, gill slits, or larval mouth parts; forelimbs continuous by perculum that is continuous with abdominal respiratory folds.
Eleutherodactylus nubicola	Damp cavities under stones	None	No gills or gill slits; vestige of larval lower lip and of operculum; tail modified as respiratory structure.

specimen, the type specimen of *Haideotriton,* was reported by Carr (1939) to be 75.6 mm in length. Pylke and Warren (1958) found that an animal grown to be 43 mm long was still sexually immature. As with *Typhlomolge,* it seems likely that if larger specimens of *Haideotriton* were treated with thyroxin they might pass through a complete metamorphic sequence. It must be conceded, however, that the' tissues of both *Typhlomolge* and *Haideotriton* are very resistant to the metamorphic action of the thyroid hormone and that they might be properly classed as permanent larvae.

When immersed in a solution of thyroxin at a concentration of 1:500,000, the Tennessee cave salamander *Gyrinophilus* palleucus was seen after about two weeks to begin metamorphosis with a regression of soft tissues at either side of the tip of the snout. The gills shrank too become mere stubs at the end of about three weeks. By this time the labial folds and tail fin were resorbed, and parasphenoid teeth, maxillary bones and teeth were formed. The formation of eyelids took several more weeks, and the differentiation of the tongue was a protracted process that took up to five or six months for completion. Rather surprisingly, in view of the length of time required for complete metamorphosis at this rather high concentration of thyroxin, a few specimens underwent spontaneous metamorphosis in ordinary springwater. The factors that stimulated this spontaneous metamorphosis have not been discovered.

Complete metamorphosis was brought about in *Eurycea tynerensis* and in *Eurycea neotines* within 18 days by immersion in a 1 : 500,000 solution of thyroxin. The other species *of Eurycea* listed in the second category have not been tested, but it seems reasonably safe to assume that because of their close relation to *E. tynerensis* and *E. neotines* they also are quite responsive to the thyroid hormone. The ease with which metamorphosis is induced in the axolotl *Siredon pisciformis is* common knowledge.

The response of the species listed in category 3 to the thyroid hormone has not been tested in all instances, but it is safe to assume that they are all quite responsive. Metamorphosis occurred quite readily in *Notophthalmus viridescens, e.g.,* when neotenic specimens were exposed to quite low concentrations (1:2,000,000) of thyroxin. *Ambystoma gracile* completes metamorphosis at 18 days in a 1:500,000 solution of thyroxin.

Thus, it is reasonably clear that the tissues of the animals in categories 2 and 3 of Table 9.1 are competent to respond to thyroid hormone. But what of their own endocrine glands? For many years it was generally believed that the thyroid gland was congenitally absent in *Typhlomolge rathbuni* , but eventually Gorbman (1957) **made** a careful histological study and found in each of two specimens around 100 loosely arranged thyroid follicles.

The thyroid of *Gyrinophilus palleucus* typically functions at a low level but produces sufficient hormone to induce metamorphosis when stimulated with exogenous thyroid stimulating hormone. The thyroid of the axolotl -induces metamorphosis when stimulated by pituitary grafts from its typically metamorphosing relative *Ambystoma tigrinum,* but *A. tigrinum* larvae retain their larval form when their pituitary glands are replaced with axolotl pituitaries. In general, these observations and others made on the thyroid glands of facultative neotines indicate that their metamorphic failure results from hypofunction of the pituitary gland.

Withdrawal from the Water

From the standpoint of evolution, several advantages have accrued to those amphibians that have taken up completely terrestrial existence. The survival value of the change is readily recognized when one becomes aware of the wide geographic distribution and the numbers of highly successful species that have acquired this mode of life. The aquatic larva is beset by greater numbers of predators than the developing terrestrial amphibian. On land, parental protection is feasible and often given. The hazards resulting from the drying up of temporary pools and the flooding of mountain streams are eliminated. Metamorphosis is apparently a traumatic process, as evidenced by the fact that in progenies of typical amphibians reared in protected laboratory situations the highest mortality rates are always observed during the metamorphic period. The amphibians that have achieved direct development avoid the rigors that attend the extensive remodelings of typical amphibian metamorphosis.

Adaptations that have resulted in various degrees of withdrawal from the water are found in both the Anura and the Urodela. The range of adaptation is broadest and **most** complete within the Anura, and we shall give first consideration to them. Gradations of withdrawal can be arranged in two series that are unsequential in the evolutionary sense. One, illustrated in Table 7.2, reaches its culmination with completely direct development in which strictly larval characters are almost entirely eliminated. The species listed in the left-hand columns of Tables 7.1 is meant to be representatives of groups of animals that have identical or very similar life histories.

Direct Development Among Anurans

Rana pipiens is representative of all those anurans that have a typical life history in which jelly-encased eggs are laid in some body of water and in which typical aquatic larvae hatch from those eggs to eventually undergo a typical metamorphic sequence. The little West Indian tree frog *Hyla septentrionalis is* representative of those forms that lay their eggs in very small volumes of water such as those found in sections of bamboo or in the cavities created by the branching of leaves from the bases of bromeliads. Their development is morphologically typical but extremely rapid. Such small deposits of water would be likely to evaporate before slowly developing larvae could metamorphose. The South American frogs *Hyla faber, H. pardalis,* and *H. rosenbergi* lay their eggs in small nests or puddles of water that are very close to or walled off from larger ponds or *pools. H. rosembergi* has an additional adaptation.' Its gills are modified for clinging to the surface film of the water in which it develops.

A large number of species from several genera and families attach themselves to vegetation that overhangs some body of water. In the South American *Hyperolius tuberillinquis* the eggs are contained within a stiff mass of jelly. Oftentimes, as in *Rhacophorus leucomvstax* from the Philippines, the nest is composed of froth beaten up from an albuminous secretion of the female by the limbs of one or both parents. Sometimes the nest remains relatively soft and sometimes it hardens superficially into a crust that resists dehydration. The female of *Chiromantis xerampolina* remains with and moistens her nest until the larvae within it are hatched, otherwise the crust becomes too hard for the larvae to break when the time comes for them to escape. Other forms such as *H. pusillus* attach their eggs individually to leaves or wrap leaves around the eggs, as do the banana frogs of the genus *Hoplophyryne.* In all of these species the larva upon hatching falls into the water and takes up the existence of a typical tadpole.

The majority of the 50-odd species of the genus *Leptodactylus* lay their eggs in froth-filled nests near small bodies of water that fluctuate in depth with rainfall. The nest sites are from time to time flooded and the larvae are routinely washed into the body of water before metamorphosis takes place. *Hylambates natalensis* and a few species from other families are known to build quite similar nests.

With her snout, the female *of Hemisus marmoratum* digs an underground nest chamber and remains with her eggs until they hatch. She then tunnels to the water and is followed by the larvae which, even though they become aquatic, do not develop external gills.

Thoropa petropolitana is representative of a few species of South American frog such as *Cyclorampus pinderi* whose tadpoles are only semiaquatic -in that they spend their larval period upon moist rocks and not actually within the water. Their mouths are especially adapted for clinging to the rock, and their tails are modified somewhat as respiratory organs, although gills do develop. *Leiopelma archeyi* from New Zealand. is occasionally semiaquatic throughout the larval period. The eggs are laid in a damp situation, but not in the water, and the young swim only if the next happens to be flooded before metamorphosis is complete. It has four pairs of open gill slits, but no gills form. As pointed out earlier, the anuran operculum is derived principally from a transverse dermal fold that grows backward from the hyoid region, but also from a low,

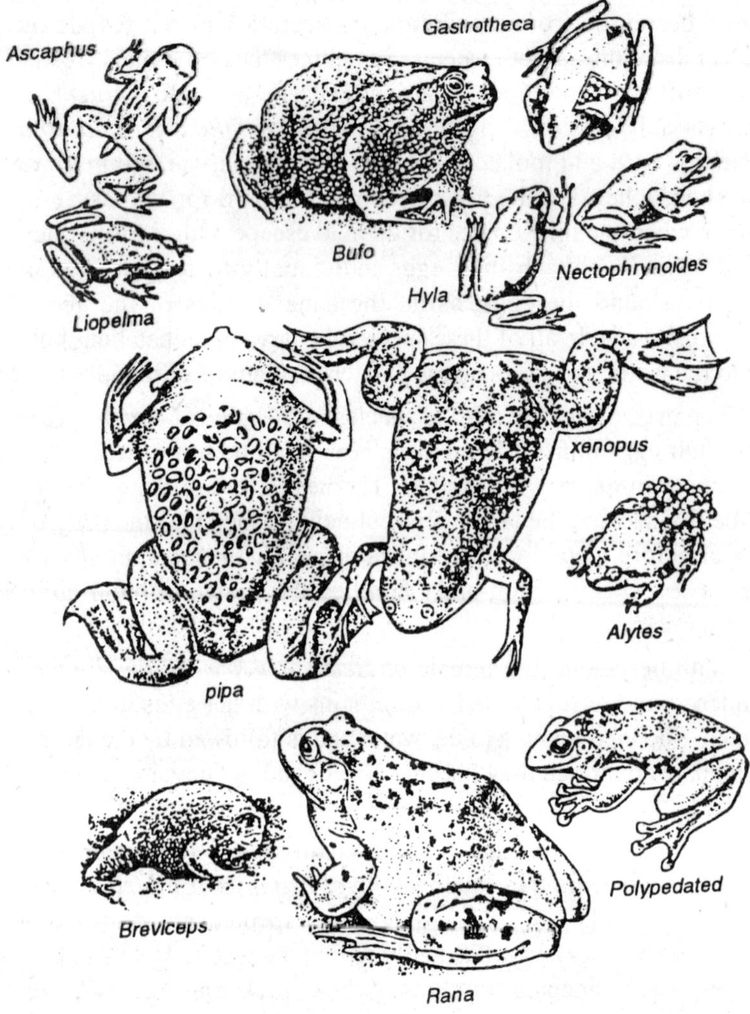

Figure 7.5 : Some of the anuran amphibians.

ridgelike fold across the anterior part of the belly just behind the forelimb, buds. In aquatic larvae these two components are fused together prior to the formation of the forelimb bud. In *Leiopelma* fusion does not take place although the forelimb buds are covered by the anterior components. The tongue forms before hatching occurs. In South American *Leptodactylus* represents a group of several species such as *Zachaenus parvulus* whose larvae are semi-aquatic, being laid and left throughout metamorphosis either in froth or in some moist situation some distance from water. In these animals essentially all larval features are retained and the metamorphic pattern is essentially unchanged. The South American frog *Arthroleptella lightfooti* has a semiaquatic larva but is considerably adapted in the direction *of* direct development with the loss *of* gills, gill slits, and larval mouth parts. It does retain the larval operculum. Its tail shows no special adaptations.

Frogs *of* the genus *Cornufer* have essentially direct development. The operculum is the only larval structure that is retained. The embryos are distinctive in that their abdominal walls bulge into huge saclike structures that are obviously adapted for respiration.

Eleutherodactylus nubicola is representative *of* the some 200 different species of over 15 other genera in which the aquatic larval period and most of the larval characters are eliminated. The young are encased within gelatinous membranes throughout the developmental period to a stage equivalent to the termination of metamorphosis. Information is fragmentary concerning most of these species, but a reasonable amount of detail is available concerning a few such as Arthroleptella rattrayi as well as six species *of-£leutherodactylus.* In these forms gills have either disappeared completely or are present in vestigial form. Gill slits never develop, and without them neither do internal gills. Among the species *of Eleutherodactylus* that have been studied, *nubicola is* the most advanced. In this species a trace *of* the lower larval lip and a small vestige *of* the posterior opercular anlage are the only larval characters that remain.' Among the other species *of Eleutherodactylus, E. portoricensis, E. nasutus,* and *E. guentheri* have evolved to a stage nearly equivalent to that of E. *nubicola,* whereas *E. inoptatus* and *E. martinicensis* have transitory vestiges of external gills. In all *of* these animals the highly vascularized tail expands into a balloonlike structure and serves as an organ *of* respiration.

Parental Care Among Anurans

Although they lack fetal membranes, anurans with direct

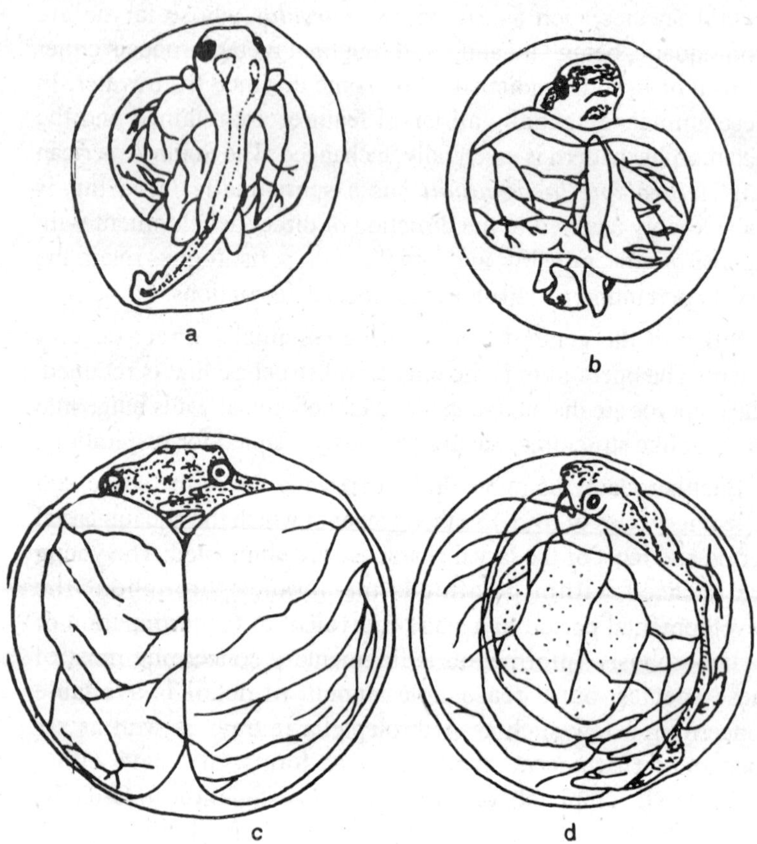

Figure 7.6 : Embryos of Cornufer peleuensis a and b are dorsal and ventral views of a young embryo, c is a ventral view of an animal nearing the hatching stage, and d is a lateral view of an advanced embryo.

development have otherwise reached a condition *of* oviparity equivalent to that typical *of* the birds and *of* many reptiles. They show a progressive increase in parental care and handling that culminates in true ovoviviparity. The "brooding" of eggs is not uncommon among those forms with direct or near direct development. A parent guards the eggs in several species of *Eleutherodactylus,* and the male of *Leiopelma* guards the eggs. It has been suggested by Jameson (1950) that the male of *Eleutherodactylus latrans* wets down the eggs that it guards with urine to prevent their dryingout. Some wetting down of the

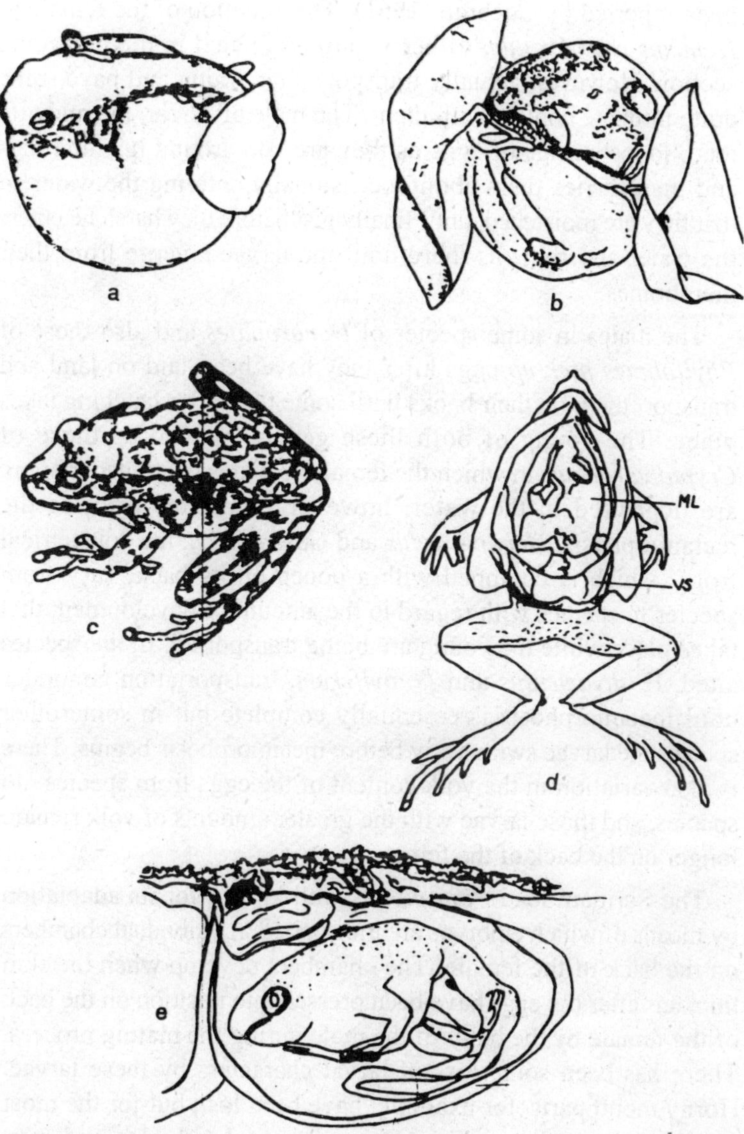

Figure 7.7 : a: Embryo of Ekutherodactylus inoptatus at early developmental stage. Advanced development stage of Gastrotheca marsupiata. c: Cryptobatrachus evani. A female carrying embryos upon her back. d: Vocal sac in male specimen of Rhinaderma darwinii e: Metamorphic individual of Pmtoplpa aspera within a maternal dorsal pocket shown in vertical section.

encrusted froth nest of *Chicomantis by a* guarding parent has also been reported by Cochran (1961). The attention of the female of *Hemisus marmoratum* to her young was noted in the preceding section. However, actually transport their young and have some quite intimate contact with them. The male of *Alytes*, the midwife toad, loops strings of eggs as they are laid around his hind legs and then carries them about, occasionally entering the water so that they are moistened, until finally just before they hatch he enters the water and remains there until the larvae emerge from their membranes.

The males in some species of *Dendrobates* and also those of *Phyllobates pick up* eggs after they have been laid on land and transport them on their backs until some time after hatching takes place. The young of both these genera as well as those of *Cryptobatrachus*, in which the female provides the transportation, are deposited in the water, however, sometime prior to the metamorphosis, *Hemiphractus* and *Gastrotheca*, the "obstetrical frog," which is equipped with a pouch on its back, vary from species to species with regard to the amount of development that takes place while the young are being transported. In the species cited, H. *divaricatus* and *G. oviferum*, transportation continues until metamorphosis is essentially complete but in some other species the larvae swim away before metamorphosis begins. There is also variation in the yolk content of the eggs from species _to species, and those larvae with the greater amounts of yolk remain longer on the back of the female.

The Surinam toad *Pipa pips* is well known for its adaptation by means of which embryos are transported in individual chambers on the back of the female. The chambers develop when the skin thickens after the eggs have been pressed into position on the back of the female by the belly of the male during the mating process. There has been some loss of larval characters by these larvae. Horny mouthparts, for example, have been lost, but for the most part they have the configuration of typical tadpoles and may actually feed on small organisms that come within their grasp during the last few weeks they are within their chambers. A similar pattern of life history is, found in two other species of *Pipa* and in

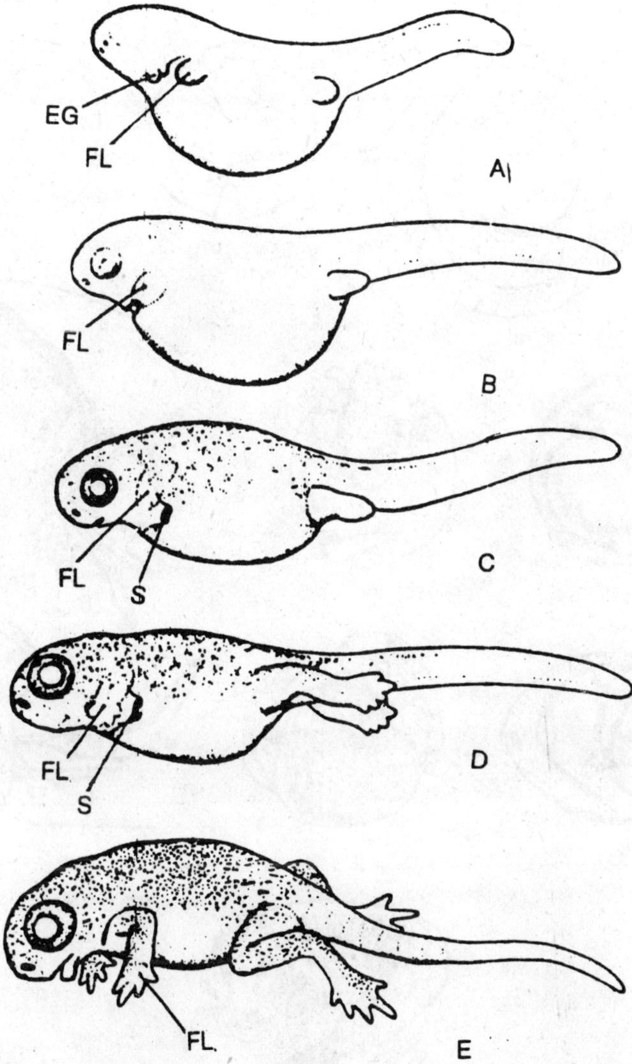

Figure 7.8 : Larvae removed from the oviduct of the ovoviviparous toad, Nectophyrnoides tornieri, at various departmental stages. In B the external gills and forelimb buds shown in A have been covered over by the developing operculum. In C operculum formation is complete and the spiracie is evident. In D metamorphosis is near as the forelimb becomes visible through the thin skin of the operculum. In E metamorphosis is underway. The forelimbs have emerged, and the tail fin has been resorbed.

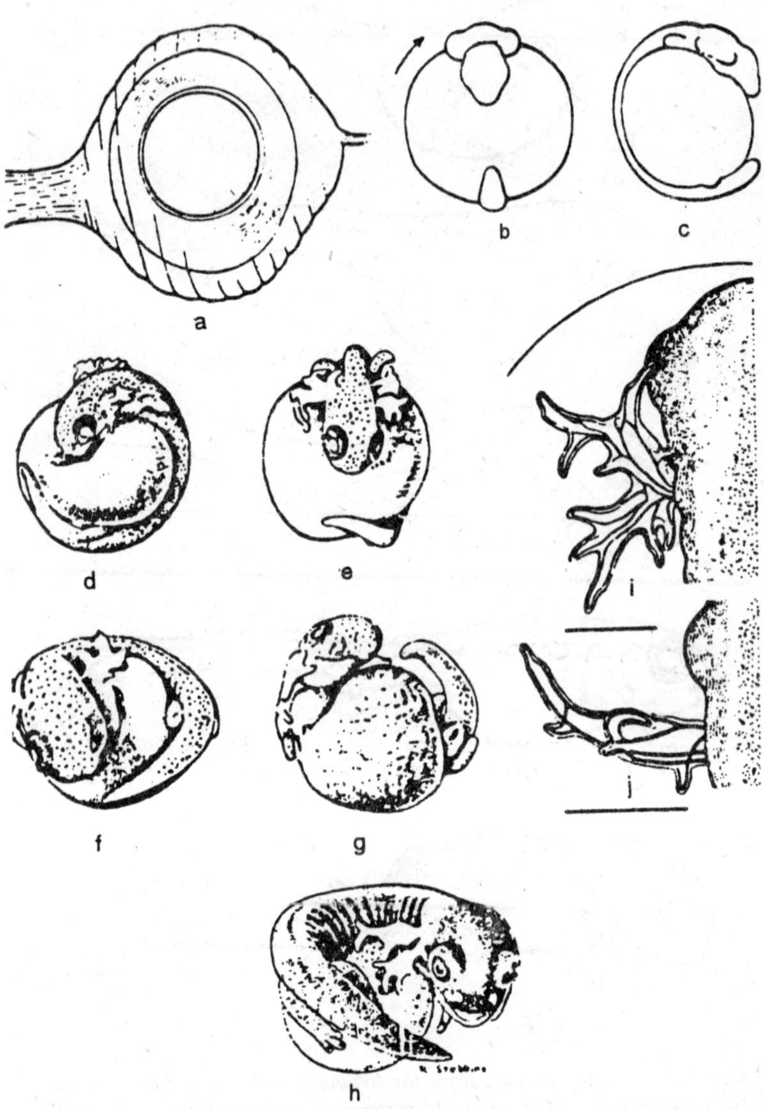

Fig. 9.9. Development of a plethodontid salamander (Batrachoseps wrighti). a: Newly laid egg with its membranes. b and c: Tail bud stage showing anlagen of limbs and gills. d to g: Stage equivalent to free swimming larva. Oral, cloacal, and nasolabial grooves shown. h: Equivalent of premetamorphic stage. Digits well formed. i and j: Details of gills. Horizontal lines each represent 1 mm.

the species of the closely related genus *Protopipa*, except that the larvae leave the female prior to metamorphosis

Hylambates brevirostris is the only amphibian known to brood its eggs in its mouth, although this behaviour pattern is encountered in several fishes. The female if H. *brevirostris* takes the fertilized eggs in her mouth and carries them there without eating until metamorphosis is complete.

The reproductive adaptation of the Chilean frog *Rhinoderma danvinii* has been known since the voyage of H.M.S., Beagle but is nonetheless striking. In this species several males gather around the eggs after they have been laid and fertilized, guarding them for a brief period of time. Then one or more of the males takes a small complement of eggs into his mouth. From the mouth the eggs are moved into the vocal sac. The vocal sac gradually enlarges as the embryos increase in size. The larvae are typical in form and undergo a typical metamorphosis with the exception that the horny teeth and beaks never harden. Although the embryos have a considerable amount of yolk, some feeding may take place toward the end of the developmental period while they are still encased within the vocal sac.

In the three species of *Nectophrynoides,* ovoviviparity is attained. The larvae are equipped with gill slits and suckers, but horny beaks and teeth are absent. The long, ratlike tail has very low fines. Although its surface area is not very great the tail is well vascularized and obviously has a respiratory function. This is quite apparent in *N. vivipara*. Here the uterus may contain as many as 100 larvae whose bodies tend to be located toward the central part of the uterus and whose elongate tails are. arranged so as to have a maximal contact with the uterine wall. Angel and Lamotte (1984) report *N. occidentalis* to be without a spiracle. Orton (1989) states that a spiracle is present in *N. tornieri* but that it is quite small.

Withdrawal from the Water by Urodeles

The movement from the water in the Urodela is roughly parallel to that in the Aruna. Several species (including, oddly enough, the neotenic and otherwise aquatic *Amphiuma)* lay their eggs on land but near water that fluctuates in level so that the embryos are swept into it prior to hatching.

Among the urodeles, direct development is accomplished only in the family Plethodontidae. The large, yolk-laden eggs are surrounded individually with heavy gelatinous membranes. In general, there is no loss of larval characters and no deviation from the typical metamorphic pattern except that the gills are larger and longer than those of aquatic larvae.

In view of its neoteny it is somewhat surprising to find that *Proteus is* often ovoviparous in the lower temperatures of its range. The European newt *Salamandra salamandra* likewise retains embryos in utero until after they hatch, sometimes apparently stimulated by low temperatures, throughout metamorphosis. *Salamandra atra* is consistently ovoviviparious, as are the plethodontids, *Hydromantes* and *Oedipus*. As in the ovoviviparous urodeles, with direct development there is no loss of larval characters in ovoviviparious urodeles. The intrauterine larvae of *Salamandra*, for example, develop rudimentary balancers and lateral line organs. The elongate gills of these creatures function in the exchange of respiratory gases between maternal and larval bloodstreams.

The Role of the Thyroid Gland in Direct Development

In a preceding section the involvement of the thyroid gland in amphibian neoteny was commented upon. Its function in direct-development is also a matter of considerable interest. As early as 1917 Hoskins and Hoskins showed that the course of typical metamorphosis was halted by removal of the thyroid gland. In 1975, Allen found some difference in *Bufo* and *Rana* in the degree to which limbs will grow in the absence of thyroid stimulation. In *Bufo* the hind limbs of thyroidectomized larvae may reach a length of *8* mm, whereas those of *Rana* remain as small buds. It is well-known that administration of thyroid hormone to normal tadpoles brings about precocious metamorphosis. It seems possible, then, that direct development may consist of a telescoping of larval stages resulting from a precocious metamorphosis brought about by an early and intensive functioning of the thyroid gland, by an usually high sensitivity of the tissues to a relatively low thyroidal activity, or by the emancipation of the tissues from the need for stimulation by the thyroid hormone. HistologicaI observations made by Lynn in 1976 indicated that in *Eleutherodactylus* the thyroid began to function early in the developmental period and therefore might be responsible for a precocious metamorphosis. Similar conclusions were reached by Brink in 1939 with regard to *Arthroleptella bicolor*, but Dent found that the thyroid differentiates late in the intraoval life of the terrestrial salamanders *Plethodon cihereus* (1982) and *Aneides anaeus (1984)*.

Embryos of neither *Plethodon* nor *Eleutherodactylus* have survived attempts to remove the anlage of the thyroid by surgical procedures. In 1987, however, Lynn treated embryos of *Plethodon chhereus* with the goitrogen thiourea, blocking thyroid function by chemical means. Those embryos completed their development except for the resorption of the long and branched gills. Similarly, Lynn (1984) and (Lynn) and Peador, in 1955 reported results of treating with goitrogens *Eleutherodactylus ricordii* and *Eleutherodactylus martinicensis*. Three metamorphic features were affected by the treatment. The pronephoroes did not degenerate, the tail was not resorbed, and the egg tooth the animals develops just prior to hatching did not drop off as it ordinarily does. Administration of thyroxin to *Eleutherodactylus martinicensis* caused precocious degeneration of the pronephroes and resorption of the tail. Thus, it seems clear that the final steps of direct development are under control of the thyroid but that in the course of evolution the greater part of the ontogenetic sequence has been freed from thyroid control in *Plethodon* and in *Eleutherodactylus*.

Environmental Factors in Metamorphosis

Dodd and Callan (1985) found sexually mature neotenic individuals within an otherwise typical population of *Triturus helveticus* congregated in a pond of the count of Fife in Scotland. As indicated in Table 7.1, neoteny has been reported to occur occasionally in several species of *Triturus*. These specimens of *T. helveticus*, however, were unique in that their thyroid glands were goiterous and tremendously enlarged. This condition could hardly be attributed to a lack of iodine in the environment since the pond is situated within a few miles of the North Sea, and the iodine content of drinking water in the nearly town of Crail in 5 gg/1. Dodd and Callan noted that kale and turnips were cultivated in fields in the vicinity of the pond. The goitrogenic effects of the brassicas is well-known. Rabbits were frequently seen in the vicinity of the pond, and rabbit feces accumulated on the slopes from which water drained into the pond. Dodd and Callan concluded that this drainage water should contain the "brassica factor" at times when the rabbits were feeding on turnips and kale and that larvae overwintering in the pond might well, as a result, become goiterous and *neotenic*. Although it is interesting, it is unlikely that this condition described by Dodd and Callan for *T. helveticus* obtains generally among other occasionally neoteni forms.

Notophthalmus viridescens is neotenic in the lowlands of Louisiana, on Cape Cod, and on *Long* Island; but the majority of the neotenous individuals among the species listed in category 3 of Table 7.1 live in lakes located at altitudes of several thousand feet, as does *Siredon pisciformis*, the axolotl cited in category 2. Snyder (1986) has made comparative study of the Pacific Coast salamander *Ambystoma gracile* from ponds found at sea level and from other ponds at high elevations (4,300 to 5,500 ft.) in Mount Ranier National Park. At sea level a high proportion of larvae transform into immature adults at one year of age, and most of the remainder transform at two years of age as sexual maturity is attained. A small number persist as neotenic larvae. Adult animals are found in the *montane* habitats, but metamorphosis appears to be rare and most of the mature animals are *neotenic*. Snyder states that among amphibians cold either inhibits the release of thyroid hormone or the ability is tissues to respond to its presence, and Huxley (1929) has demonstrated that below 50°F the tissues of tadpoles are not stimulated by thyroidal material. Frieden has studied this effect extensively. Snyder states further that younger larvae respond more readily than older animals to the metamorphic effects of the thyroid hormone. This *contention* is supported by observation of Lipchina (1979) made on the axolotl. At high elevations the annual period of activity and growth lasts only about three months, whereas at sea level larvae may be active and feeding throughout the year. Snyder suggests that since the montane larvae reach metamorphic size at a later age they are possibly less responsive to the thyroid hormone or perhaps produce less thyroid hormone and thus do not metamorphose. The presence some neotenic animals at sea level is accounted for by Snyder on the grounds that eggs are laid over a period of five to six weeks and that perhaps the last eggs give rise to animals that overwinter as larvae and reach the age at which they are resistant to the thyroid hormone. Some brief experiments of a preliminary nature appeared to give support to this hypothesis, but further studies should be made.

From an evolutionary point of view its seems reasonable that the selective pressures would be greater on the barren icy borders of a mountain lake than within its waters. Similarly, in the caves inhabited by most of the animals of category 2 in Table 7.1 it is usually quite apparent that food is more abundant and other conditions are more favourable to the salamander within the water than outside of it. Very likely it is these selective pressure that have brought about the rise of neoteny in caves and in mountain lakes.

Pedogenesis has never been found to occur among the Anura, but the larval period in *some* frogs varies greatly in *length*. Temperature appears to be the predominant factor involved. *Rana clamitans*, the green frog, is usually said to metamorphose after spending one winter as a larva, but Ting (1981) showed that tadpoles of *R. clamitans* metamorphosed in 92 days in the laboratory, and Martof (1982) found that great numbers of larvae metamorphosed in August from . a pond that had been dry the preceding summer. He thought that overwintering larvae come from eggs laid late in the season. The bullfrog *Rana catesbeiana* also has a larval period of variable length, which is taken from a paper by Willis, Moyle. and Baskett (1986). These figures indicate that the larval period increases with the length and severity of winters.

TABLE 7.3 : AGE OF BULLFROG TADOLES AT TRANSFORMATION IN VARIOUS PARTS OF THE UNITED STATES.

Locality	Number of Winters of Life Before Transformation				Reference
	0	1	2	3	
New York			X	X	Wright (1914)
Iowa			X	X	Carlander et al. (1950)
California			X		Storer (1922)
Iowa		X			Klimstra (1949)
Florida		X			Fla, D. Ag. (1952)
Louisiana	X	?			George (1940)
Gulf States	X	X			Viosca (1934)

The length of the larval period may also be increased in urodeles without the occurrence of paedogenesis. Many individuals of *Eurycea bislineata* metamorphose in their second year, but some (presumably those from eggs laid late in the first year) metamorphose in the third year. In southern Europe *Triturus vulgaris* metamorphoses in the fall of its first summer, but in northern Russia it hibernates for one winter as a larva , no doubt because the summers in the latter region are not long enough or warm enough for it to complete its larval development in one of them.

In looking about for environmental features that may be responsible for neoteny in any given group of amphibians one always given- consideration to the iodine content of the water. Actually, no one has yet reported finding neotenous larvae in water with an iodine content too low to support metamorphosis in other amphibian species. Elair (1981) reported that one of two specimens of neotenic *Gyrinophilus palleucus* metamorphosed after three months in a rather strong solution of sodium iodide, but the other was still uncharged after six months, and as was pointed out earlier bent and Kirby-Smith (1993) found that specimens of this species occasionally metamorphose spontaneously in spring water under laboratory conditions. Although the induction of metamorphosis in the axolotl by the application of iodine has been reported, the amount given was relatively large. It seems safe to conclude that low iodine content of water is not ordinarily a cause of neoteny.

It is to be expected that larvae deprived of food would soon stop growing and differentiating. As far back as 1888 Yung reported that amphibian larvae are highly susceptible to nutritional deficiency and that their development is conditioned by the nature of the food. In 1897, Barfurth noted that under certain conditions the development of tadpoles was accelerated by starvation. This phenomenon was investigated in detail by D'Angelo, Gordon and Charipper (1981). They found that up to a critical period occurring in the early stages of hind-limb development metamorphic progress is slowed down and then halted by inanition so that tadpoles can be held for considerable periods of time in a "stasis" condition. Having passed the critical stage, the rate of metamorphosis indeed is increased by inanition. Possibly *inanition* accelerates the degenerative phases of metamorphosis. D'Angelo, Gordon, and Charipper observed that the thyroid and pituitary glands of starved animals underwent atrophic and degenerative changes. Stasis tadpoles metamorphose readily after either immersion in thyroxin solutions or injection with pituitary material. The thyroid glands of stasis animals that are metamorphosing after treatment with thyroxin are histologically inactive, but those of pituitaryinjected tadpoles give histological evidence of marked activity. On the basis of these observations it was concluded that the failure of starved animals to metamorphose is directly related to a decreased production and release of thyrotropic hormone from the anterior hypophysis.

Any naturally occurring inanition would be likely to be associated with crowding, and crowding itself appears to have a direct effect on the growth of amphibian larvae. It was Yung (1885), again, who first made observations on the relation of crowding to the delay in tadpole metamorphosis. His work was followed by that of others;

notably, Adolph in 1971 and more recently Richards (1988 and 1992), Rose (1990) and Akin (1996). Adolph saw that uncrowded animals reaches a much larger size than crowded ones and that they metamorphosed in a much briefer period of time. Rose observed that whenever a group of R. *pipiens* embryos were put in a rather confined space all began to grow after hatching, but at different rates. Those that grew more rapidly at first and became larger than their bowl mates continued to grow if the water was changed daily, whereas those that lagged behind stopped growing and failed to eat even when abundant food was supplied to them. On the other hand, the stunted animals grew if they were removed and put into other containers, giving greater "lebensraum." Richards (1988) showed that if small tadpoles were put into culture water in which large tadpoles had been *growing* the growth of the small tadpoles was completely or almost completely inhibited, indicating that some sort of inhibitory product is thrown off into the medium by the larger tadpoles. Further, the inhibitory effect could be removed by heating the culture water to 60°, by centrifugation, by sonification, or by filtration. Thus, the inhibitory product is a rather large particle.

In an aquarium where both large and small animals were present and the small ones were growing poorly and dying out, the largest animals were just as large as large animals that had been growing in isolation (Rose, 1990). This indicates that the large animals were unaffected by anything produced by *the* small tadpoles or that the small ones were neither producing stimulatory nor inhibitory substances. The growth of small tadpoles was supported, on the other hand, by culture water from large tadpoles after it had been treated with a proteinase. At least some of the inhibitory material, then, must be a protein. Richards (1992) reported that the inhibitory agent is associated with a type of algal cell in R. *pipiens*. Akin (1996) showed that the agent is elaborated by the posterior half of the gut in the growing tadpole. The algae pass through the gut and apparently transport the agent to the water. Akin also confirmed earlier reports that the agent is largely species-specific.

There are not reports of the inhibitory effects of crowding in nature, but such effects must exist since in the laboratory one rapidly growing large tadpole can appreciably retard the growth of small tadpoles in as much as 75 liters of water.

There have been reports that various electrolytes have accelerating or inhibitory effect on metamorphosis. Lynn and Wackowski (1981), however, are of the opinion that these apparent electrolytic effects are caused by changes in the hydrogen ion concentration of the medium rather than by any specific effects of the ion in question. Marzulli in 1971 confirmed earlier observations of Rosen (1978) to the effect that acidity below pH 4.8 and alkalinity above pH 11.0, respectively accelerate and retard the metamorphosing action of thyroxin. Marzulli further demonstrated that if thyroxin is injected its effects are not dependent on the pH of the culture medium.

He concluded that the greater effectiveness of thyroxin dissolved in an acid culture medium results from the fact that it is taken up more actively by the tissues at acid rather than alkaline pH levels. For further discussion of the uptake of thyroxin.

Disclos (1989) reported increased metamorphic rates among tadpoles of *Alytes obstetricans* given supplemental illumination, and Guyetant (1994) found that growth and metamorphosis were accelerated in larvae of *R. temporaria* maintained in constant illumination at *2,000* and 4,000 lux, whereas tadpoles kept in permanent darkness grew more slowly. It seems likely that the effects of illumination upon development will be found to be quite complex. Possibly they are mediated through the neuro-secretory pathways of the hypothalamus. This area of investigation is relatively untouched and may be the source of very interesting results in the future.

8

Endocrine Regulation

If instead of reviewing the published endocrine studies *on* amphibian metamorphosis we ask questions concerning the endocrine control of the process from the viewpoint o:f developmental physiology, we become impressed more with the lacunae *in* our knowledge than with the strength of the separate threads. In any event the general endocrine interrelations *in* this field have been reviewed in some detail Here we propose to examine metamorphosis from the viewpoint of the physiology of animal development rather than to inquire into the role of the separate endocrine glands. Before we can do that, however, we must summarize the main outlines of the **endocrine** relations among vertebrates generally in order to provide the framework within which we can ask our questions concerning control of metamorphic change by the hormones.

Endocrine Relationships

No detailed citations to the literature will be given for this discussion *of* endocrine interrelationships, but such references can be found in recent summaries of the field such as the *recent* volumes on *Neuroendocrinology* and *The Pituitary Gland* and in standard textbooks of endocrinology.

The thyroid hormones (TH) are iodine-containing derivatives of tyrosine. The principal hormone is thyroxine. The *thyroid* gland has an iodine-trapping mechanism whose efficiency *as* determined with radioiodine (1^{131}) is one measure of thyroid activity.. The histological picture presented by the thyroid is also a clear indicator of its physiological state. Abundant cytoplasm and release of colloid from the follicles indicate active glands. However, where iodine uptake is prevented by goitrogens, a histological picture of activity is associated with the failure to release potent hormone.

The thyroid gland can function autonomously at a low level, but higher levels of activity are dependent upon activation by a hormone, thyrotropin, or thyroid-stimulating hormone (TSH), produced by the anterior lobe of the pituitary. The level of activity of the pituitary-thyroid (PT) axis is under control through two known mechanisms.

One of these is by way of feedback of thyroid hormones that inhibit the activity of the TSH cells, thus stabilizing the PT axis at a particular level. There is good evidence that this negative feedback of TH upon TSH production operates primarily at the pituitary level, directly inhibiting the TSH cells.

The.second mode of regulating TSH activity is by way of a thyrotropin releasing factor (TRF) produced in the hypothalamus. TRF is presumed to be a neurosecretory material reaching the anterior pituitary by way of the pituitary portal veins that drain the median eminence of the hypothalamus. At present the chemical nature of TRF has not been clarified nor have the neural cells from which it arises been identified. It is believed, however, to differ from the peptides that constitute the classical neurosecretory substances produced in hypothalamic nuclei (preoptic nucleus in amphibians) and stored in the neural lobe of the pituitary. In stimulating TSH production, TRF may be thought to act by partially desensitizing the pituitary to the negative feedback action of TH and thereby permitting the level of the TP axis, the so-called thyrostat, to rise.

A word of clarification is needed with regard to the concept of neurosecretion. This has undergone marked development in recent years Originally neurosecretion was identified by characteristic, although not specific, staining reactions in light microscopy, i.e., neuronal granules positive to aldehyde fuchsin or chrome alum haematoxylin. Physiological, histochemical, and electronmicroscopical evidence has compelled the recognition that such material is related primarily to the pars nervosa although also occurring in the median eminence (Oota and. This latter region, however, has been shown, to be rich in monoamines and in peptides differing from those of the nervoasa. In the present discussion the neurosecretory system will be considered to include in addition to the classical neurosecretory pathway to the posterior lobe of the pituitary:

1. Neurons that produce other specific chemicals released into the bloodstream in the median eminence.

2. The median eminence with its primary capillary bed intimately related to neurosecretory fibers.

3. The portal veins that drain blood from the primary capillary bed of the median eminence into the secondary capillary bed of the pars anterior of the pituitary.

These endocrine and neuroendocrine interrelations are applicable to amphibian metamorphosis. As early as 1912, Gudernatch reported that the feeding of thyroid-gland preparations to young tadpoles precipitated metamorphic changes. It was soon demonstrated - particularly by M. Allen, Hoskins, and Hoskins and P. E. Smith - that the pituitary gland of the tadpole controls thyroid activity and that the latter is the immediate agent of metamorphic change. The neuroendocrine relations governing metamorphosis were worked out more recently. The evidence is convincing here, too, that the hypothalamus influences pituitary TSH activity by way of a TRF passed into the capillaries of the median eminence.

Another pituitary hormone that recently assumed a role in our understanding of metamorphosis is prolactin, which like TSH is a protein product of the anterior lobe of the pituitary. It is known to be active in stimulating body growth in several vertebrates and has recently been found to have antithyroid activity in tadpoles. In mammals and probably in amphibians prolactin appears to be under inhibitory rather than stimulatory control by the hypothalamus.

The Metamorphosis in a Typical Anuran

However, the endocrine analysis with which we are concerned

here has been carried out largely on a few species of anurans. To follow this analysis t will be most useful to have a more exact and quantitative delineation of the developmental pattern relative to metamorphosis in a typical Rapid, Rana *pipiens.* The principal points to be noted here are as follows. The first post-embryonic period characterized by much growth with very little change in form. This is here designated the growth or premetamorphic period and lasts about seven weeks at conventionᴦl room temperatures (22 to 25°C). This is followed by the period designated prometamorphosis and characterized by differential growth of the hind legs. During this period of about three weeks, the legs grow from about 2 mm to about 20 mm, whereas the body growth increases only from about 55 mm total length (body length, 18 mm; tail length, 37 mm) to 65 mm body length, 21 mm; tail length, 44 mm). It is easy to follow the progress of the animal through prometamorphosis by nothing the ratio of hind-leg length to body length (HL/BL).

The animal has definitely entered prometamorphosis when the HLJBL ratio exceeds 0.2 and it reaches the end of that period when this ratio approaches 1.0. During the latter part of prometamorphosis certain minor morphological changes may be observed in the intact animal. For example, the resorption of the anal canal piece of ACP (the basal lobe of the ventral fin that carries the anal opening out into the left side of the tail) occurs when the HL/BL ratio is about 0.6 In a day or two thereafter at a ratio of about 0.8 the first signs of the degeneration of the opercular skin over the gill chambers (the skin window for the forelegs, SWFL) can be seen on the right side. The corresponding change on the left is the reduction of the tubular wall of the spiracular opening from the gill chamber. In one or two days thereafter the forelegs emerge, usually within a few hours of each other, and the changes from the narrow tadpole mouth to the wide frog mouth begin with the shedding of horny teeth and beaks. The emergence of the forelegs and loss of tadpole mouthparts constitute the last phase of prometamorphosis and the beginning of metamorphic climax.

As noted in described in terms of the numbered stages of Taylor and Kollors (1986), Nieuwkoop and Faber (1996), and Gosner

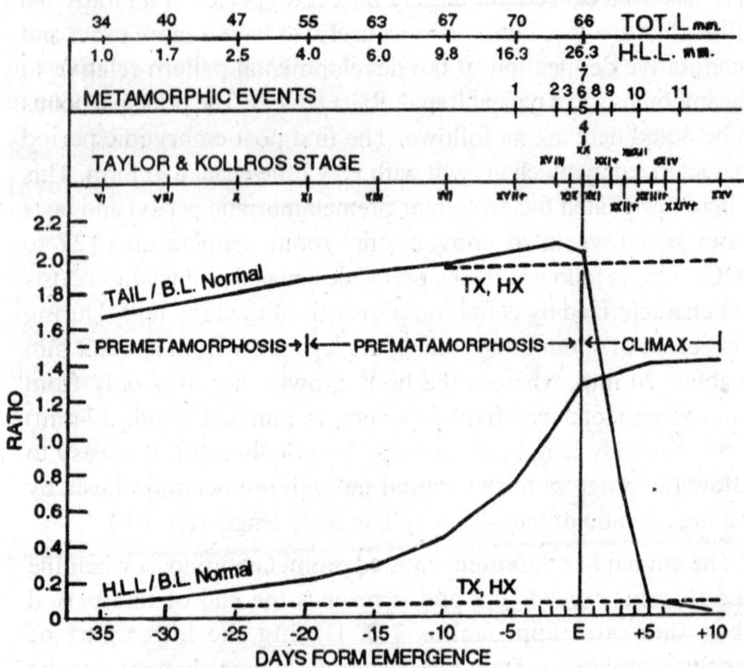

Figure 9.1 : Pattern of metamorphosis in Rana* pipiens. *Data from one batch of normal animals raised at 23°C = 1 shown by solid line. Comparable data for thyroidectomized animals (TX) and hypophysectomized animals (HX) are shown by broken lines. The metamorphic events indicated in the figure by number are as follows: 1. Anal canal piece-first definite reduction. 2. Anal canal piece reduction completed. 3. Skin window for the forelegs clearly apparent. 4. Loss of 2d (both) beaks. In experimental animals this is the most satisfactory criterion for the beginning in climax. 5. Emergence of first foreleg to appear. 6. Emergence of second foreleg (E). 7. Mouth widened to level of nostril. Events 4, 5, 6 and 7 usually occur within a period of 24 hours. 8. Mouth widened to level between nostril and eye. 9. Mouth widened to level of anterior edge of eye. 10. Mouth widened past level of middle of eye. 11. Tympanum definitely recognizable. By use of the data of this table it is possible to classify individual animals in terms of days before or after the beginning of climax (E).

(1960). However, for the experimental analysis it is important to recognize the exact quantitative and temporal relations of metamorphic changes as depicted. By use of the information in this figure it is possible to derive the concept of slowly accelerating metamorphic activity during prometamorphosis with climax recognizable as a burst of morphological change. In the design of experiments it is possible by use of these tables to select animals at particular stages and to predict the course of events to be expected in normal animals.

It should be noted that the widely used stages of Taylor and Kollros describe the entire range of tadpole development and are not directed at the analysis of metamorphosis per se. They do not recognizc the differential acceleration of hind-leg growth as the initiation of metamorphosis but regard this process as beginning in what we designate here as late prometamorphosis. They also do not differentiate a climax phase. Descriptively, the procedure of Taylor and Kollros is highly useful, but it obscures the experimental analysis. As will be seen later, early leg growth (stage XII to XVIII) is dependent upon activation of the myroid gland and is thus considered here to be part of metamorphosis. Furthermore, the endocrine balance undergoes a profound change at the beginning of climax so that the precise delineation of this phase is essential for an adequate understanding of the hormonal control of metamorphosis.

The most important consideration that emerges from this analysis is that the postembryonic developmental cycle of a typical anuran involves three phases: (1) a growth phase characterized by rapid growth and little morphological change, (2) a prometamorphic phase with reduced body growth rate and with morphological changes proceeding at a progressively accelerating pace, and finally (3) a phase of metamorphic climax in which body growth has ceased and differentiative changes proceed with extreme rapidity. We may center our analytic discussions, therefome, upon the special endocrine characteristics of each phase and the regulation of the transition from one to the next.

The Role of the Endocrines in the Growth Phase of Tadpole Development

It is obvious that at least morphologically all the elements necessary for metamorphic activity are present in the early tadpole, the hypothalamus, the pituitary, the thyroid, and the tissues. We may then ask Why does not the animal transform immediately?

Many possibilities suggest themselves, and we may consider the more plausible of these seriatum:

1. Are the tissues initially insensitive or relatively insensitive to thyroid hormone? Such a change in sensitivity might determine the time of initiation of metamorphic activity. The evidence, however, seems to indicate clearly that this is not the case. It is indeed true that the tissues of the embryo seem to be insensitive to thyroxin as seen in the often repeated observation that embryos develop normally in thyroxin solution and do not show metamorphic change (e.g., leg growth or tail resorption) until reaching the definitive tadpole stage (stage I)-for earlier literature see Etkin, 1985. On the other hand, it is also clear, as in Gudernatch's original experiments, that the postembryonic tadpole's tissue is capable of giving metamorphic responses to thyroid hormone. In a brief study reported only in abstract form, Etkin (1980) attempted to determine more precisely just when the tissues acquire thyroxin sensitivity. He did this by exposing embryos of R. pipiens to immersion in strong thyroxin solutions (or implantation of thyroxine crystals), beginning at successively later stages. He observed that embryos exposed before embryonic stage, S-23 did not develop metamorphic changes any earlier than did those whose exposure began at stage S-23. On the other hand, those exposed at later stages showed the first evidence of response at successively later periods. He concluded, therefore, that the tissues first became sensitive at about stage S-23 and are not influenced by exposure at earlier stages. There is a latent period of about three days in *the* appearance of metamorphic change, even when late tadpoles are exposed to strong thyroxine-1 part per million (ppm). The first changes do not appear in the above experiment until the animals are in stage S-25. Recent experiments by Prahlad and De Lanney (1995) with embryos of the axolotl likewise indicate early acquisition of thyroxine sensitivity. Furthermore, the pattern of change in the embryos of R. pipiens exposed at stage S-23 is the same as that in animals exposed, later. This suggests that the general tissues, as observed. externally; acquire sensitivity at the same time and approximately to the final degree.

There have been many attempts to show that sensitivity of

tissues to thyroxin increases during tadpole development. However, the present author does not regard the evidence available on this point as satisfactory for two reasons: (1) When, as in the experiments that claim to demonstrate changes in sensitivity, normal tadpoles of different ages are compared in their reactivity, the older animals start from a more advanced baseline since their tissues have been exposed for a longer time to conditioning by low levels of thyroid hormone present in the tadpole. (2) The differences in sensitivity reported are small, less than a factor of two times and therefore as compared to the changes in thyroid level can play only a minor role in determining normal metamorphic change. In some cases differences in time of first appearance of metamorphic change in animals treated as embryos have been interpreted as indicating differences in time of acquisition of sensitivity. However, such differences may represent merely differences in latent period of response. In summary, then, except for certain nervous structures, the tadpole's tissues appear to be ready to respond to the metamorphic stimulus throughout the growth phase of development. Changes in sensitivity play a minor, if any, role in determining metamorphic pattern.

2. A second possibility to be considered is that the thyroid gland may not be capable of forming the necessary hormone during the growth phase. However, the earliest studies have shown that the thyroid gland differentiates normally in the absence of the absence of the pituitary. In the normal animal, moreover, the gland forms detectable levels of T_4 in the early tadpole stage (16 mm total length in R. pipiens), as shown by Flickinger (1994). The tadpole's thyroid also responds to pituitary TSH at all stage of tadpole development and even in the embryo. Therefore, there is no reason to suspect that the thyroid of the tadpole is incapable of responding appropriately to a metamorphic stimulus during any part of the growth phase. We must look higher than the thyroid in the hypothalamuspituitary-thyroid axis for the explanation of the failure of the tadpole to metamorphose during this period.

If we ask next whether the pituitary is capable of effective levels of TSH production during this period, we must again answer that it is. The most direct and satisfactory evidence for this would be the demonstration of the responsiveness of the tadpole pituitary to a hypothalamic TRF factor. However, as is discussed below, evidence from this source is not yet available. But other evidence does indicate clearly that the tadpole's pituitary is capable of producing an effective TSH during tadpole life. One such bit of evidence is the demonstration that when the pituitary (adenohypophyseal) primordium an thyroid primordium are placed close together in the embryo, the thyroid is precociously activated. This shows that even at early stages the pituitary is capable of producing an effective TSH. The evidence derived from the effects of goitrogens in tadpoles further demonstrates that this capacity for producing TSH continues through tadpole life. The administration of such goitrogens leads to hypertrophy of the thyroid. This action, like the similar action in mammals, works by preventing the iodination of the molecule in the gland and, therefore; renders its hormone production ineffective. The lack of thyroid hormone in the goitrogen-treated tadpole removes the feedback inhibition normally exerted by thyroid hormone upon TSH production. The excess TSH produced by the pituitary of the goitrogen-treated tadpole. stimulates the thyroid to increased growth and to the abundant secretion of its physiologically ineffective product. We have recently found this goitrogen effect to obtain even in the early tadpole (unpublished results). Thus, we are led to regard the pituitary of the early tadpole as capable of producing the TSH necessary for the induction of metamorphosis but restrained from doing so because of the inhibition of its TSH-secreting cells by negative feedback from thyroxine produced by the thyroid. The premetamorphic period may be regarded as one in which the pituitary-thyroid axis is maintained in a steady state at an extremely low level of activity because of the great sensitivity of the TSH cells of the pituitary to negative thyroid feedback. The level of this steady state is so low that the amount of thyroid hormone produced is not sufficient to make the normal animal deviate perceptibly from the thyroid-ectomized one.

As the growth curve of the animal suggests, and as has been recognized and emphasized by Gudernatch and other early workers in the field, there is a reciprocal relation between the rate of overall body growth and the rate of metamorphic change. Therefore, we may inquire as to the significance of the endocrine factors in maintaining the high growth rate of the premetamorphic period. It was recognized early that thyroid treatment inhibits growth even as it promotes metamorphosis. Steinmetz (1982 and 1984) studied this phenomenon quantitatively by measuring the growth rate of tadpoles immersed in various concentrations of thyroxine and treated with the goitrogen, propothiouracil (PTU). He showed that distinct inhibition of the growth rate occurs at the lowest concentration of thyroxine measurably affecting leg growth and that the goitrogen stimulates the tadpole's growth. From this he' inferred that the level of thyroid hormone in the remetamorphic animal is maintained at an extremely low level, less than that equivalent to one part thyroxine per billion parts of water. Our own unpublished work with thyroxine concentration applied to normal tadpoles fully confirms Steinmetz's results. Thus, it is clear that the low steady state of the PT axis is an essential factor in maintaining the characteristic high growth rate of the premetamorphic period.

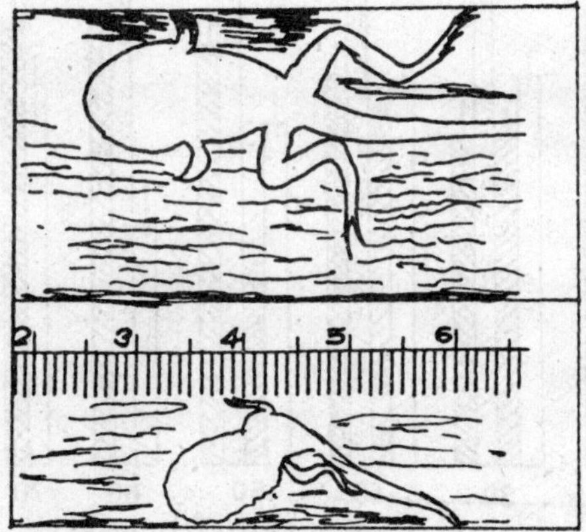

Figure 9.2 : Normal animal (above) compared to experimental animal raised in 3 to 9 ppb thyroxin.

In recent years it has come to be realized that prolactin (or a prolactinlike molecule) plays a significant role in amphibian physiology. Berman et al. (1994) and Nicoll *et* al. (1995) reported a stimulation of growth in normal tadpoles by prolactin, and Etkin

(1994) and Etkin and Gona (1997) reported such stimulation in hypophy-sectomized animals. These studies indicate an antagonism between thyroid hormone and prolactin. The antithyroid activity of prolactin has been found at low doses to act peripherally and to act as a goitrogen at high dosage level. In any case it appears that the retardation of growth to be seen in the hypophysectomized tadpole is to be ascribed at least in part to the absence of the prolactinlike factor. Further support of this concept of derived from the report of Etkin and Lehrer (1990). They found that the transplanted pituitary reduces growth in hypophysectomized hosts in excess of that of the normal. This suggests that the production of a prolactinlike hormone in the amphibian, like its production in the mammal, is under inhibitory control by the hypothalamus.

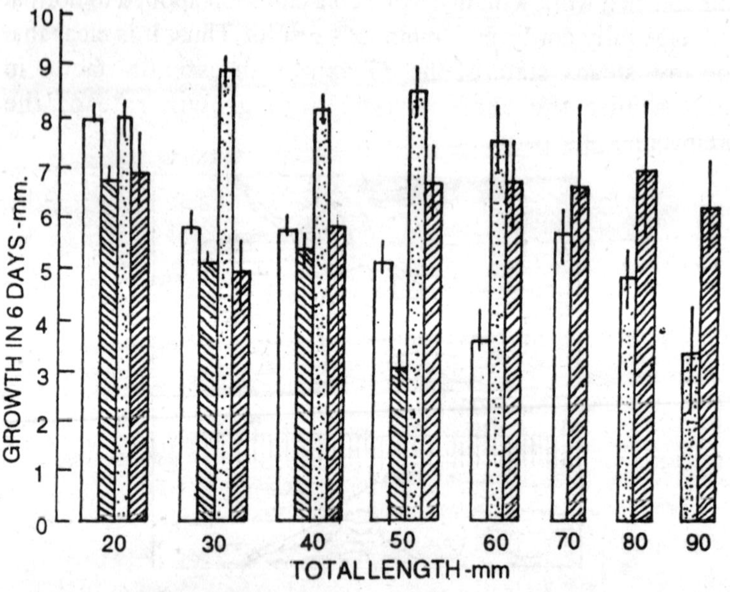

Figure 9.3 : Rate of growth of tadpoles of Rana* pipiens. *All animals of ,same batch. Individual growth curves kept for each animal and amount of growth in a six-day period as derived from these growth curves is plotted at different stages of development. Controls entered metamorphic climax at 65 to 70 mm. Hypophysectomized animals generally failed to grow above 60 mm.

The concept of the neuroendocrine relationships responsible for the high growth rate and the low metamorphic tendency in the premetamorphic tadpole that emerges from this evidence may be summarized as follows. The hypothalamus is only minimally active in producing a TRF or a prolactin-inhibiting factor. By this activity it only partially retards prolactin production and does not appreciably stimulate T5H production. Consequently, the negative feedback of thyroxine upon the activity of the TSH cells prevails and keeps the PT axis at a very low level. The high level of prolactin and low level of thyroid hormone favour a high growth rate and no appreciable metamorphic change during this period.

The Regulation of the Pattern of Tissue Response

The concept of the low-level steady state of the metamorphic mechanism during the growth phase of the tadpole's life raises most directly the question of how this system is disrupted to permit metamorphosis to take place. Betore we can examine this question, however, it is necessary to arrive at some understanding of endocrine activity during metamorphosis so that we can appreciate what the nature of the transition from one condition to the other might be. The clue to this was given by the analysis of the pattern of thyroid activity in relation to the pattern of metamorphic change.

It will be recalled from a preceding section that the prometamorphic period is characterized by rapid growth of the hind legs and other less conspicuous changes that are spread over about three weeks in R. pipiens. This is followed by about a week of climax, during which profound changes in morphology occur. The relation of developmental and histological changes in the thyroid gland to. these events was early subjected to extensive studies. The results in different anuran species indicate that during the period of, prometamorphosis the relative growth rate of the thyroid is high and the gland reaches a maximum size at the end of this period. The histological picture of moderate increase in cell height accompanied by enlargement of follicles indicates cell activity and storage of hormone. In early climax, however, the epithelium reaches a maximum height and the follicles show a reduction of colloid which, particularly in smaller species,brings on partial collapse of the follicles. This picture was early interpreted as indicating an increasing release of thyroid hormone during prometamorphosis and a very high level of activity at climax. At the end of climax the histological picture shows a return to a flat epithelium and to follicles distended with colloid, thus indicating a deactivation of the thyroid.

Modern studies have attempted to apply recently developed techniques to the analysis of thyroid activity in relation to metamorphosis. These have included chemical studies with and without radioiodine electrical conductivity measurements and enzyme studies. In a general qualitative way these studies have supported the morphological investigations mentioned above since most authors interpret their findings in terms of increasing activity with the approach of metamorphic climax. However, the quantitative refinement that one could wish for from such studies was not forthcoming. For example, Saxen et al. found no clear increase in protein-bound iodine in prometamorphosis and only a twofold increase at climax. Whereas these authors and Kaye reported a large increase in I^{131} uptake, this uptake peaked in mid-or late prometamorphosis rather than at climax. Similarly, the conductivity measurements of Gorbman and Ueda indicated the greatest change in midprometamorphosis and a return to the premetamorphosis level at climax. Flickinger was able to detect thyroxine in peripheral tissues only at climax. Yamamoto followed t_4 deiodinase activity through preisely defined stages of metamorphosis and reported a great increase during prometamorphosis peaking at climax, falling abruptly thereafter. Although the physiological significance of this deiodination is not dear, the parallelism to metamorphic activity is suggestive of changes of hormone level. Unfortunately, the results of Dowling and Razevska are not in agreement with the findings of Yamamoto's study. The reason for this difference remains unexplained. Needless to say, each of these techniques has its complexities of interpretation, the analysis of which would take us far afield at this point. Therefore, without going into detail, the present author may summarize his interpretation that these studies reinforce the concept that prometamorphosis is marked by an increase in thyroid activity, much of which goes into storage of hormone in follicles. However, they fail to clarify in any quantitative way the changes of level of effective hormone. Particularly, they fail to define the effective hormone level responsible for climax changes. It is to be hoped that this admittedly personal evaluation of the results of these methods constitutes a challenge to a critical application of biochemical and biophysical methods to.this problem. There is as much to be gained in !heislarification of the methods as well as in the understanding of thyroid action in metamorphosis by such a study. A most promising application of modem biochemical methodology to this problem is the attempt of measure T_4 and T_3 levels in the blood directly by chromatographic separation. Preliminary results by this method support the concept of increasing concentration of thyroid hormone during prometamorphosis to a maximal at climax with a decrease thereafter. But a more precise qualification of hormone level is not yet available.

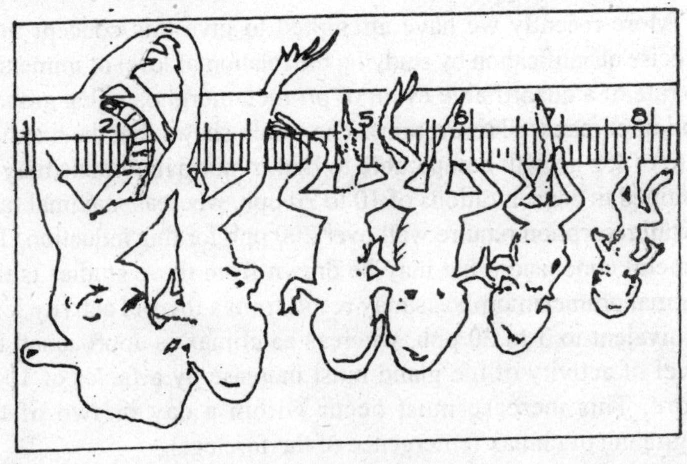

Figure 9.4 : Tadpoles of R. pipiens. Second from right is an untreated control fixed three days after emergence of forelegs when tail resorption is half completed. The maximal size attained by this animal was 68 mm. The animal at right was a thyroidectomized animal induced to metamorphose by a patterned application of increasing concentrations of thyroxine after reaching 90 mm. To the left are a series of normal animals similarly treated beginning at various early stages and fixed at middimax. Note the normal morphology induced by the pattern of increasing concentration of hormone in contrast to the abnormalities induced by single concentrations.

An indirect method for evaluating thyroid function quantitatively is that of studying metamorphic change in young tadpoles,. prekrably thyroidectomized animals, during immerskn in thyroxine solutions of various concentrations. An early study demonstrated that low concentrations (3 to 10 parts thyroxine per billion parts of water) yielded good leg growth, but later metamorphic change was protracted at this hormone level. Higher concentrations (100 to 1,000 ppb) on the other hand yielded climax events at near normal rates but did not permit sufficient time for leg growth to attain normal dimensions before tail resorption was induced. The general inference drawn from these studies was that a normal pattern of metamorphic change could be induced only by an extended period of treatment with a low concentration of T_4 followed by immersion in high concentration. This inference has been repeatedly confirmed in many subsequent studies in this laboratory.

More recently we have attempted to give this concept more precise quantification by studying the relation of level of immersion to rate of a quantifiable event of prometamorphosis (leg growth) and of climax (tail resorption). The-graph shows that the maximal rate of leg growth comparable to that in normal animals may be attained in concentrations of 10 to 20 ppb, whereas maximal rates of tail resorption require well over 200 ppb for this induction. The general conclusion that may be drawn from these studies is that normal prometamorphosis may result from a thyroid activity level equivalent to 3 to 20 ppb, whereas as climax is approached the level of activity of the gland must increase by a factor of 10 or more. This increase must occur within a day or two of the beginning of climax (emergence of the forelegs).

It should be noted parenthetically that Frieden advocates the application of thyroxine by injection rather than immersion because he finds a low level of absorption of the hormone from the medium. We cannot agree with this view-point for two reasons: (1) the equilibrium level of absorption is irrelevant as long as it varies with the external level and (2) after injection the internal level does not remain constant since loss by excretion and degradation are rapid, as shown by his own studies. Of course, immersion studies do not tell us directly what the equilibrium level of hormone is within the animal's body, but Kollros (1963) has shown that the hormone's concentration is maintained at a highly constant level by the immersion method.

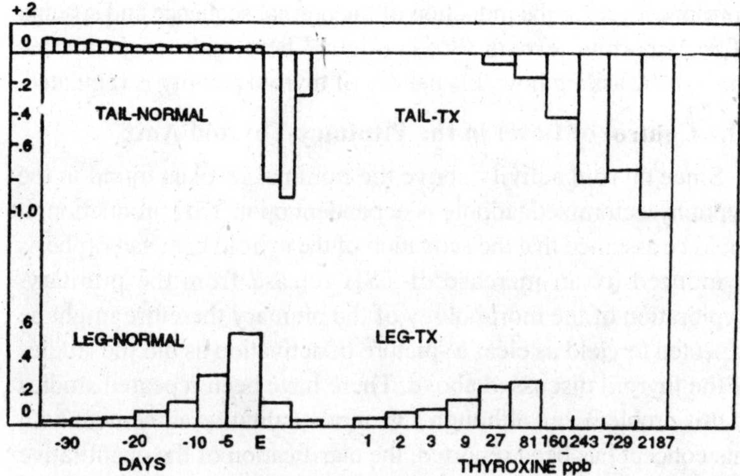

Figure 9.5 : Results of an experiment (right) to test the effect of different concentrations of thyroxine (Tx) on hind-leg growth and tail resorption in half-grown normal tadpoles. For comparison the rates of change of leg and tail in normal metamorphosis are shown at the left. The rates of change are expressed as proportions of body (snout to anus) length make the data of smaller experimental animals comparable controls. Each bar for the tail shows the ratio change over two-day period in normal animals and for days 3 to 5 after posure to Tx for the experiments. Leg ratios are shown for five periods in normals and days 3 to 8 in experimentals. It may be noted that in the normals the legs grow most rapidly in tine fiveday period before climax begins (E), and tail reduction begins after R and drops by 0.8 of the body length in each of the next two-day periods. In the experimental animals it can be seen that the rate of leg growth produced by 27 ppb thyroxin is about maximum. Animals in concentration higher than 81 ppb do not survive long enough to pro de adequate data, although observations shows that their legs do not grow faster than those in animals at 27 ppb. The tail, on the other hand, does not show its maximal rate f reduction until the concentration of 243 ppb is reached. It may be concluded that maximal leg growth such as occurs during late prometamorphosis requires a Tx concentration about one tenth that necessary for the maximal rate of tail resorption.

This type of evidence then leads to the concept that the level of thyroid hormone action rises progressively during prometamorphosis and undergoes an explosive increase by a factor of at least 10 times at climax. The most immediate question raised by this concept is that of the significance of this changing thyroid hormone level for the induction of the normal sequence and spacing of metamorphic events. We continued here with the endocrine analysis by asking how this pattern of thyroid activity is regulated.

The Control of Level in the Pituitary-Thyroid Anix

Since thyroid activity above the minimal level as found in the hypophysectomized tadpole is dependent upon TSH production, it could be assumed that the activation of the thyroid in metamorphosis is induced by an increase of TSH release from the pituitary. Explbration of the morphology of the pituitary therefore might be expected to yield as clear a -picture of activation as did the studies of the thyroid discussed above. There have been repeated studies of this problem, but although a general qualitative agreement with this concept has been reported, the clarification of the quantitative interrelations is not impressive. Recent studies by Kerr (1996) in *Xenopus* and by Kiremidjian and Ortman (1996) in *R. pipiens* have indicated an increase in the supposed TSH cells (identified as Aldehyde fuchsin positive basophils). Yet the amount of the increase, even admitting that the level of activity of a cell is not readily inferred from its staining reaction, does not seem entirely consistent with the inference from the thyroid pattern. Kerr emphasizes that there is no evidence of hormonal discharge in the pituitary at the time of metamorphic climax. The identification of the TSH cell as a basophil is itself uncertain. Several authors have presented evidence pointing to an acidophil as the source of THS. The study of this problem at the electron microscope level by Dent and Gupta (1997) again indicates some increase in the supposed TSH cells but not as great a change at climax as was to be anticipated. The recent finding of the antithyroid activity of prolactin suggests that instead of a simple increase in TSH there may be a shift in proportion of TSH to prolactin production that accounts for the activation of the thyroid gland. Indeed, the criteria for identifying the TSH cell (response to goitrogens, thyroxine, etc.) will have to be reconsidered in the light of a possible role for prolactin in controlling thyroid activity. In any case, it is apparent that further quantitative work will be required before we can specify the. nature of the change in the 'pituitary activity that is responsible for the patterning of thyroid activity› during metamorphosis.

But whatever may be the precise nature of the change in the pituitary, it is clear that the signal initiating and controlling the pattern of metamorphosis must come from the pituitary. Therefore, we may ask whether the pituitary is autonomous, i.e., whether it determines its own rate of activity by some sort of built-in' clock mechanism or whether it is subject to some external control. The remarkable fact that throughout the vertebrates, however diverse their brain-pituitary morphology may be, the connection between the two structures is always maintained suggests that the pituitary is under control by the CNS. Furthermore, the clarification of the morphological relationship by the demonstration of the neurosecretory system and the pituitary portal system of blood vessels strongly reinforces this viewpoint. Before the nature of the neurosecretory system was understood, this problem had been attacked in relation to anuran metamorphosis by isolating the gland from the brain. In 1978, Etkin showed that if a tadpole's own pituitary were transplanted in the embryo the animal would usually grow very well but would show at best a retarded and protracted metamorphosis. Nonetheless, the capacity of at least the most successful cases for inducing prometamorphosis was taken to indicate the essential independence of the pituitary from its connection to the brain, a connection then thought of in terms of conventional innervation. In 1980, Uyematsu reported the converse experiment in a toad, removing the region of the embryonic neural plate that gives rise to the infundibular lobes of the hypothalamus and thereby isolating the epithelial pituitary. He also reported his animals to show prometamorphosis, but he found them unable to complete climax changes. This failure he ascribed to a degeneration of the isolated gland at climax. But despite this evidence, which speaks for the concept of an autonomous clock mechanism in the pituitary as the controlling factor in metamorphosis, when the nature of the neurosecretory and the pituitary portal system and hypothalamic influence on TSH production was elucidated in mammals, the need to reexamine this question was recognized. We were able to confirm out earlier work with embryonic grafts and extended it to grafts of differentiated glands placed into hypophysectomized hosts. In these studies the animals were maintained into climax, and it was found that the hosts to successful grafts, though often completing prometamorphic development, invariably entered a metamorphic stasis at climax. Clearly, then, graft activity was 'capable of activating the thyroid to the low levels responsible for prometamorphic change but not to the high level necessary for climax events. It was apparent that the failure at climax was not due to a degeneration of the gland at that time since the gland was found to be maintained morphologically and also was seen to continue the production of its growth and pigmentation-regulating factors in spite of the metamorphic stasis. We were also able to confirm Uyematsu's findings of similar capacities in pituitaries isolated by removing part of the embryonic hypothalamic region.

There have been many reports in the last 10 years confirming the necessity of the presence of the hypothalamus for the completion of metamorphosis. However, Guardabassi (1991) reported completion of metamorphosis after removal of the hypothalamus. It should be understood that failure of metamorphosis in short-term experiments or in experiments in which the animals fail to grow vigorously does not necessarily imply hypothalamic control of TSH function since injury or starvation by themselves can inhibit metamorphosis. However, in our experiments and those of Remy and Bounhiol there can be no doubt of the vigour of the animals since many achieved gigantic size without completing metamorphosis. At least in these experiments, then, it is clear that isolation of the pituitary from the hypothalamus specifically inhibits it from attaining a high level of TSH activity. It is possible that the discordant results reported by Guardabassi are the consequence of inmmpl removals accompanied by regenerative repair, which is possible in the tadpole's nervous system. In the opinion of this author it appears to be clearly established that the high level of thyroid activity necessary for metamorphic climax can be maintained by a pituitary gland only if it has its normal connection with the brain. In urodeles also it' is clear that the metamorphic process that corresponds to climax in anurans depends upon normal hypothalamic relations with the pituitary. A barrier inserted between these two structures (see frontispiece D) effectively prevents metamorphosis, provided it completely separates them. A low prometamorphic level, however, can be maintained by the isolated pituitary in anurans.

On the other hand, some evidence indicates a considerable measure of independence of the pituitary TSH production from hypothalamic control in amphibians. Dent (1996) reported that molting in the newt, in which this process is known to be dependent upon the thyroid, is maintained by pituitaries isolated from the brain. Iodine metabolism, though reduced in-toads with pituitary grafts, is higher than in hypophysectomized animals. We regard such evidence as consistent with that derived from metamorphic studies where the isolated pituitary is found to sustain prometamorphic change. It is possible that the role of thyroid in the molting of these amphibians is merely permissive. Though necessary at a minimal level, it does not determine the rhythm of molting by its variation.

One is tempted to infer from the evidence given above that the pituitary TSH system is autonomous for low levels of activity and requires hypothalamic cooperation only for the highly activated state. However, if we think of the hypothalamicpituitary interrelationship in terms of neurosecretion rather than conventional innervation it is apparent that inference is not justified. Presumably, the significance of the pituitary portal venous system lies in the greater efficiency it provides for the transfer of chemicals produced in hypothalamic neurons to the cells of the anterior pituitary. Thus, it appears likely that though this system of direct transfer of neurosecretion may be essential for maximal stimulation of the pituitary,. a lower level of TSH activity may be maintained by the transfer of neurosecretion through the systemic circulation. Such a low level of stimulation could reach a graft wherever, it was located. The evidence on brain removal mentioned above either does not include the areas presumed to contain the relevant pericarya or is too fragmentary and incompletely analyzed

(Voitkevich and Guardabassi) to permit judgment. Further studies should clarify this critical point. At present it appears most logical to accept the possible transfer of hypothalamic substances in diluted form through the systemic circulation as the explanation of the low and moderate levels of TSH' function reported in isolated pituitaries.

Of course, a most direct approach to this question could be derived from experiments with extracts of the hypothalamus that have thyrotropin-releasing properties (TRF). Such TRF preparations have been developed for mammals in several laboratories. However, Bowers and Schally, working with their TRF preparatidn, failed to find evidence of TSH release in the tadpole (personal communication). In our laboratory, work with a TRF prepared by Dr. Roger Guillemin that was potent in tests on rodents likewise failed to elicit activation of metamorphosis, even when large amounts were injected directly into the heart. Presumably the chemistry of the amphibian TRF must differ from that in mammals, but no adequate studies of an amphibian TRF are yet available. The possibility should also kept in mind that a shift in the prolactin-TSH balance rather than a simple release of TSH may be necessary for metamorphic activity.

Our consideration of the hypothalamic-pituitary-thyroidtissue axis in relation to metamorphosis thus leads us to the concept that at the beginning of prometamorphosis the hypothalamus initiates the changes, in some way stimulating the pituitary-thyroid axis. This activation process builds up during prometamorphosis to a subtotal activation of the axis by the beginning of climax. At the end of metamorphosis the hypothalamus apparently stops its stimulation of the PT axis since the latter becomes inactive, although we have no direct evidence on this point. Such a concept raises the question of the. control. of the hypothalaints.Does it, rather than the pittritary, contain the "clock" mechanism that determines the timing and pattern of metamorphosis?

The Activation of the Metamorphic Mechanism

Sine the evidence indicates that the control of the metamorphic process depends upon the hypothalamic neurosecretory apparatus, it was desirable to investigate the development of this mechanism.

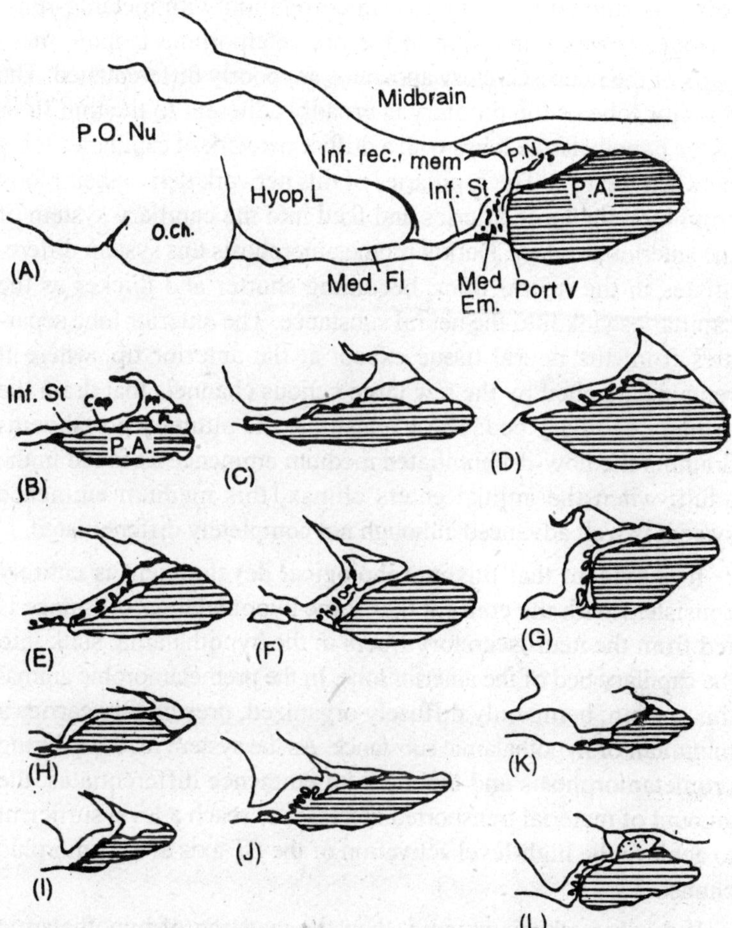

Figure 9.6 : Camera lucida drawings of sagittal sections of the pituitary region. A: Adult frog, B: premetamorphosis; C: early prometamorphosis; D: late prometamorphosis; E: beginning of climax; F: midclimax. G: post-climax. A to G show Rana pipiens. H: Early prometamorphosis; I: late prometamorphosis; J: one day before E. H to J show Rana sylvatica. K: midprometamorphosis; L: early climax. K to L show Bufo americanum.

Wilson et al. (1957) reported on the morphology of this system in the western tree frog *(Hyla regilla)* and showed that the classical neurosecretory material of the posterior lobe (see above) appears early in development. However, they did not follow the differentiation of the portal vessels and medium eminence in detail. When this was studied in *R. pipiens.* in correlation with metamo-rphic change, it was found that in the premetamorphic tadpole these parts of the neurosecretory apparatus are poorly differentiated. The anterior lobe of the pituitary is broadly adherent to the thin floor of the hypothalamic lobes with a diffuse network of capillaries lying between the two. The capillaries of this network derive their blood from hypothalamic arteries and feed into the capillary system of the anterior pituitary. During prometamorphosis this system differe-ntiates in the neural floor, becoming shorter and thicker as the capillaries sink into the neural substance. The anterior lobe separ-ates from the neural tissue except at the anterior tip, where it remains attached by the few large venous channels that drain the primary capillary bed. These constitute the pituitary portal veins draining the now-differentiated medium eminence as found in the adult; when the animal enters climax, this medium eminence system is well advanced although not completely differentiated.

It is evident that this morphological development is entirely consistent with the concept that some hypothalamic substance is fed from the neurosecretory fibers in the hypothalamic stalk into the capillary bed of the anterior lobe. In the premetamorphic animal this system, being only diffusely organized, presumably carries a minimum of hypothalamic substance. As the system matures during prometamorphosis and the medium eminence differentiates, the amount of material transported increases to reach a level sufficient to achieve the high-level activation of the PT axis at metamorphic climax.

If this hypothesis is valid, then the question of hypothalamic control could be studied by examining the differentiation of the median eminence region in the thyroidectomized larva. If the hypothalamus is autonomous in its differentiated, the median eminence should mature in spite of the failure of the thyroidless larva to metamorphose. The examination of this question showed that this was not so. In the thyroidectomized larva the median eminence region retains its larval character (see frontispiece B). However, if such a larva is artificially induced to metamorphose in a normal pattern by the application of graded concentrations of thyroxine, the median eminence is seen to differentiate as in the normally transforming animal. Thus, it is apparent that the median eminence, part of the hypothalamic mechanism that is presumed to control the PT axis, is itself controlled by thyroid hormone. Evidently, then, there is a circular mechanism involving a positive feedback of thyroid hormone to the hypothalamus. This suggests that the differentiation of the hypothalamic mechanism is gradually brought about by the action of thyroid hormone. This feedback process starts in the early larva at an extremely slow rate because of the low level of thyroid activity in the premetamorphic period. Since it contains a positive feedback element, however, this circular system accelerates slowly at first then more rapidly and finally ends in a burst of activity as any circular system with positive feedback must.

This intriguing possibility could be tested in a number of *ways.* One such test is to expose early larvae to low concentrations of thyroxine (1 to 9 ppb) for sometime. Such exogenous thyroxine in this hypothesis, should, accelerate the maturation of the endogenous hypothalamic mechanism responsible for activating the animal's own PT axis. Animals thus treated should metamorphose earlier than controls and should show a normal pattern of climax events. Repeated attempts in which different concentrations of exogenous hormone were applied in various combinations however, failed, to produce an acceleration of metamorphosis. Of course, the thyroxin-treated animals were smaller at metamorphosis than controls because the hormone inhibited their growth rate, as explained above. This result raised the possibility that the hypothalamic system, as certain other neural elements, does not acquire its sensitivity to thyroxine until late in the premetamorphic period. An experimental analysis of this point showed that it was indeed so. Animals *(R. pipiens)* treated with graded concentrations of thyroxine from early larval stages and thus brought into mid-climax much earlier than normal failed to show any metamorphological advance of the median eminence region over the larval condition. On the other ha , animals that were so treated as to be only slightly precoci us did show such development. Thus, it is clear that until a short time before the normal animals cnter prometamorphosis, the median eminence region, and presumably the rest of the hypothalamic neurosecretory apparatus, is sensitive to positive thyroid feedback. The feedback cycle thus begins about a week before a commencement of metamorphosis in normal development and builds up quickly through prometamorphosis to climax.

Thus, we are led to consider that the timing of the beginning of metamorphosis is regulated by a clock mechanism in the hypothalamus that times the acquisition of hormone sensitivity in that organ. On the other hand, the pattern of thyroid hormone build up that, as we have seen previously, determines the pattern of metamorphic change is determined by the positive feedback system of thyroxine to the hypothalamus. In order to form a more comprehensive picture of the mechanism regulating development in larval life of the frog we must now add the newly acquired knowledge of the role of prolactin in promoting body growth and inhibiting metamorphosis in tadpoles as discussed above. Since prolactin is under inhibitory control by the hypothalamus, the positive feedback of T_4 to the neurosecretory system presumably inhibits prolactin activity while at the same time stimulating the PT axis. In Fig. 10.9 an attempt is made to depict the interaction of these elements in the life history of the anuran larva.

Metamorphosis as a Development Pheomenon

I propose in this section to speculate more broadly than, in the stress of scientific investigation and writing, scientists commonly permit themselves to do. Since the ideas expressed are very general, no detailed documentation will be offered.

Evolution and Developmental Mechanisms in Amphibians

Although a few fossil larvae are known, they contribute little to an understanding of the evolution of metamorphosis beyond the fact that it was present is paleozoid labyrinthodonts. General biological considerations, however, permit some reasonable speculations. Metamorphosis in urodeles is a developmental adaptation permitting the change from water to land environment. The basic mode of feeding by predation and the associated locomotor mechanisms, however, remain unchanged. Presumably this was the situation is primitive amphibians. In anurans, on the other hand, the larva generally feeds as a free-swimming scavenger, herbivore, or filter feeder. In metamorphosis it changes to a predator which depends upon powerful leg action for its saltatory locomotion. The significance of the prometamorphic phase in anuran transformation appears to lie chiefly in providing time for the legs, whose development had been repressed during the larval phase, to grow before the transition to land is made at metamorphic climax. It urodeles the limbs develop in the way usual among vertebrates, during embryonic stages, and are not involve in metamorphosis.

This evolutionary process must, of course, have operated through modification of the mechanics of development. From this point of view, the changes of prometamorphosis, principally limb growth, have been brought into the metamorphic picture by the evolution of a developmental mechanism separating limb differentiation from the general embryonic processes and suppressing it during the premetamorphic period. The action of thyroid hormone, then, appears as the factor which removes this initial inhibition of limb development. We see here an example of a phenomenon appearing frequently in the mechanics of development. This is that control of development is effected by a balance between inhibiting and disinhibiting factors operating on a protoplasmic mechanism with very broad developmental capacities. We see this type of development control in gene action at the molecular level, in fertilization phenomena, and in field effects in organ determination.

At the level of endocrine action we again see that developmental control is effected by a balance between inhibition and disinhibition rather than by simple stimulation. The PT axis is kept at a low level of activity in the growth phase of the tadpole's development by negative feedback, and at metamorphosis its activation is brought about by disinhibition of this feedback by hypothalamic action. It is possible that the hypothalamic controlling mechanism of the pituitary has been inhibited for the duration of the larval period by some evolutionary change in the genome. In that case what we have described above as the positive feedback of thyroxine to the hypothalamus would be another instance of the disinhibition of development by thyroxine.

The complexity of the push-pull type of interaction in governing metamorphosis is further emphasized by the discovery of the role of prolactin as a thyroid antagonist in amphibian development. Whether this substance acts at the peripheral level or as a goitrogen or in both ways its role again emphasizes that development is controlled by a dynamic balance of plus and minus factors. A fascinating aspect of this particular interaction is the manner in which it appears to have been seized upon as the mechanism for the evolution of the "second metamorphosis" in the common newt.' After a first metamorphosis that produces the land form, this animal returns to the water for breeding in a second period of transformation (see frontispiece A). This second metamorphosis has been shown to be under the influence of prolactin. We must now view this change as a shift in the balance between the pituitary factors, prolactin and TSH, rather than as an activation of one of them. First metamorphosis is induced by a shift in favour of TSH, second metamorphosis by a return to the predominance of prolactin. What brings on this second shift is yet to be explored.

Insect and Amphibian Metamorphosis

The analogy between insect metamorphosis and that of amphibians has often been commented upon. In both, the brain acting through a neuro-secretary mechanism controls the endocrine apparatus which governs tissue response through hormone release. Until recently one feature of the insect system seemed to be lacking in vertebrates. In insects the hormone of the corpus allatum acts as a modulator inhibiting the action of ecdysone. We now see, however, that there is an analogous situation in amphibians, with prolactin playing the role of modular to thyroid activity. Perhaps the analogy will suggest ways in which factors that are found to regulate balance in one system can be applied to the other.

Metamorphosis and Puberty

A final area of speculation deserving comment is the analogy between amphibian metamorphosis and puberty in mammals. There is striking similarities in the mechanism of sexual regulation and metamorphosis. In each, the hypothalamic neurosecretory system appears dominant, controlling the pituitary (gonadotropin or TSH) which controls the basic endocrine gland (gonal or thyroid). This is turn regulates the response of the peripheral tissues. Within this system, likewise, there is a negative feedback relation which makes this, too, a balanced system.

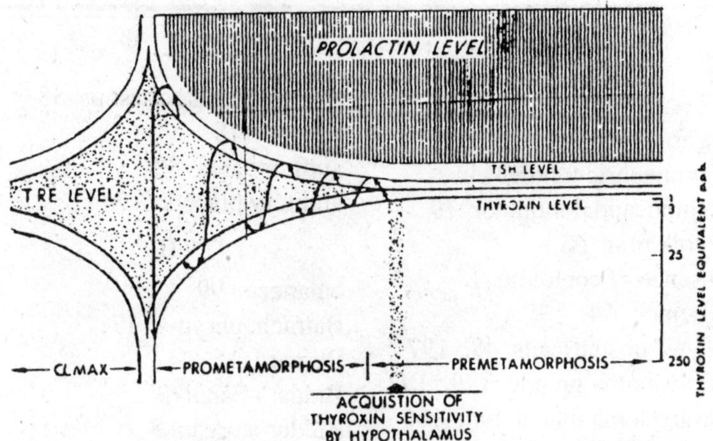

Figure 9.7 : Diagram illustrating the interaction of endocrine factors in determining the time and pattern of anuran metamorphosis.

In the prepuberal mammal in the amphibian larva the lower levels of the control sequence are capable of response much before they are actually called upon to act. Thus, the sex accessories and secondary sex characters can respond to gonadal stimulation long before puberty in most mammals. Likewise the gonads and the pituitary show early responsiveness. The critical factor determining the time of puberty then lies in the activation of the hypothalamus just as it does in metamorphosis. Beyond this point, however, the analogy appears to break down. Property placed lesions in the hypothalamus have been shown to accelerate puberty so that the hypothalamic gonadotropic releasing mechanism appears to be under inhibitory control of other neural centers. This has never been shown to apply to amphibian metamorphosis. On the other hand no positive feedback system of hormones to the hypothalamus has been described for the mammal as it has for the amphibian larva. Could this be because the possibilities suggested by the analogy have never been explored?

Index